Witnesses to a Massacre

Polyp • Schlunke • Poole

Peterloo
Witnesses to a Massacre

First published in 2019 by
New Internationalist
The Old Music Hall
106-108 Cowley Road
Oxford OX4 1JE
newint.org

Printed and bound in the Czech Republic on paper produced from sustainable
sources by PBtisk, who hold environmental accreditation ISO 14001.

British Library Cataloguing-in-Publication Data
A catalogue record for this book is available from the British Library.
Library of Congress Cataloging-in-Publication Data
A catalog record for this book is available from the Library of Congress.

ISBN 978-1-78026-475-2

Artwork: Polyp

Script Editor: Eva Schlunke

Historian: Robert Poole

Additional Research: Peter Castree

With many thanks to:

Mike Christodoulou
Rafe Conn and Steven Tennant
Matt Hill and Glossop Labour Club
Forever Manchester
The Free Radicals
Chris Mills
Maxine Peake
Julie Dalkin, Jeremy Hicks Associates
Jane Angel
Linda Mercer
Simon Thomas
Paul Harnett and Chorlton Socialists
Stockport Trades Union Council
Ed Glinert
Kelzo
Salford Star
Karen Shannon and Manchester
   Histories Festival
Michael Powell
UNITE retired members branch Salford
Karen Heatley and Sarah Hodgkinson,
   Rochdale Touchstones Museum
Dawn Taylor
Jenna Bowyer
David Fitzgerald and Paul Smith
Sean Rorke, Hot Bed Press
Laura Mackey
The Portico Library

Peterloo Memorial Campaign
Ocean Cad
Janette Martin, John Rylands Library,
   University of Manchester
Donna Sherman, University of
   Manchester Library
Peter Castree
Stuart Cooper
Harriet Monkhouse
Martin Gittins
Sean Baggaley
Elizabeth and Stuart Bailey
Elizabeth Sibbering
Nick Mansfield
Steve Roman
Jacqui Carroll
Mark Hodgkinson
Leah Graham
Helen Wakeford
Gabriel Radakovitch
Greg Falvey
Gabriel Falvey
Paul Monaghan
Rob Harrison
David Schlunke

And, of course, our colleagues at New
Internationalist and Myriad Editions.

Dedicated to the memory of...

WILLIAM FILDES age 2, knocked from his mother's arms by yeoman's horse.

ARTHUR NEILL age 40, from Manchester, truncheoned and crushed.

JOHN RHODES age 22, from Hopwood, sabred.

WILLIAM BRADSHAW age 19, from Lily Hill near Bury, sabred.

THOMAS BUCKLEY age 62, from Baretrees, Chadderton, bayoneted and sabred.

EDMUND DAWSON age 19, from Saddleworth, sabred.

JAMES CROMPTON from Barton-upon-Irwell, trampled by cavalry.

MARY HEYES from Manchester, trampled by cavalry, died giving birth to a premature baby.

JOHN ASHTON age 41 from Cowhill, near Oldham, sabred and trampled.

MARTHA PARTINGTON age 38, from Eccles, thrown into a cellar and crushed.

JOSEPH WHITWORTH age 19, from Hyde, shot at New Cross on the evening of the 16th August.

UNBORN CHILD OF ELIZABETH GAUNT mother beaten by constables and mistreated in custody.

JOHN LEES age 21, from Oldham, beaten by constables.

THOMAS JOHN ASHWORTH special constable from Manchester, trampled.

ROBERT CAMPBELL age 57, special constable from Manchester, beaten in revenge attack on the 17th August.

And to those believed dead, but whose fate is unknown...

MARGARET DOWNES from Manchester, severely sabred and supposed dead.

SAMUEL HALL cotton spinner from Hulme, sabred and trampled.

WILLIAM EVANS from Hulme, carter and special constable, trampled, last seen in a dying state.

I

NED LUDD DID IT

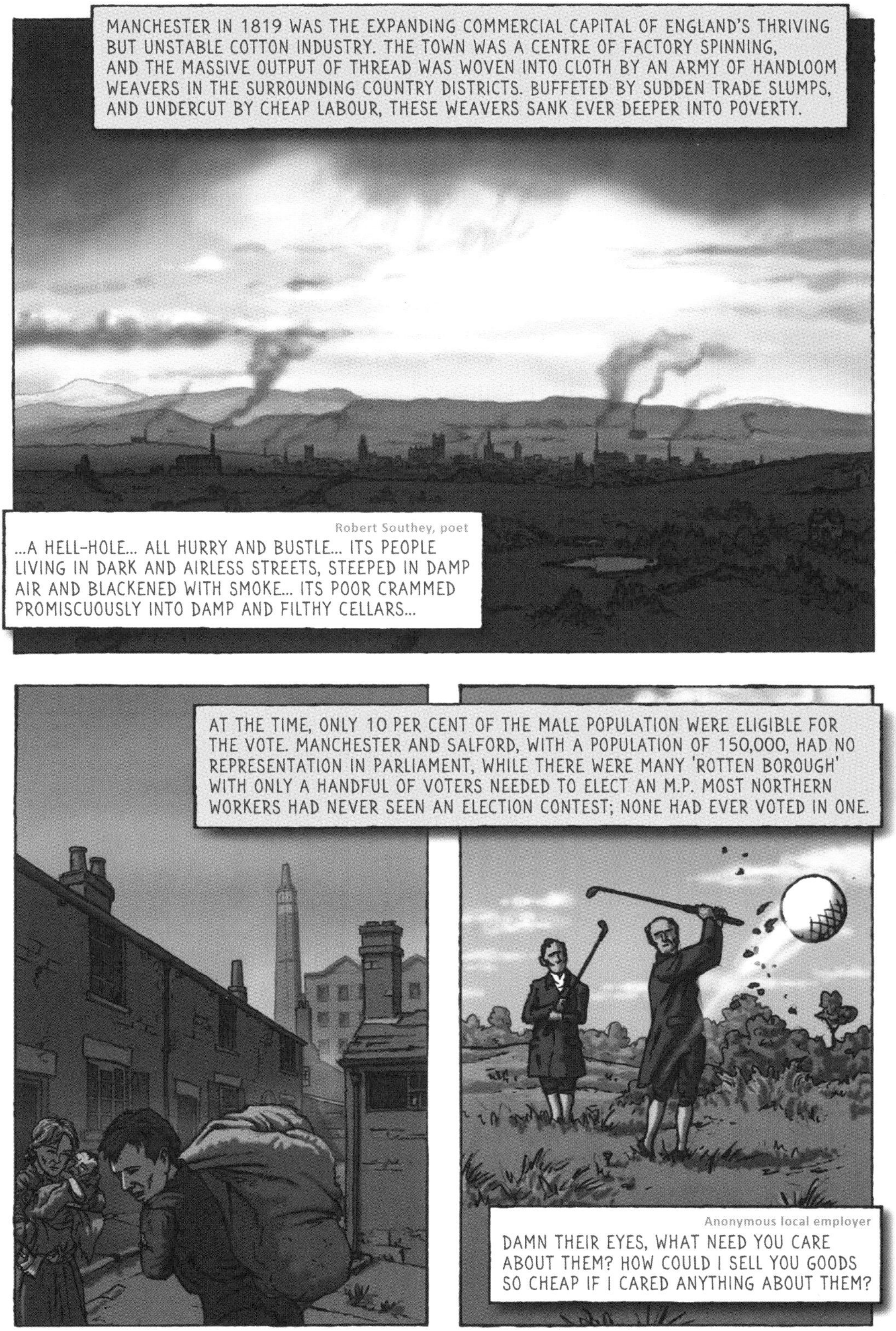
MANCHESTER IN 1819 WAS THE EXPANDING COMMERCIAL CAPITAL OF ENGLAND'S THRIVING BUT UNSTABLE COTTON INDUSTRY. THE TOWN WAS A CENTRE OF FACTORY SPINNING, AND THE MASSIVE OUTPUT OF THREAD WAS WOVEN INTO CLOTH BY AN ARMY OF HANDLOOM WEAVERS IN THE SURROUNDING COUNTRY DISTRICTS. BUFFETED BY SUDDEN TRADE SLUMPS, AND UNDERCUT BY CHEAP LABOUR, THESE WEAVERS SANK EVER DEEPER INTO POVERTY.
Robert Southey, poet
...A HELL-HOLE... ALL HURRY AND BUSTLE... ITS PEOPLE LIVING IN DARK AND AIRLESS STREETS, STEEPED IN DAMP AIR AND BLACKENED WITH SMOKE... ITS POOR CRAMMED PROMISCUOUSLY INTO DAMP AND FILTHY CELLARS...
AT THE TIME, ONLY 10 PER CENT OF THE MALE POPULATION WERE ELIGIBLE FOR THE VOTE. MANCHESTER AND SALFORD, WITH A POPULATION OF 150,000, HAD NO REPRESENTATION IN PARLIAMENT, WHILE THERE WERE MANY 'ROTTEN BOROUGH' WITH ONLY A HANDFUL OF VOTERS NEEDED TO ELECT AN M.P. MOST NORTHERN WORKERS HAD NEVER SEEN AN ELECTION CONTEST; NONE HAD EVER VOTED IN ONE.
Anonymous local employer
DAMN THEIR EYES, WHAT NEED YOU CARE ABOUT THEM? HOW COULD I SELL YOU GOODS SO CHEAP IF I CARED ANYTHING ABOUT THEM?

THE TERRORS OF THE FRENCH REVOLUTION STILL HAUNTED THE BRITISH AUTHORITIES. THEY CLAIMED THAT 'SUBVERSIVE' DEMOCRATIC IDEAS LIKE THOSE IN THOMAS PAINE'S 1791 BOOK *RIGHTS OF MAN* WOULD LEAD TO OPEN REBELLION. BRITAIN WENT TO WAR WITH FRANCE CAUSING SEVERE ECONOMIC HARDSHIP. FOOD RIOTS BROKE OUT ACROSS THE COUNTRY.

Captain W Chippendale, Oldham
THE SPIRIT OF TURBULENCE HAS ASSUMED A NEW CHARACTER SINCE JACOBINISM WAS INFUSED INTO THE LOWER ORDERS, AND IS NOW BECOME PERFECTLY INFERNAL.

THIS WAS THE AGE OF THE 'LUDDITES': NETWORKS OF ARTISAN TEXTILE WORKERS WHO ORGANIZED TO ATTACK THE EMPLOYERS AND MACHINERY WHICH THEY BLAMED FOR DRIVING THEM AND THEIR FAMILIES TOWARDS STARVATION. THEY WERE NAMED AFTER THEIR FICTIONAL LEADER, KING NED LUDD, WHO WAS SAID TO LIVE IN SHERWOOD FOREST.

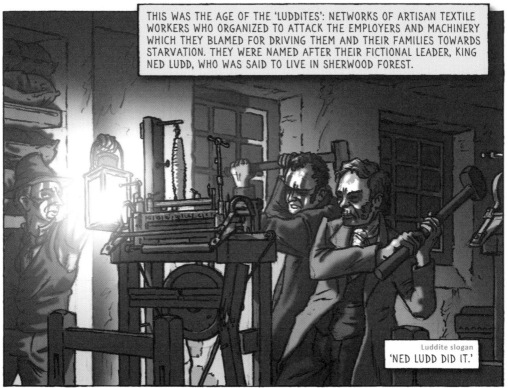

Luddite slogan
'NED LUDD DID IT.'

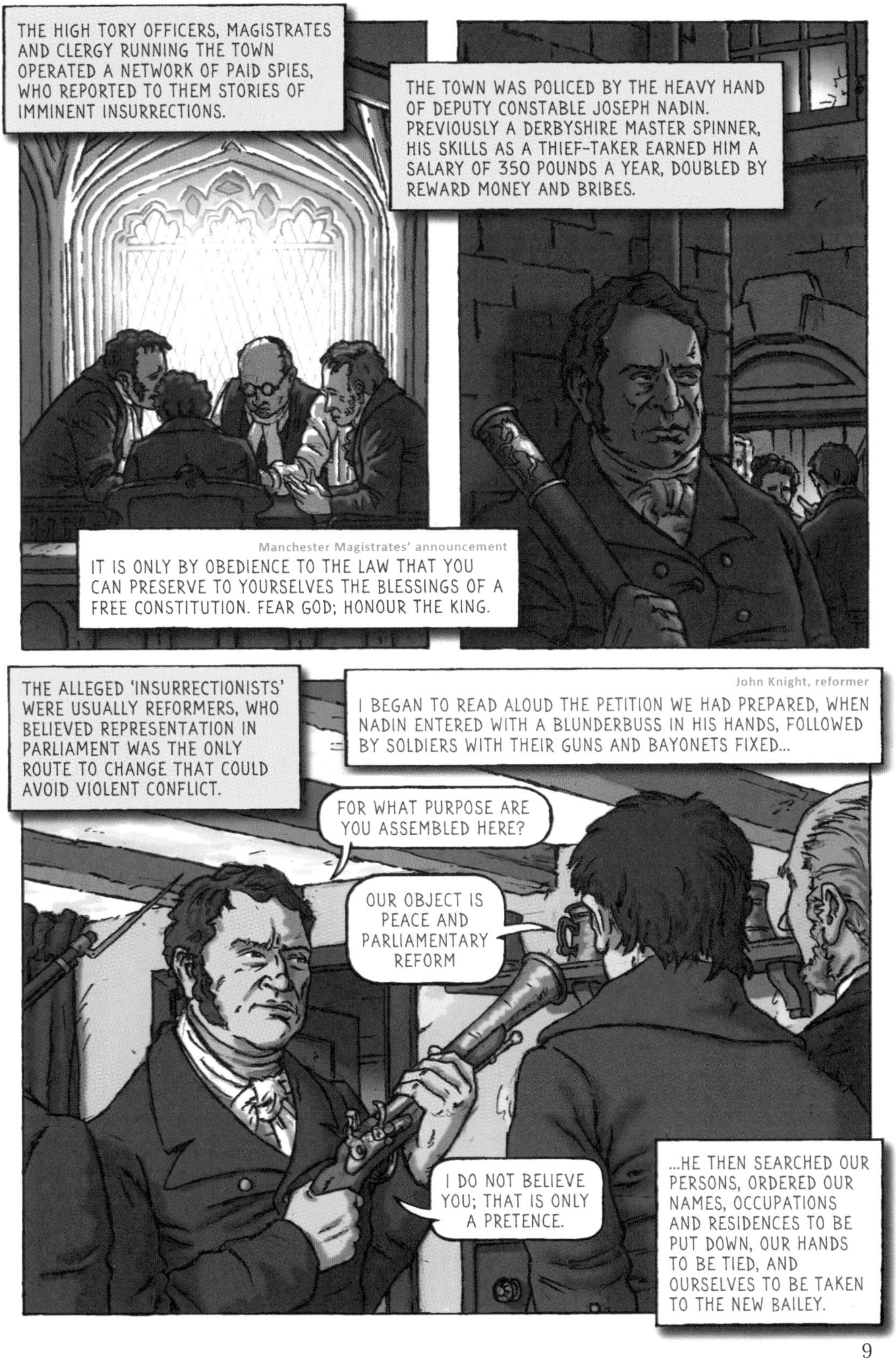
THE HIGH TORY OFFICERS, MAGISTRATES AND CLERGY RUNNING THE TOWN OPERATED A NETWORK OF PAID SPIES, WHO REPORTED TO THEM STORIES OF IMMINENT INSURRECTIONS.
THE TOWN WAS POLICED BY THE HEAVY HAND OF DEPUTY CONSTABLE JOSEPH NADIN. PREVIOUSLY A DERBYSHIRE MASTER SPINNER, HIS SKILLS AS A THIEF-TAKER EARNED HIM A SALARY OF 350 POUNDS A YEAR, DOUBLED BY REWARD MONEY AND BRIBES.
Manchester Magistrates' announcement
IT IS ONLY BY OBEDIENCE TO THE LAW THAT YOU CAN PRESERVE TO YOURSELVES THE BLESSINGS OF A FREE CONSTITUTION. FEAR GOD; HONOUR THE KING.
THE ALLEGED 'INSURRECTIONISTS' WERE USUALLY REFORMERS, WHO BELIEVED REPRESENTATION IN PARLIAMENT WAS THE ONLY ROUTE TO CHANGE THAT COULD AVOID VIOLENT CONFLICT.
John Knight, reformer
I BEGAN TO READ ALOUD THE PETITION WE HAD PREPARED, WHEN NADIN ENTERED WITH A BLUNDERBUSS IN HIS HANDS, FOLLOWED BY SOLDIERS WITH THEIR GUNS AND BAYONETS FIXED...
FOR WHAT PURPOSE ARE YOU ASSEMBLED HERE?
OUR OBJECT IS PEACE AND PARLIAMENTARY REFORM
I DO NOT BELIEVE YOU; THAT IS ONLY A PRETENCE.
...HE THEN SEARCHED OUR PERSONS, ORDERED OUR NAMES, OCCUPATIONS AND RESIDENCES TO BE PUT DOWN, OUR HANDS TO BE TIED, AND OURSELVES TO BE TAKEN TO THE NEW BAILEY.

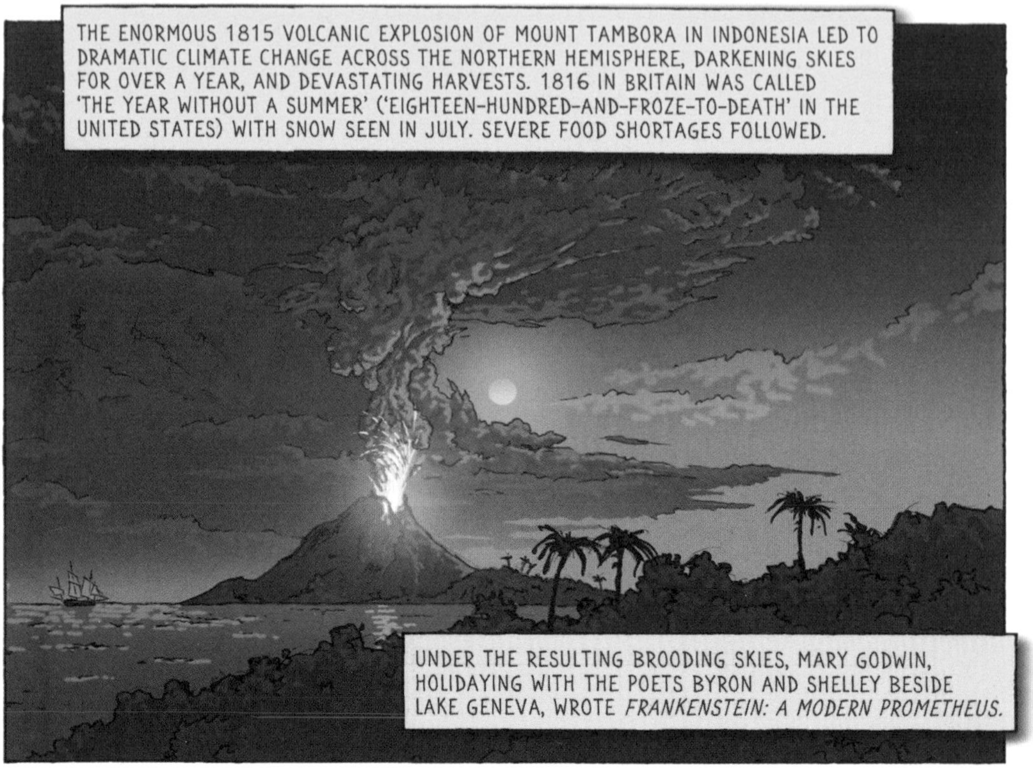
THE ENORMOUS 1815 VOLCANIC EXPLOSION OF MOUNT TAMBORA IN INDONESIA LED TO DRAMATIC CLIMATE CHANGE ACROSS THE NORTHERN HEMISPHERE, DARKENING SKIES FOR OVER A YEAR, AND DEVASTATING HARVESTS. 1816 IN BRITAIN WAS CALLED 'THE YEAR WITHOUT A SUMMER' ('EIGHTEEN-HUNDRED-AND-FROZE-TO-DEATH' IN THE UNITED STATES) WITH SNOW SEEN IN JULY. SEVERE FOOD SHORTAGES FOLLOWED.
UNDER THE RESULTING BROODING SKIES, MARY GODWIN, HOLIDAYING WITH THE POETS BYRON AND SHELLEY BESIDE LAKE GENEVA, WROTE *FRANKENSTEIN: A MODERN PROMETHEUS.*

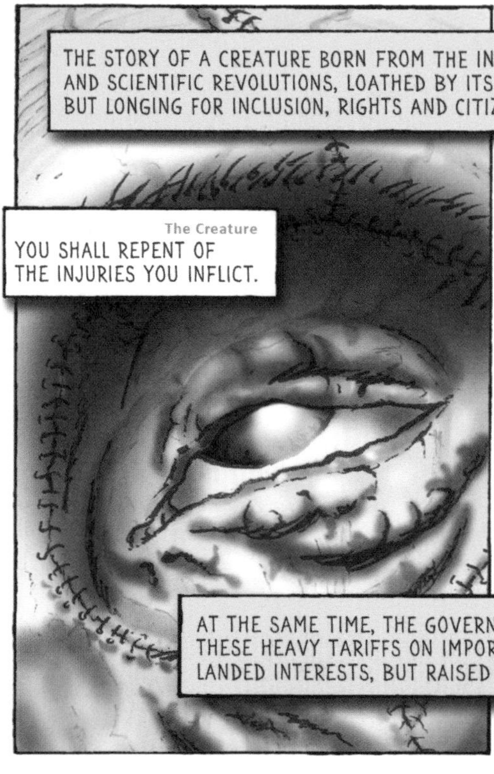
THE STORY OF A CREATURE BORN FROM THE INDUSTRIAL AND SCIENTIFIC REVOLUTIONS, LOATHED BY ITS CREATOR BUT LONGING FOR INCLUSION, RIGHTS AND CITIZENSHIP.
The Creature
YOU SHALL REPENT OF THE INJURIES YOU INFLICT.

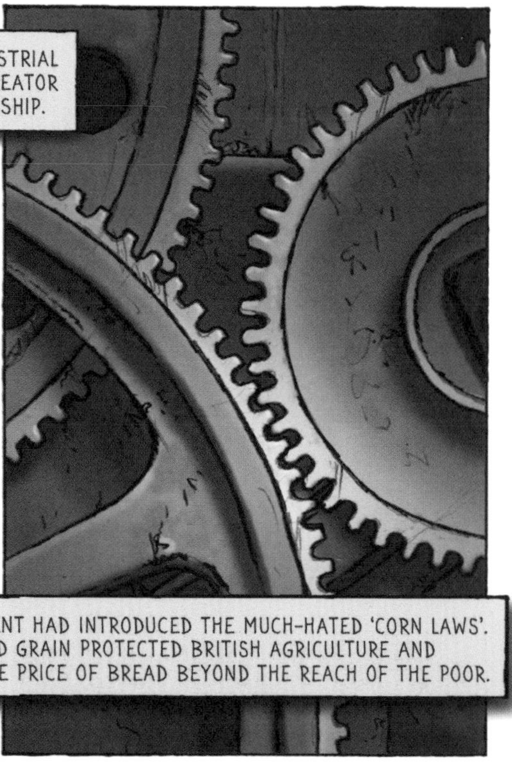
AT THE SAME TIME, THE GOVERNMENT HAD INTRODUCED THE MUCH-HATED 'CORN LAWS'. THESE HEAVY TARIFFS ON IMPORTED GRAIN PROTECTED BRITISH AGRICULTURE AND LANDED INTERESTS, BUT RAISED THE PRICE OF BREAD BEYOND THE REACH OF THE POOR.

THE LONG WARS AGAINST FRANCE SAW AROUND ONE IN FIVE ADULT MALES IN UNIFORM, AS VOLUNTEERS, MILITIA OR REGULARS. THE COST OF THE CONFLICT LED TO AN IMMENSE NATIONAL DEBT, HIGHER TAXES, AND A HUGE STRAIN ON THE 'POOR RELIEF' SYSTEM.

London handbill

FOUR MILLION IN DISTRESS!!!
HALF-A-MILLION LIVE IN SPLENDID LUXURY!!!
DEATH WOULD NOW BE A RELIEF TO MILLIONS!!!
ARROGANCE, FOLLY AND CRIMES HAVE BROUGHT AFFAIRS TO THIS CRISIS!!!

'Advice Addressed to the Lower Ranks of Society'

REMEMBER THAT BY THUS COMING FORWARD TO AID YOUR RICHER SUPERIORS, THEY WILL CONTRACT TO YOU A DEBT OF GRATITUDE, WHICH, AFTER THE CONTEST IS OVER, THEY WILL NOT FAIL TO REPAY.

Petition to the Prince Regent

YOUR POOR SUBJECTS AND FAMILYS THAT HAS SO GALLANTLY FOUGHT FOR YOUR FATHERS FAMILY ALL THIS WAR, AND COME HOME TO THERE NATIVE COUNTRY TO BE STARVED TO DEATH WITH THERE FAMILYS FOR WANT OF BREAD.

Prime Minister to Home Secretary

I SEE NO DIFFICULTY IN YOUR DECLINING TO PRESENT PETITIONS TO HIS MAJESTY. SAY NOTHING ABOUT THEM, UNLESS ASKED, AND IF ASKED, SAY THEY WERE NOT FIT TO BE PRESENTED.

IN JANUARY 1817 THE PRINCE REGENT'S CARRIAGE WAS ATTACKED AS HE RETURNED FROM OPENING PARLIAMENT. A COACH WINDOW WAS SMASHED: SOME SAID BY A BULLET, OTHERS SAID BY A POTATO.

20 YEARS OF WAR ENDED IN 1815 WITH THE BATTLE OF WATERLOO. 350,000 EX-SERVICEMEN GLUTTED ENGLISH LABOUR MARKETS.

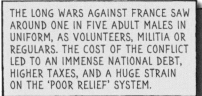

ON THE 10th OF MARCH 1817, 5,000 'BLANKETEER' REFORMERS ATTEMPTED A MARCH TO LONDON FROM ST PETER'S FIELD, MANCHESTER. THEY PLANNED TO PRESENT ANOTHER PETITION DIRECTLY TO THE PRINCE REGENT, IMPLORING HIM TO RELIEVE THEIR POVERTY AND INSTALL A NEW GOVERNMENT. THEY WERE INTERCEPTED ON ROUTE BY SOLDIERS. MASS ARRESTS FILLED THE LOCAL GAOLS.

Samuel Drummond, blanketeer
WE WILL LET THEM SEE IT IS NOT RIOT AND DISTURBANCE WE WANT, IT IS BREAD WE WANT.

IN JUNE 1817, THE MANCHESTER AND SALFORD YEOMANRY CAVALRY WAS CREATED: A PRIVATE MILITIA OF PROPERTIED CITIZENS, CLAIMING TO DEFEND THE TOWNS AGAINST INSURRECTION. IT WAS CAPTAINED BY LOCAL MILL OWNER HUGH HORNBY BIRLEY.

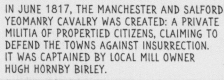

Manchester Observer
A SET OF GREASY PIG-BUTCHERS, ODOROUS TALLOW-CHANDLERS... AND SUNDRY OTHERS NOT A WHIT MORE RESPECTABLE.

Thomas Wooler, journalist
A FEW FOOLS AND A GREATER PROPORTION OF COXCOMBS, WHO IMAGINE THEY ACQUIRE CONSIDERABLE IMPORTANCE BY WEARING REGIMENTALS.

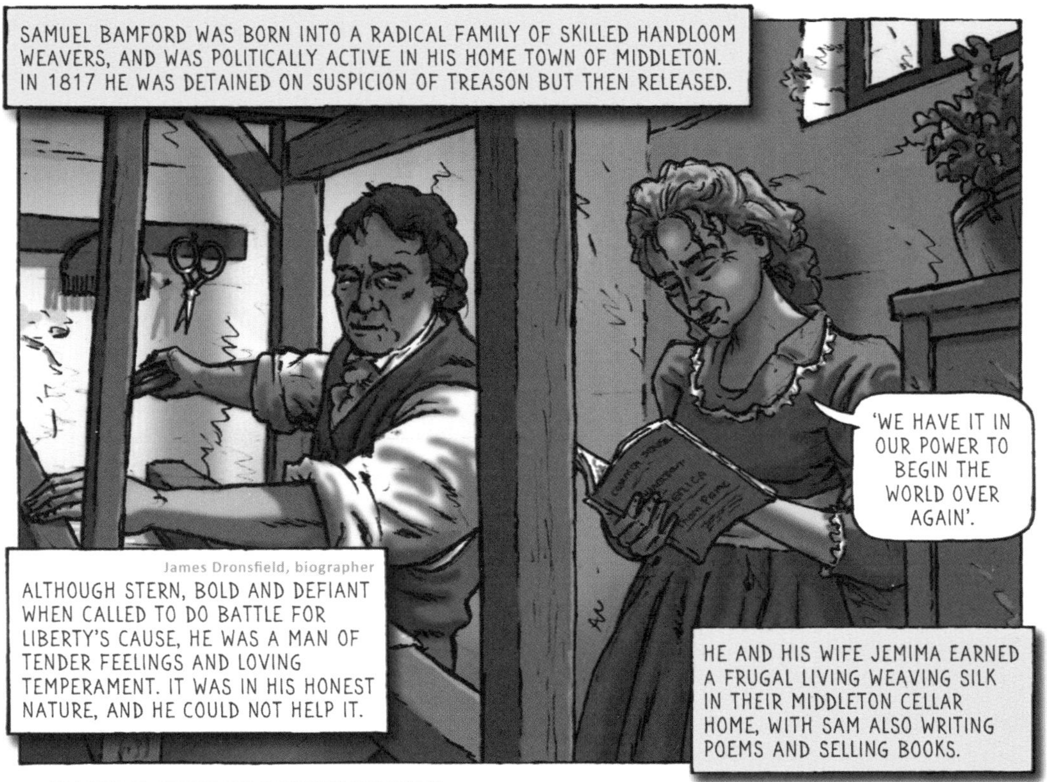
SAMUEL BAMFORD WAS BORN INTO A RADICAL FAMILY OF SKILLED HANDLOOM WEAVERS, AND WAS POLITICALLY ACTIVE IN HIS HOME TOWN OF MIDDLETON. IN 1817 HE WAS DETAINED ON SUSPICION OF TREASON BUT THEN RELEASED.
'WE HAVE IT IN OUR POWER TO BEGIN THE WORLD OVER AGAIN'.
James Dronsfield, biographer
ALTHOUGH STERN, BOLD AND DEFIANT WHEN CALLED TO DO BATTLE FOR LIBERTY'S CAUSE, HE WAS A MAN OF TENDER FEELINGS AND LOVING TEMPERAMENT. IT WAS IN HIS HONEST NATURE, AND HE COULD NOT HELP IT.
HE AND HIS WIFE JEMIMA EARNED A FRUGAL LIVING WEAVING SILK IN THEIR MIDDLETON CELLAR HOME, WITH SAM ALSO WRITING POEMS AND SELLING BOOKS.

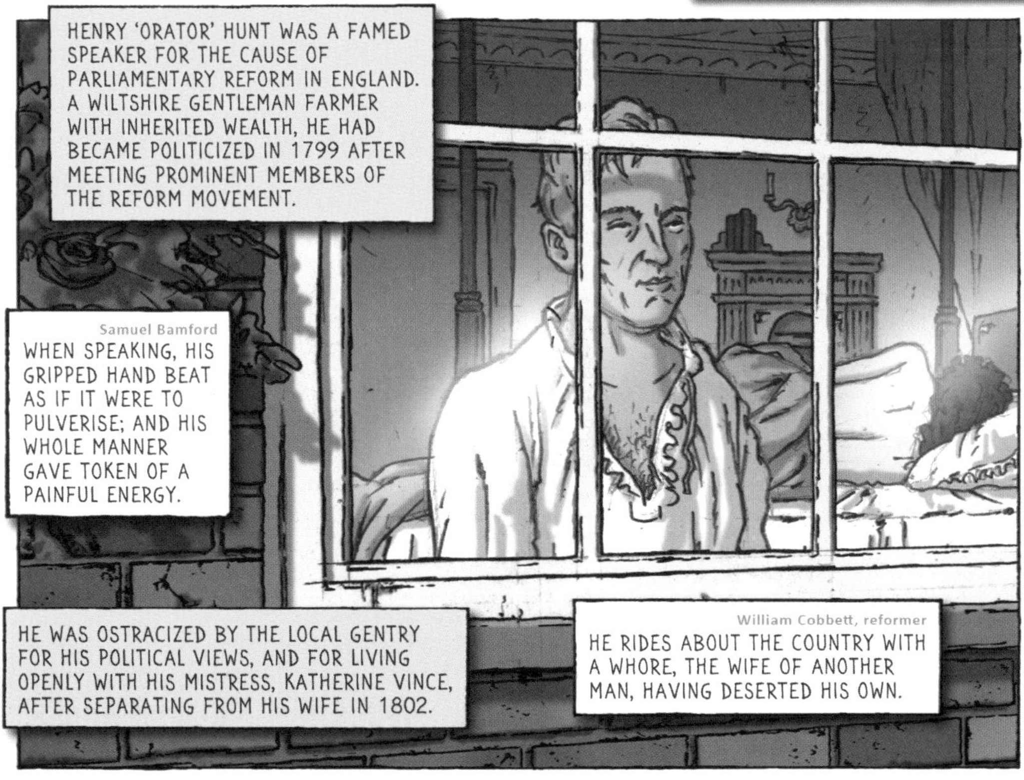
HENRY 'ORATOR' HUNT WAS A FAMED SPEAKER FOR THE CAUSE OF PARLIAMENTARY REFORM IN ENGLAND. A WILTSHIRE GENTLEMAN FARMER WITH INHERITED WEALTH, HE HAD BECAME POLITICIZED IN 1799 AFTER MEETING PROMINENT MEMBERS OF THE REFORM MOVEMENT.
Samuel Bamford
WHEN SPEAKING, HIS GRIPPED HAND BEAT AS IF IT WERE TO PULVERISE; AND HIS WHOLE MANNER GAVE TOKEN OF A PAINFUL ENERGY.
HE WAS OSTRACIZED BY THE LOCAL GENTRY FOR HIS POLITICAL VIEWS, AND FOR LIVING OPENLY WITH HIS MISTRESS, KATHERINE VINCE, AFTER SEPARATING FROM HIS WIFE IN 1802.
William Cobbett, reformer
HE RIDES ABOUT THE COUNTRY WITH A WHORE, THE WIFE OF ANOTHER MAN, HAVING DESERTED HIS OWN.

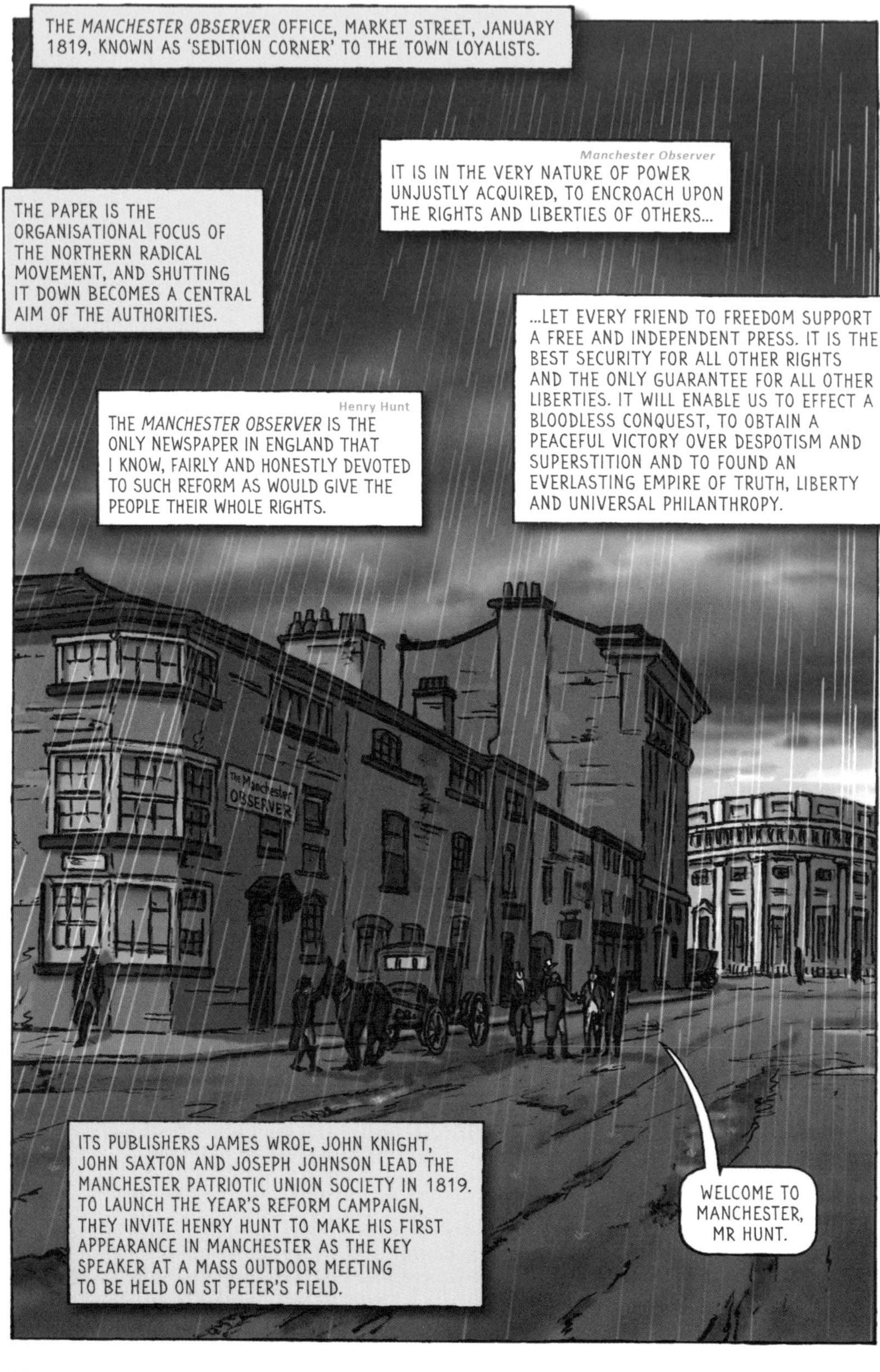
THE *MANCHESTER OBSERVER* OFFICE, MARKET STREET, JANUARY 1819, KNOWN AS 'SEDITION CORNER' TO THE TOWN LOYALISTS.
Manchester Observer
IT IS IN THE VERY NATURE OF POWER UNJUSTLY ACQUIRED, TO ENCROACH UPON THE RIGHTS AND LIBERTIES OF OTHERS...
THE PAPER IS THE ORGANISATIONAL FOCUS OF THE NORTHERN RADICAL MOVEMENT, AND SHUTTING IT DOWN BECOMES A CENTRAL AIM OF THE AUTHORITIES.
...LET EVERY FRIEND TO FREEDOM SUPPORT A FREE AND INDEPENDENT PRESS. IT IS THE BEST SECURITY FOR ALL OTHER RIGHTS AND THE ONLY GUARANTEE FOR ALL OTHER LIBERTIES. IT WILL ENABLE US TO EFFECT A BLOODLESS CONQUEST, TO OBTAIN A PEACEFUL VICTORY OVER DESPOTISM AND SUPERSTITION AND TO FOUND AN EVERLASTING EMPIRE OF TRUTH, LIBERTY AND UNIVERSAL PHILANTHROPY.
Henry Hunt
THE *MANCHESTER OBSERVER* IS THE ONLY NEWSPAPER IN ENGLAND THAT I KNOW, FAIRLY AND HONESTLY DEVOTED TO SUCH REFORM AS WOULD GIVE THE PEOPLE THEIR WHOLE RIGHTS.
The Manchester OBSERVER
ITS PUBLISHERS JAMES WROE, JOHN KNIGHT, JOHN SAXTON AND JOSEPH JOHNSON LEAD THE MANCHESTER PATRIOTIC UNION SOCIETY IN 1819. TO LAUNCH THE YEAR'S REFORM CAMPAIGN, THEY INVITE HENRY HUNT TO MAKE HIS FIRST APPEARANCE IN MANCHESTER AS THE KEY SPEAKER AT A MASS OUTDOOR MEETING TO BE HELD ON ST PETER'S FIELD.
WELCOME TO MANCHESTER, MR HUNT.

II

If we give him
much more
he'll die.

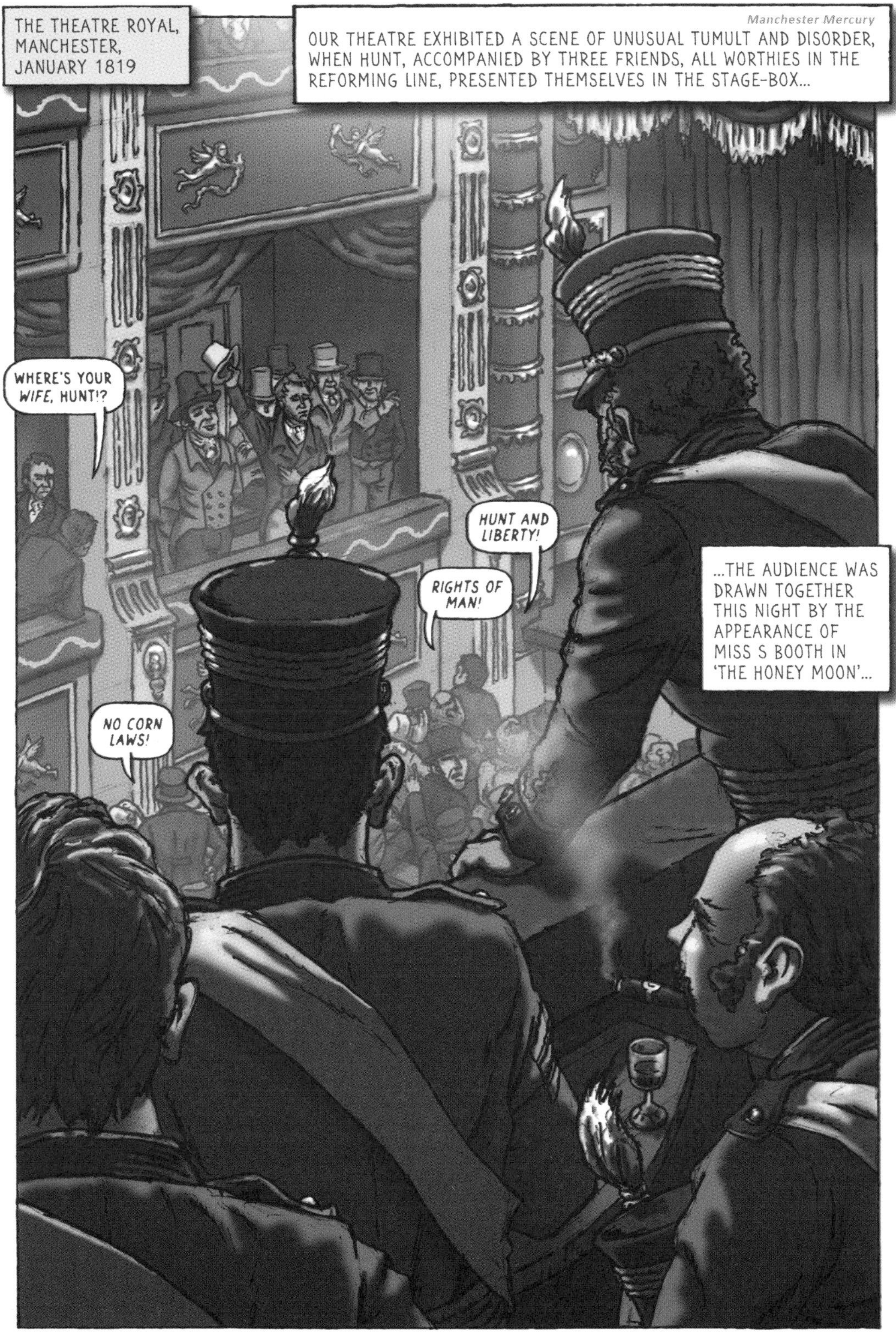
THE THEATRE ROYAL, MANCHESTER, JANUARY 1819
Manchester Mercury
OUR THEATRE EXHIBITED A SCENE OF UNUSUAL TUMULT AND DISORDER, WHEN HUNT, ACCOMPANIED BY THREE FRIENDS, ALL WORTHIES IN THE REFORMING LINE, PRESENTED THEMSELVES IN THE STAGE-BOX...
WHERE'S YOUR WIFE, HUNT!?
HUNT AND LIBERTY!
RIGHTS OF MAN!
NO CORN LAWS!
...THE AUDIENCE WAS DRAWN TOGETHER THIS NIGHT BY THE APPEARANCE OF MISS S BOOTH IN 'THE HONEY MOON'...

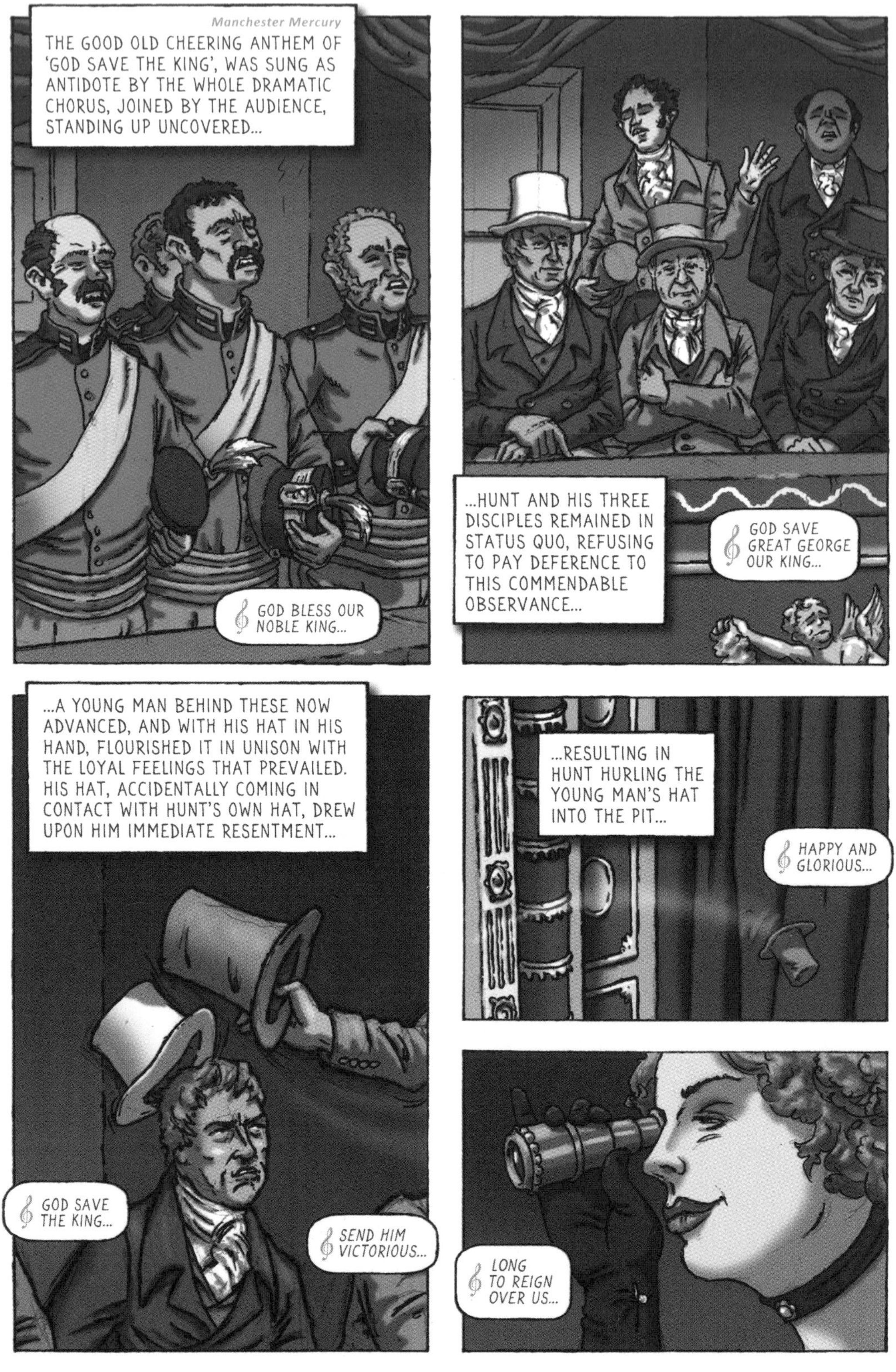
Manchester Mercury
THE GOOD OLD CHEERING ANTHEM OF 'GOD SAVE THE KING', WAS SUNG AS ANTIDOTE BY THE WHOLE DRAMATIC CHORUS, JOINED BY THE AUDIENCE, STANDING UP UNCOVERED...
GOD BLESS OUR NOBLE KING...
...HUNT AND HIS THREE DISCIPLES REMAINED IN STATUS QUO, REFUSING TO PAY DEFERENCE TO THIS COMMENDABLE OBSERVANCE...
GOD SAVE GREAT GEORGE OUR KING...
...A YOUNG MAN BEHIND THESE NOW ADVANCED, AND WITH HIS HAT IN HIS HAND, FLOURISHED IT IN UNISON WITH THE LOYAL FEELINGS THAT PREVAILED. HIS HAT, ACCIDENTALLY COMING IN CONTACT WITH HUNT'S OWN HAT, DREW UPON HIM IMMEDIATE RESENTMENT...
GOD SAVE THE KING...
SEND HIM VICTORIOUS...
...RESULTING IN HUNT HURLING THE YOUNG MAN'S HAT INTO THE PIT...
HAPPY AND GLORIOUS...
LONG TO REIGN OVER US...

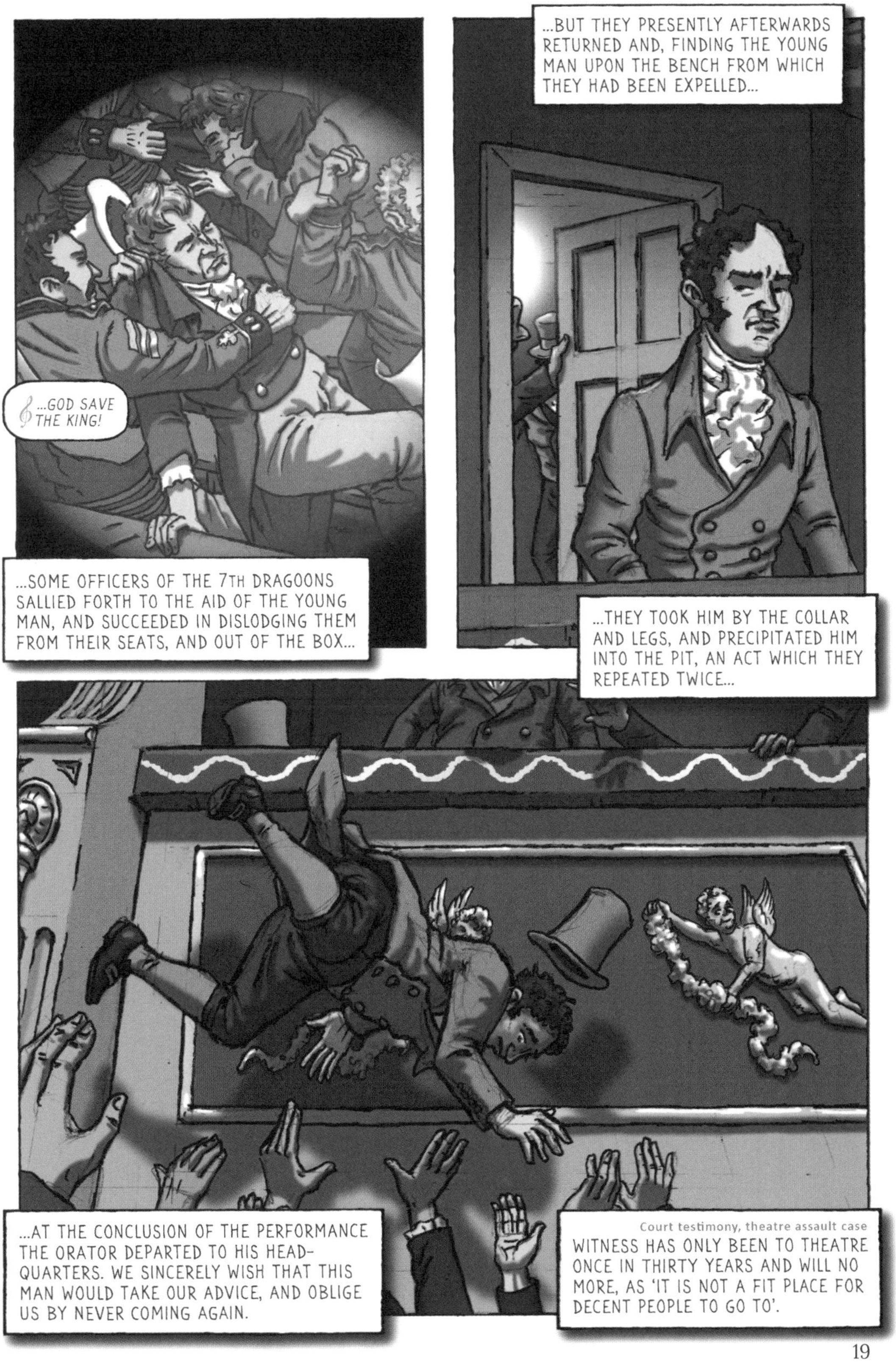
...GOD SAVE THE KING!
...SOME OFFICERS OF THE 7TH DRAGOONS SALLIED FORTH TO THE AID OF THE YOUNG MAN, AND SUCCEEDED IN DISLODGING THEM FROM THEIR SEATS, AND OUT OF THE BOX...
...BUT THEY PRESENTLY AFTERWARDS RETURNED AND, FINDING THE YOUNG MAN UPON THE BENCH FROM WHICH THEY HAD BEEN EXPELLED...
...THEY TOOK HIM BY THE COLLAR AND LEGS, AND PRECIPITATED HIM INTO THE PIT, AN ACT WHICH THEY REPEATED TWICE...
...AT THE CONCLUSION OF THE PERFORMANCE THE ORATOR DEPARTED TO HIS HEAD-QUARTERS. WE SINCERELY WISH THAT THIS MAN WOULD TAKE OUR ADVICE, AND OBLIGE US BY NEVER COMING AGAIN.
Court testimony, theatre assault case
WITNESS HAS ONLY BEEN TO THEATRE ONCE IN THIRTY YEARS AND WILL NO MORE, AS 'IT IS NOT A FIT PLACE FOR DECENT PEOPLE TO GO TO'.

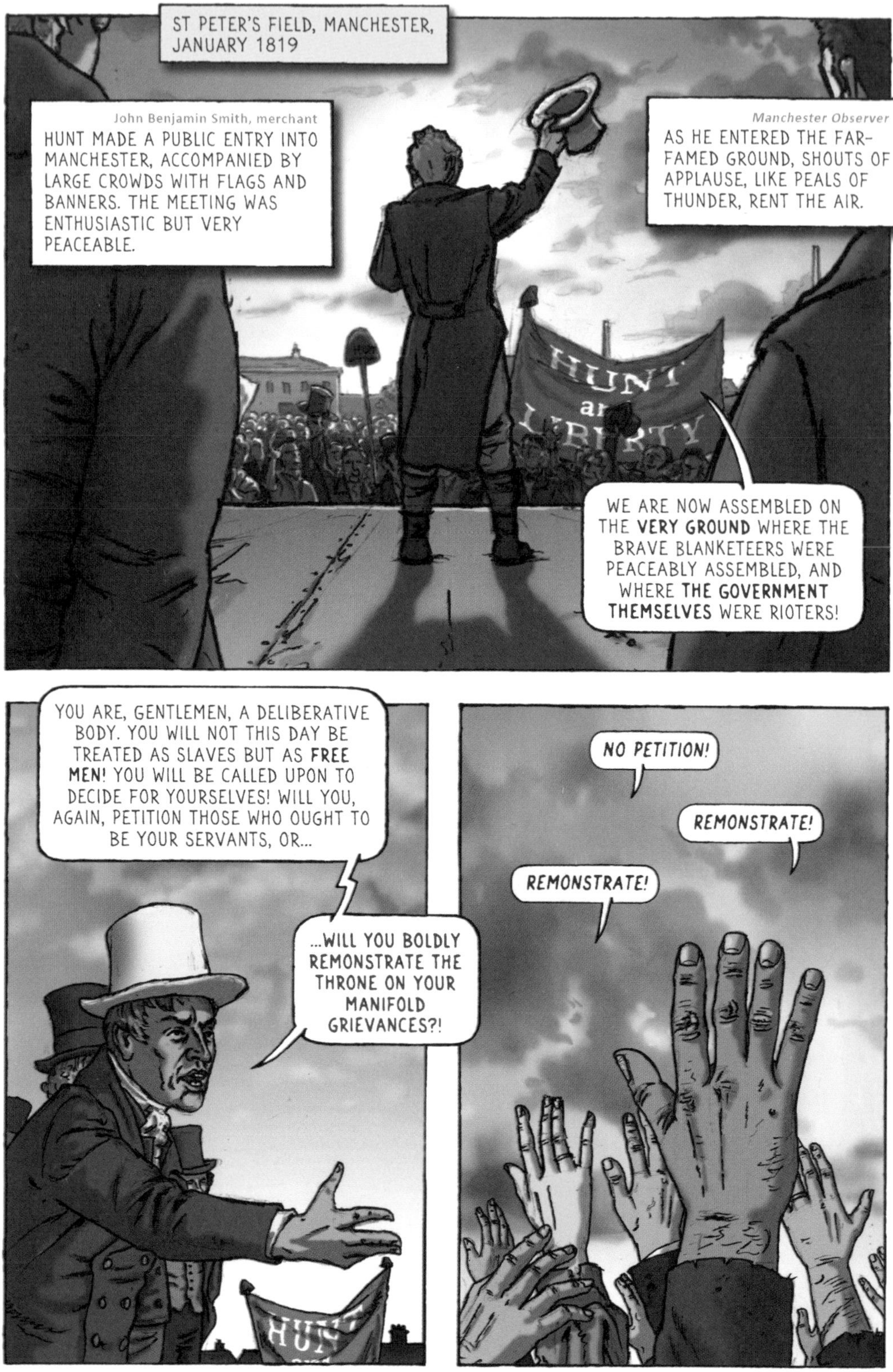
ST PETER'S FIELD, MANCHESTER, JANUARY 1819
John Benjamin Smith, merchant
HUNT MADE A PUBLIC ENTRY INTO MANCHESTER, ACCOMPANIED BY LARGE CROWDS WITH FLAGS AND BANNERS. THE MEETING WAS ENTHUSIASTIC BUT VERY PEACEABLE.
Manchester Observer
AS HE ENTERED THE FAR-FAMED GROUND, SHOUTS OF APPLAUSE, LIKE PEALS OF THUNDER, RENT THE AIR.
WE ARE NOW ASSEMBLED ON THE **VERY GROUND** WHERE THE BRAVE BLANKETEERS WERE PEACEABLY ASSEMBLED, AND WHERE **THE GOVERNMENT THEMSELVES** WERE RIOTERS!
YOU ARE, GENTLEMEN, A DELIBERATIVE BODY. YOU WILL NOT THIS DAY BE TREATED AS SLAVES BUT AS **FREE MEN**! YOU WILL BE CALLED UPON TO DECIDE FOR YOURSELVES! WILL YOU, AGAIN, PETITION THOSE WHO OUGHT TO BE YOUR SERVANTS, OR...
...WILL YOU BOLDLY REMONSTRATE THE THRONE ON YOUR MANIFOLD GRIEVANCES?!
NO PETITION!
REMONSTRATE!
REMONSTRATE!

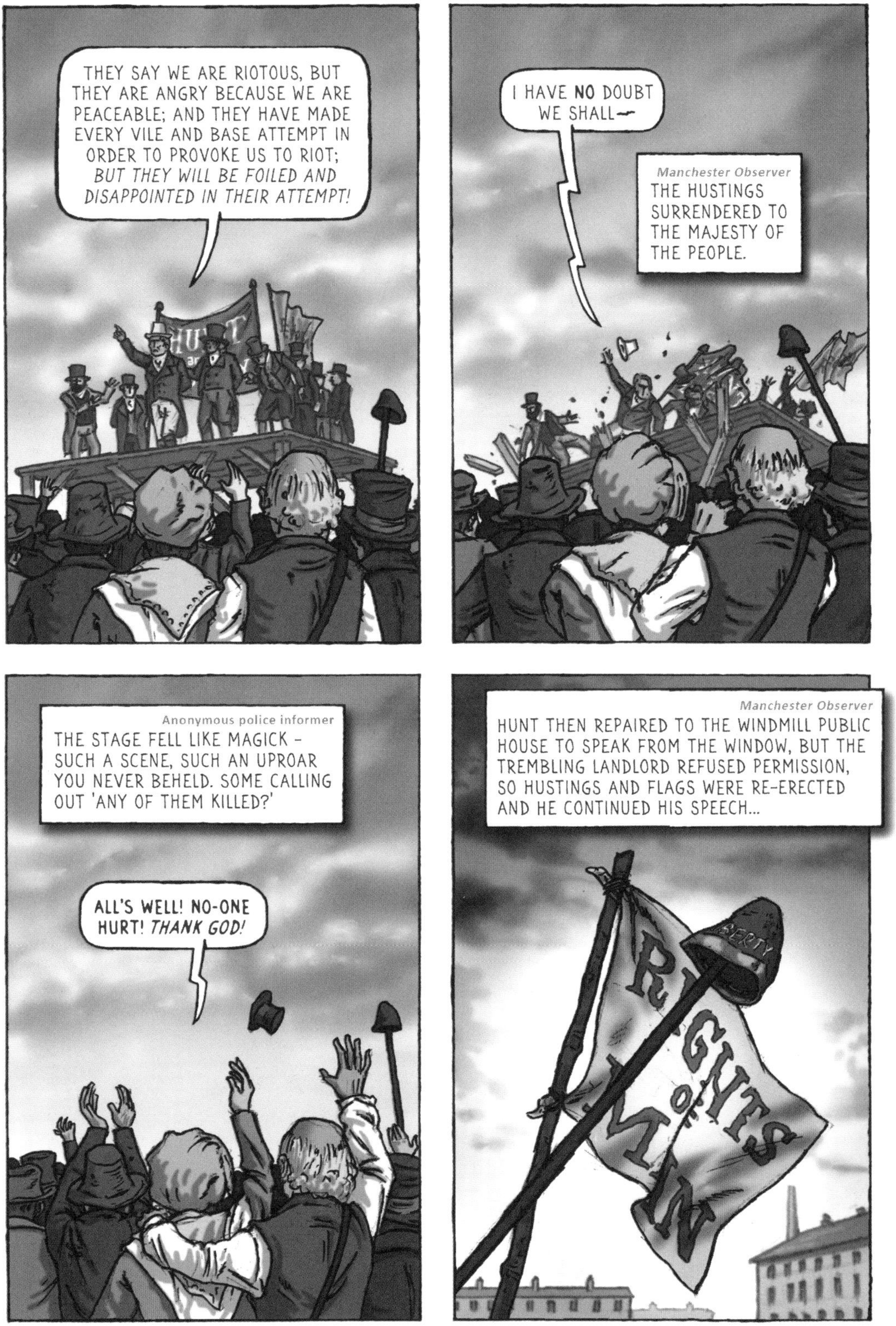
THEY SAY WE ARE RIOTOUS, BUT THEY ARE ANGRY BECAUSE WE ARE PEACEABLE; AND THEY HAVE MADE EVERY VILE AND BASE ATTEMPT IN ORDER TO PROVOKE US TO RIOT; *BUT THEY WILL BE FOILED AND DISAPPOINTED IN THEIR ATTEMPT!*
I HAVE **NO** DOUBT WE SHALL—
Manchester Observer
THE HUSTINGS SURRENDERED TO THE MAJESTY OF THE PEOPLE.
Anonymous police informer
THE STAGE FELL LIKE MAGICK - SUCH A SCENE, SUCH AN UPROAR YOU NEVER BEHELD. SOME CALLING OUT 'ANY OF THEM KILLED?'
ALL'S WELL! NO-ONE HURT! *THANK GOD!*
Manchester Observer
HUNT THEN REPAIRED TO THE WINDMILL PUBLIC HOUSE TO SPEAK FROM THE WINDOW, BUT THE TREMBLING LANDLORD REFUSED PERMISSION, SO HUSTINGS AND FLAGS WERE RE-ERECTED AND HE CONTINUED HIS SPEECH...

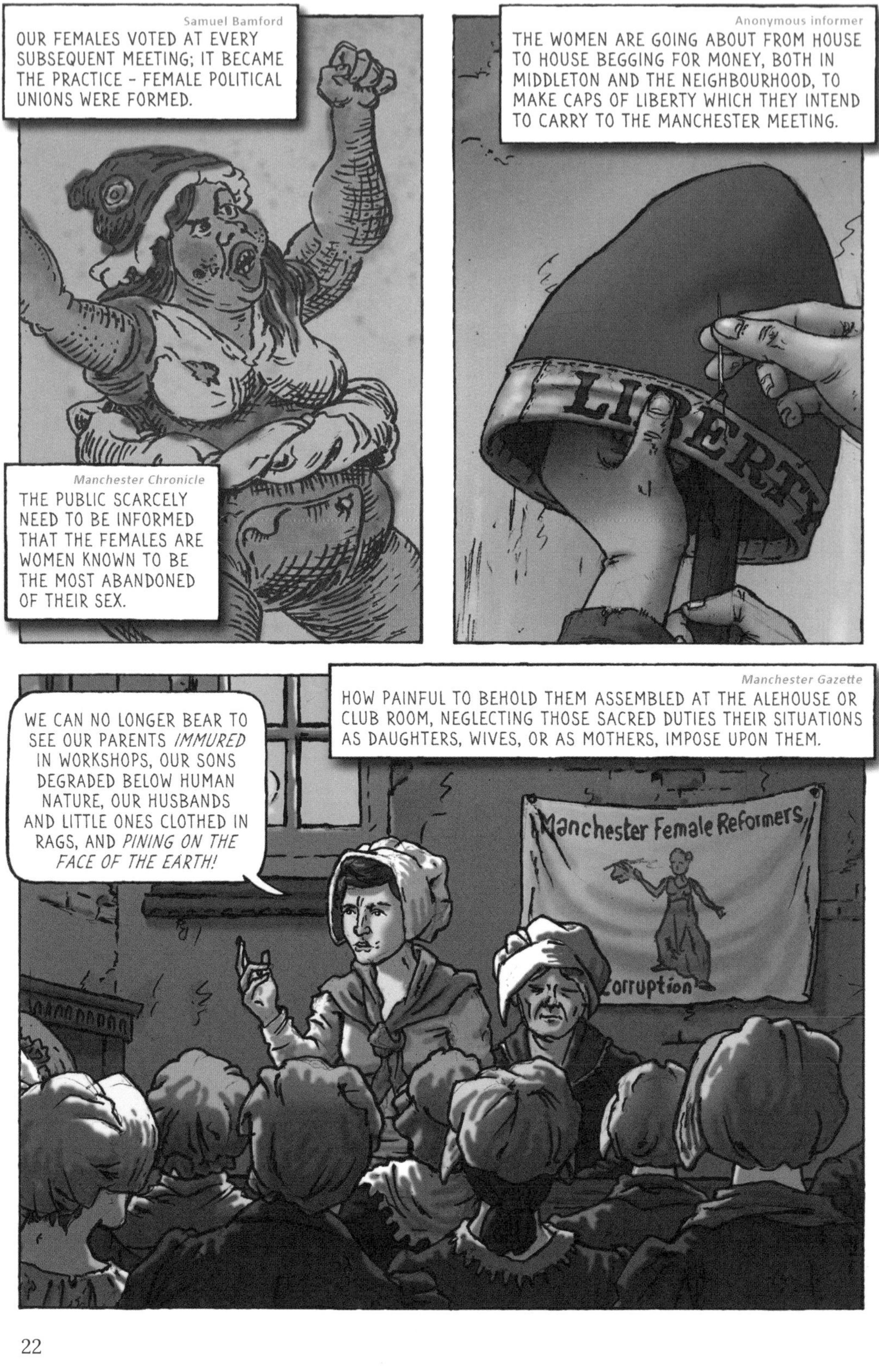
Samuel Bamford
OUR FEMALES VOTED AT EVERY SUBSEQUENT MEETING; IT BECAME THE PRACTICE – FEMALE POLITICAL UNIONS WERE FORMED.
Manchester Chronicle
THE PUBLIC SCARCELY NEED TO BE INFORMED THAT THE FEMALES ARE WOMEN KNOWN TO BE THE MOST ABANDONED OF THEIR SEX.
Anonymous informer
THE WOMEN ARE GOING ABOUT FROM HOUSE TO HOUSE BEGGING FOR MONEY, BOTH IN MIDDLETON AND THE NEIGHBOURHOOD, TO MAKE CAPS OF LIBERTY WHICH THEY INTEND TO CARRY TO THE MANCHESTER MEETING.
LIBERTY
Manchester Gazette
HOW PAINFUL TO BEHOLD THEM ASSEMBLED AT THE ALEHOUSE OR CLUB ROOM, NEGLECTING THOSE SACRED DUTIES THEIR SITUATIONS AS DAUGHTERS, WIVES, OR AS MOTHERS, IMPOSE UPON THEM.
WE CAN NO LONGER BEAR TO SEE OUR PARENTS *IMMURED* IN WORKSHOPS, OUR SONS DEGRADED BELOW HUMAN NATURE, OUR HUSBANDS AND LITTLE ONES CLOTHED IN RAGS, AND *PINING ON THE FACE OF THE EARTH!*
Manchester Female Reformers,
Corruption

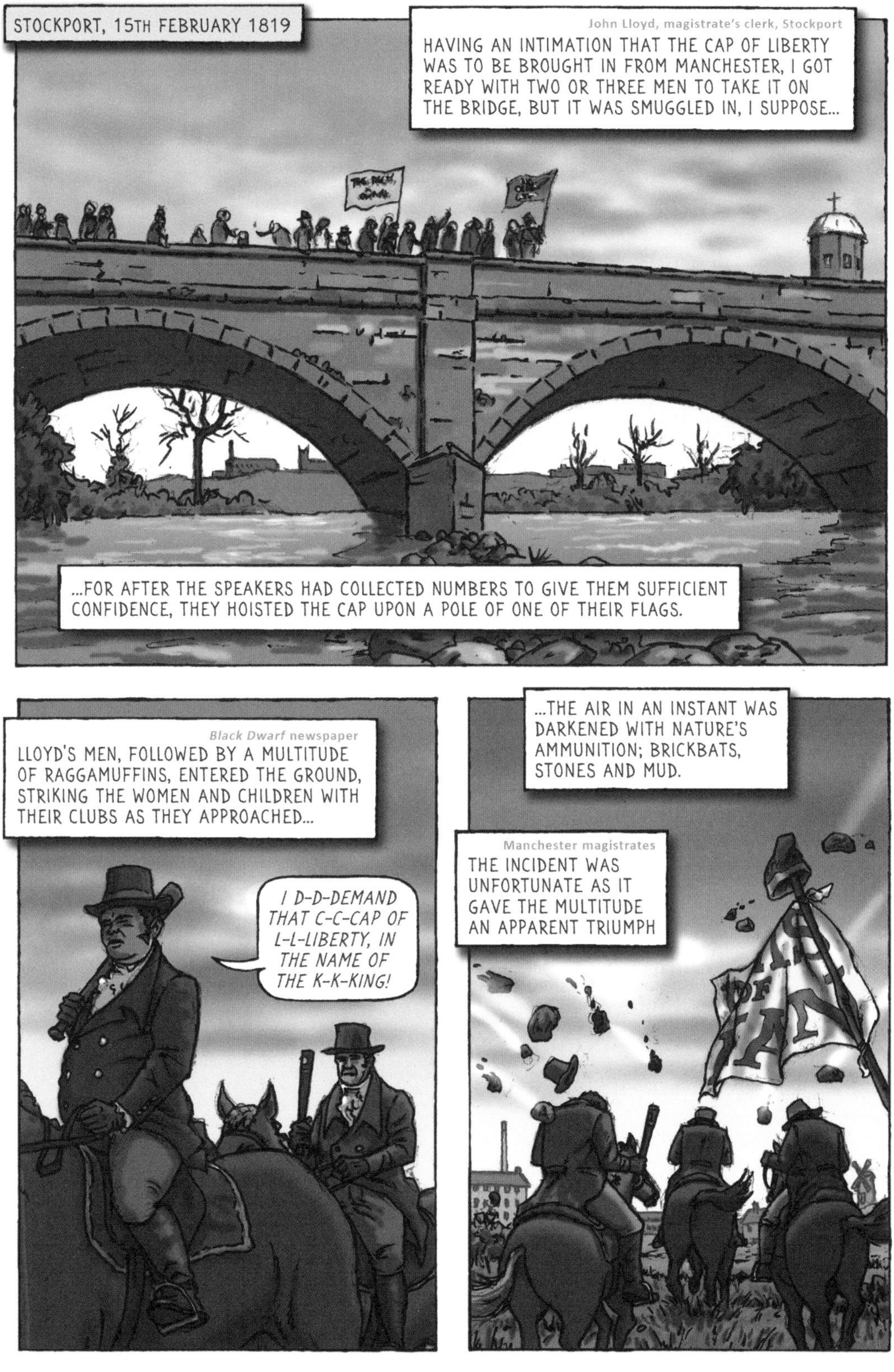
STOCKPORT, 15TH FEBRUARY 1819
John Lloyd, magistrate's clerk, Stockport
HAVING AN INTIMATION THAT THE CAP OF LIBERTY WAS TO BE BROUGHT IN FROM MANCHESTER, I GOT READY WITH TWO OR THREE MEN TO TAKE IT ON THE BRIDGE, BUT IT WAS SMUGGLED IN, I SUPPOSE...
...FOR AFTER THE SPEAKERS HAD COLLECTED NUMBERS TO GIVE THEM SUFFICIENT CONFIDENCE, THEY HOISTED THE CAP UPON A POLE OF ONE OF THEIR FLAGS.
Black Dwarf newspaper
LLOYD'S MEN, FOLLOWED BY A MULTITUDE OF RAGGAMUFFINS, ENTERED THE GROUND, STRIKING THE WOMEN AND CHILDREN WITH THEIR CLUBS AS THEY APPROACHED...
I D-D-DEMAND THAT C-C-CAP OF L-L-LIBERTY, IN THE NAME OF THE K-K-KING!
...THE AIR IN AN INSTANT WAS DARKENED WITH NATURE'S AMMUNITION; BRICKBATS, STONES AND MUD.
Manchester magistrates
THE INCIDENT WAS UNFORTUNATE AS IT GAVE THE MULTITUDE AN APPARENT TRIUMPH

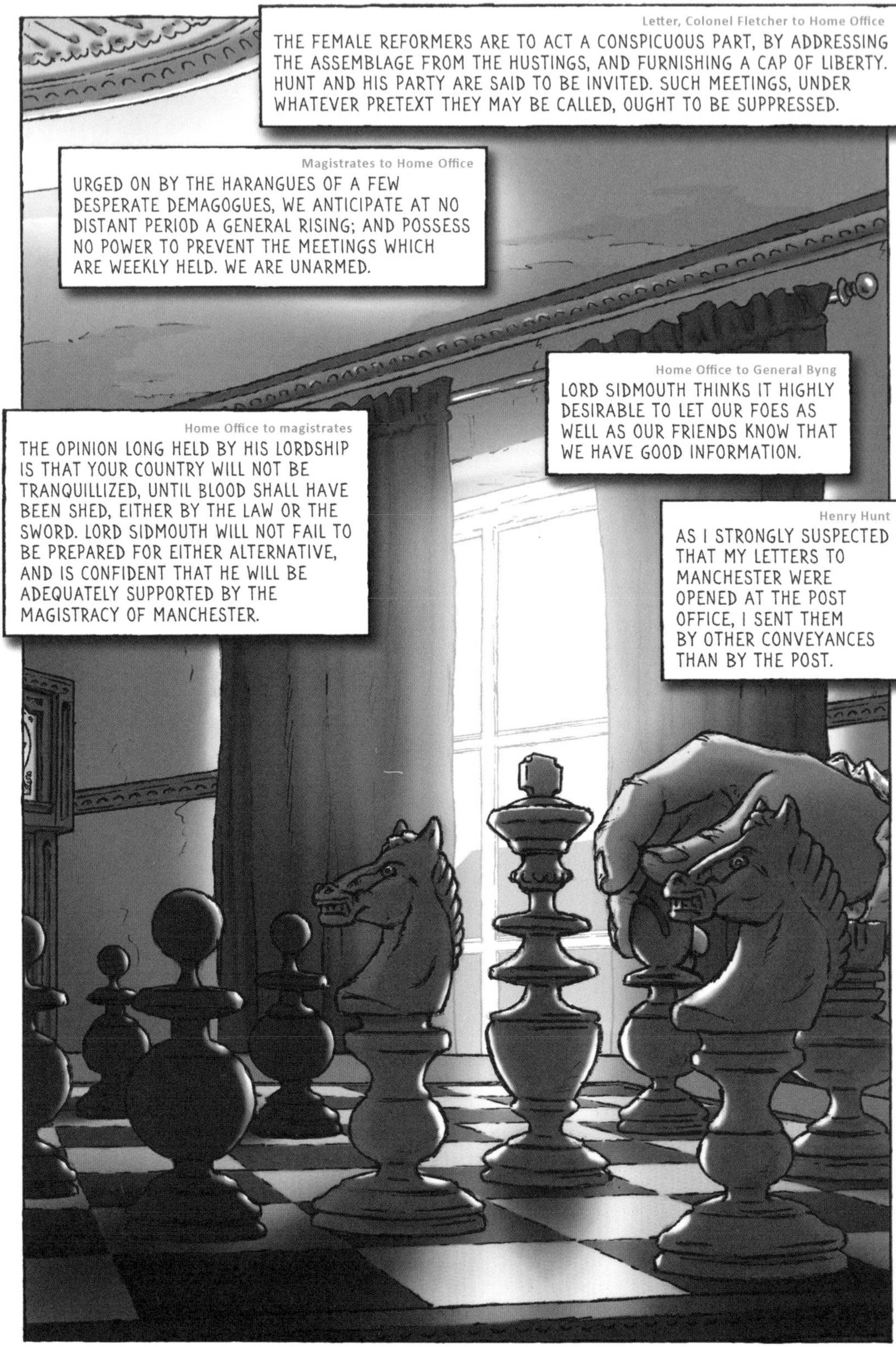
Letter, Colonel Fletcher to Home Office
THE FEMALE REFORMERS ARE TO ACT A CONSPICUOUS PART, BY ADDRESSING THE ASSEMBLAGE FROM THE HUSTINGS, AND FURNISHING A CAP OF LIBERTY. HUNT AND HIS PARTY ARE SAID TO BE INVITED. SUCH MEETINGS, UNDER WHATEVER PRETEXT THEY MAY BE CALLED, OUGHT TO BE SUPPRESSED.
Magistrates to Home Office
URGED ON BY THE HARANGUES OF A FEW DESPERATE DEMAGOGUES, WE ANTICIPATE AT NO DISTANT PERIOD A GENERAL RISING; AND POSSESS NO POWER TO PREVENT THE MEETINGS WHICH ARE WEEKLY HELD. WE ARE UNARMED.
Home Office to General Byng
LORD SIDMOUTH THINKS IT HIGHLY DESIRABLE TO LET OUR FOES AS WELL AS OUR FRIENDS KNOW THAT WE HAVE GOOD INFORMATION.
Home Office to magistrates
THE OPINION LONG HELD BY HIS LORDSHIP IS THAT YOUR COUNTRY WILL NOT BE TRANQUILLIZED, UNTIL BLOOD SHALL HAVE BEEN SHED, EITHER BY THE LAW OR THE SWORD. LORD SIDMOUTH WILL NOT FAIL TO BE PREPARED FOR EITHER ALTERNATIVE, AND IS CONFIDENT THAT HE WILL BE ADEQUATELY SUPPORTED BY THE MAGISTRACY OF MANCHESTER.
Henry Hunt
AS I STRONGLY SUSPECTED THAT MY LETTERS TO MANCHESTER WERE OPENED AT THE POST OFFICE, I SENT THEM BY OTHER CONVEYANCES THAN BY THE POST.

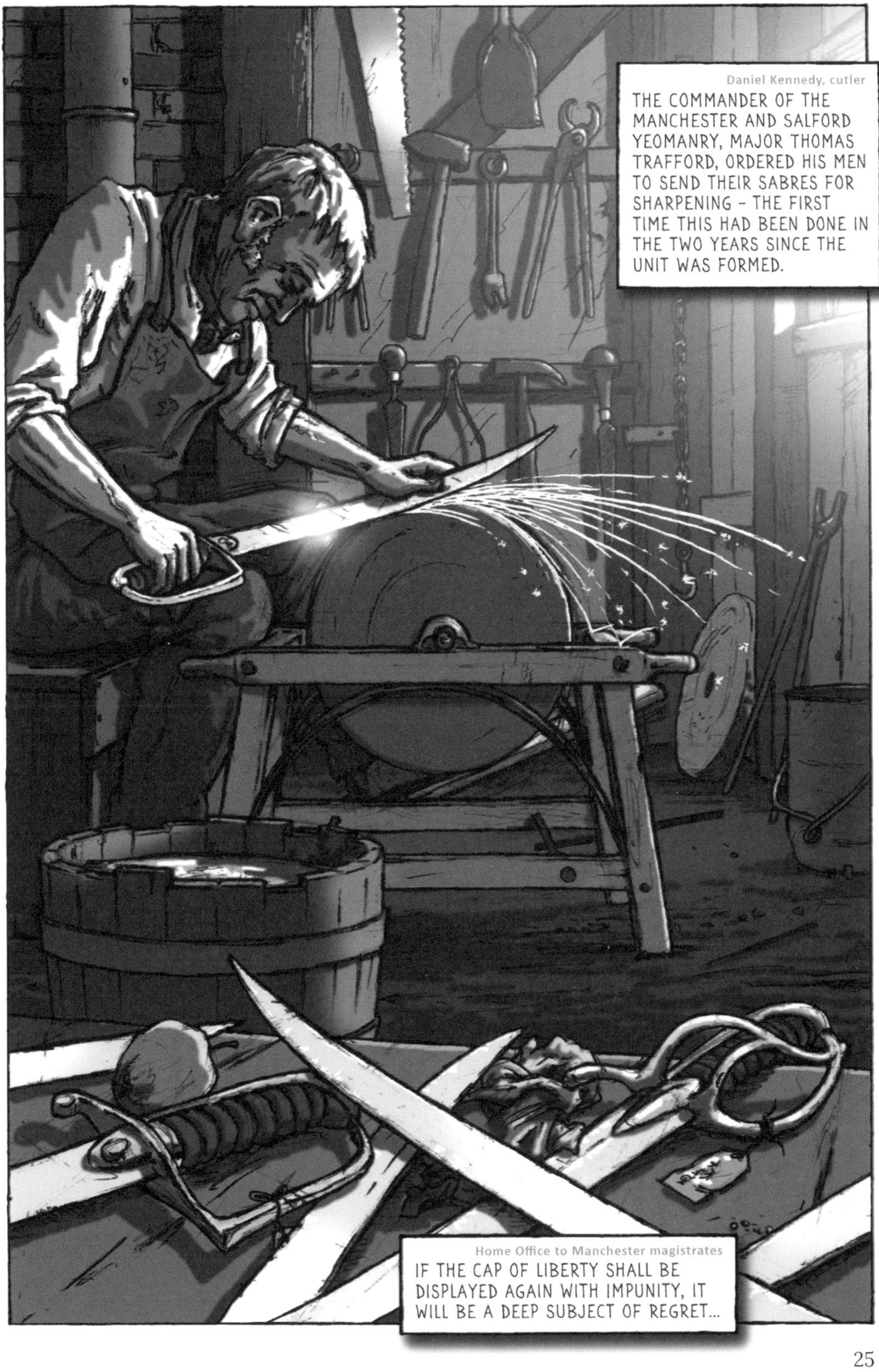
Daniel Kennedy, cutler
THE COMMANDER OF THE MANCHESTER AND SALFORD YEOMANRY, MAJOR THOMAS TRAFFORD, ORDERED HIS MEN TO SEND THEIR SABRES FOR SHARPENING - THE FIRST TIME THIS HAD BEEN DONE IN THE TWO YEARS SINCE THE UNIT WAS FORMED.
Home Office to Manchester magistrates
IF THE CAP OF LIBERTY SHALL BE DISPLAYED AGAIN WITH IMPUNITY, IT WILL BE A DEEP SUBJECT OF REGRET...

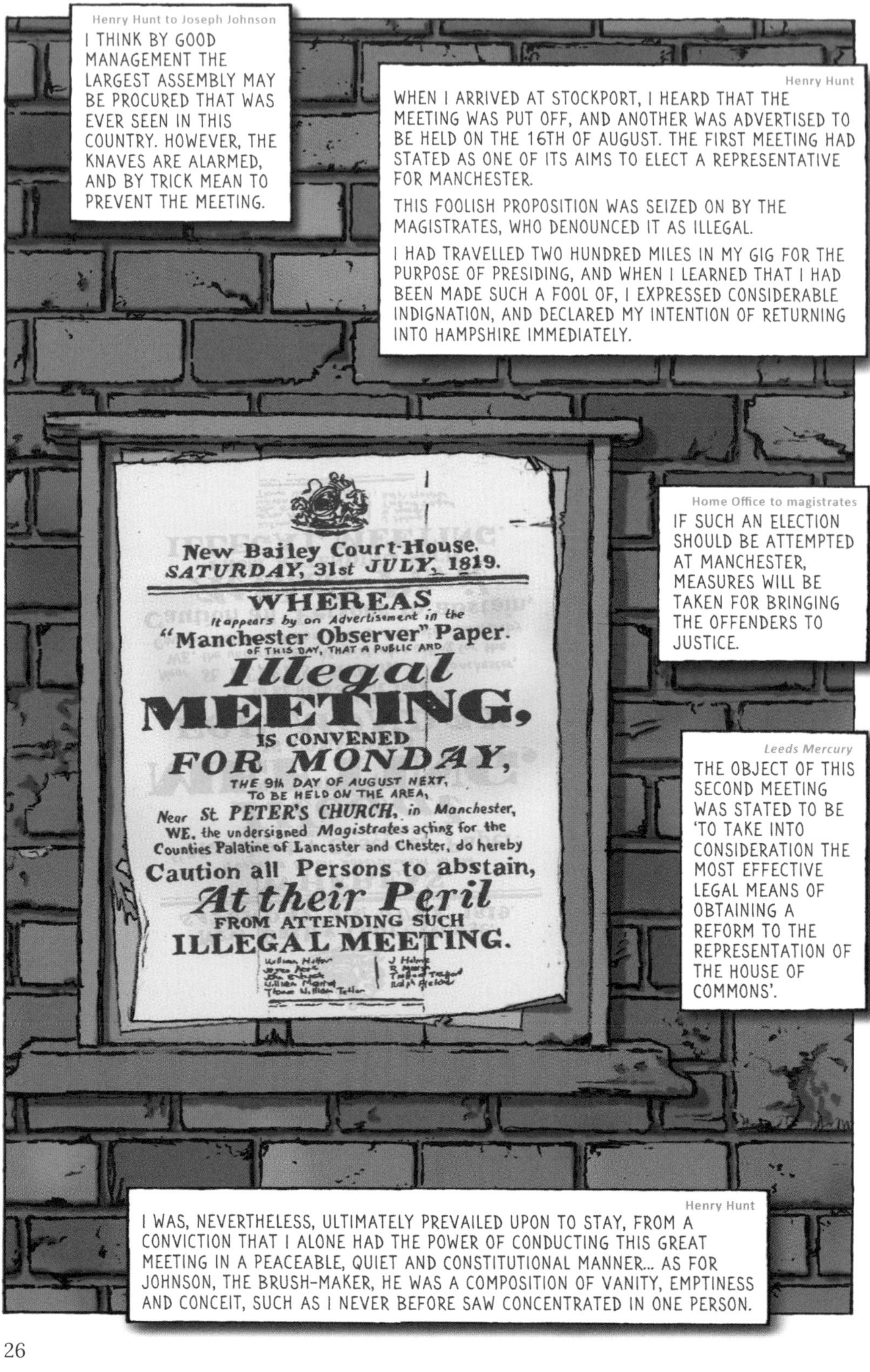
Henry Hunt to Joseph Johnson
I THINK BY GOOD MANAGEMENT THE LARGEST ASSEMBLY MAY BE PROCURED THAT WAS EVER SEEN IN THIS COUNTRY. HOWEVER, THE KNAVES ARE ALARMED, AND BY TRICK MEAN TO PREVENT THE MEETING.
Henry Hunt
WHEN I ARRIVED AT STOCKPORT, I HEARD THAT THE MEETING WAS PUT OFF, AND ANOTHER WAS ADVERTISED TO BE HELD ON THE 16TH OF AUGUST. THE FIRST MEETING HAD STATED AS ONE OF ITS AIMS TO ELECT A REPRESENTATIVE FOR MANCHESTER.
THIS FOOLISH PROPOSITION WAS SEIZED ON BY THE MAGISTRATES, WHO DENOUNCED IT AS ILLEGAL.
I HAD TRAVELLED TWO HUNDRED MILES IN MY GIG FOR THE PURPOSE OF PRESIDING, AND WHEN I LEARNED THAT I HAD BEEN MADE SUCH A FOOL OF, I EXPRESSED CONSIDERABLE INDIGNATION, AND DECLARED MY INTENTION OF RETURNING INTO HAMPSHIRE IMMEDIATELY.
New Bailey Court-House,
SATURDAY, 31st JULY, 1819.
WHEREAS
It appears by an Advertisement in the
"Manchester Observer" Paper.
OF THIS DAY, THAT A PUBLIC AND
Illegal
MEETING,
IS CONVENED
FOR MONDAY,
THE 9th DAY OF AUGUST NEXT,
TO BE HELD ON THE AREA,
Near St. PETER'S CHURCH, in Manchester,
WE, the undersigned Magistrates acting for the Counties Palatine of Lancaster and Chester, do hereby
Caution all Persons to abstain,
At their Peril
FROM ATTENDING SUCH
ILLEGAL MEETING.
Home Office to magistrates
IF SUCH AN ELECTION SHOULD BE ATTEMPTED AT MANCHESTER, MEASURES WILL BE TAKEN FOR BRINGING THE OFFENDERS TO JUSTICE.
Leeds Mercury
THE OBJECT OF THIS SECOND MEETING WAS STATED TO BE 'TO TAKE INTO CONSIDERATION THE MOST EFFECTIVE LEGAL MEANS OF OBTAINING A REFORM TO THE REPRESENTATION OF THE HOUSE OF COMMONS'.
Henry Hunt
I WAS, NEVERTHELESS, ULTIMATELY PREVAILED UPON TO STAY, FROM A CONVICTION THAT I ALONE HAD THE POWER OF CONDUCTING THIS GREAT MEETING IN A PEACEABLE, QUIET AND CONSTITUTIONAL MANNER... AS FOR JOHNSON, THE BRUSH-MAKER, HE WAS A COMPOSITION OF VANITY, EMPTINESS AND CONCEIT, SUCH AS I NEVER BEFORE SAW CONCENTRATED IN ONE PERSON.

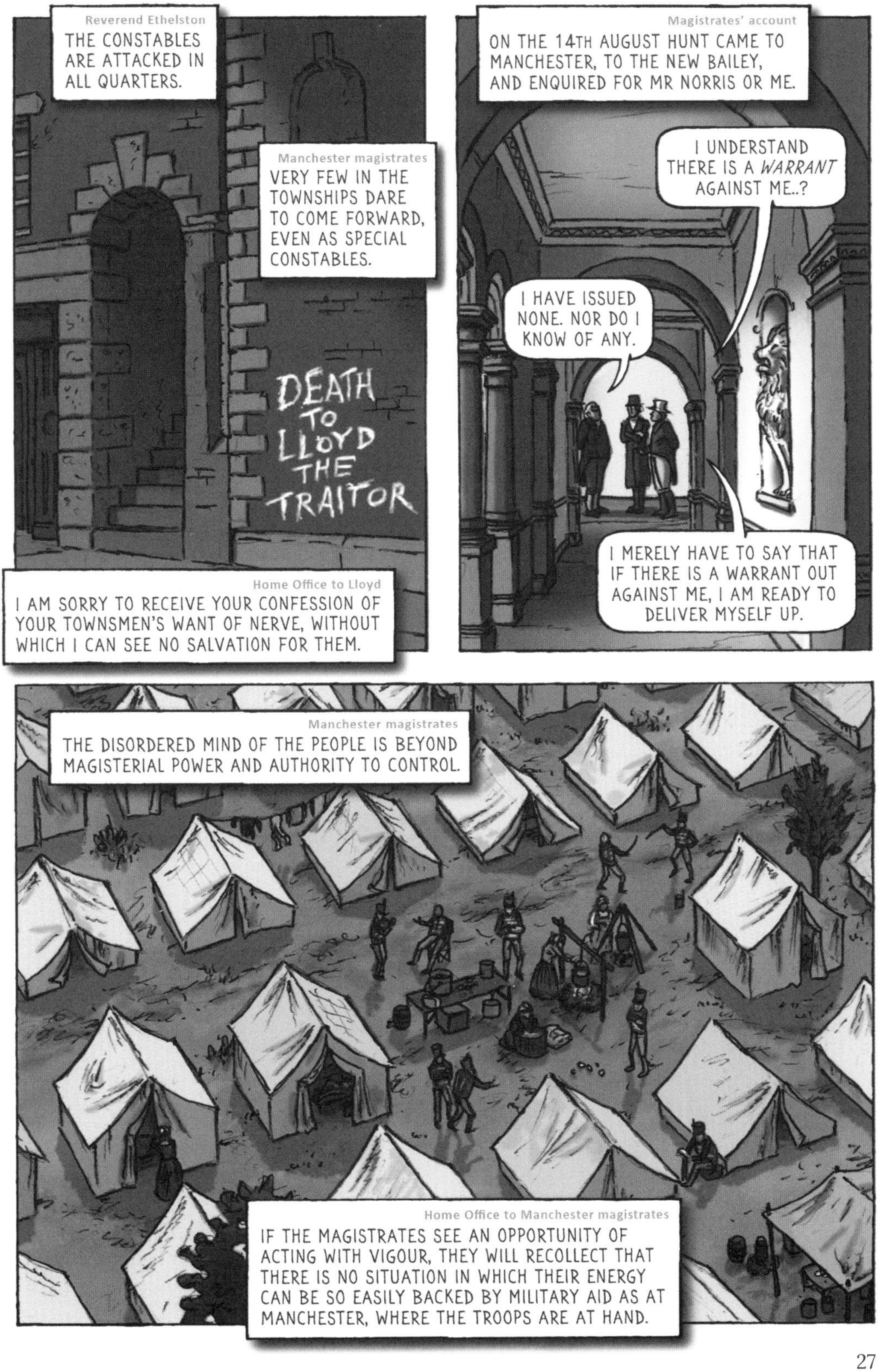
Reverend Ethelston
THE CONSTABLES ARE ATTACKED IN ALL QUARTERS.
Manchester magistrates
VERY FEW IN THE TOWNSHIPS DARE TO COME FORWARD, EVEN AS SPECIAL CONSTABLES.
DEATH TO LLOYD THE TRAITOR
Home Office to Lloyd
I AM SORRY TO RECEIVE YOUR CONFESSION OF YOUR TOWNSMEN'S WANT OF NERVE, WITHOUT WHICH I CAN SEE NO SALVATION FOR THEM.
Magistrates' account
ON THE 14TH AUGUST HUNT CAME TO MANCHESTER, TO THE NEW BAILEY, AND ENQUIRED FOR MR NORRIS OR ME.
I UNDERSTAND THERE IS A *WARRANT* AGAINST ME..?
I HAVE ISSUED NONE. NOR DO I KNOW OF ANY.
I MERELY HAVE TO SAY THAT IF THERE IS A WARRANT OUT AGAINST ME, I AM READY TO DELIVER MYSELF UP.
Manchester magistrates
THE DISORDERED MIND OF THE PEOPLE IS BEYOND MAGISTERIAL POWER AND AUTHORITY TO CONTROL.
Home Office to Manchester magistrates
IF THE MAGISTRATES SEE AN OPPORTUNITY OF ACTING WITH VIGOUR, THEY WILL RECOLLECT THAT THERE IS NO SITUATION IN WHICH THEIR ENERGY CAN BE SO EASILY BACKED BY MILITARY AID AS AT MANCHESTER, WHERE THE TROOPS ARE AT HAND.

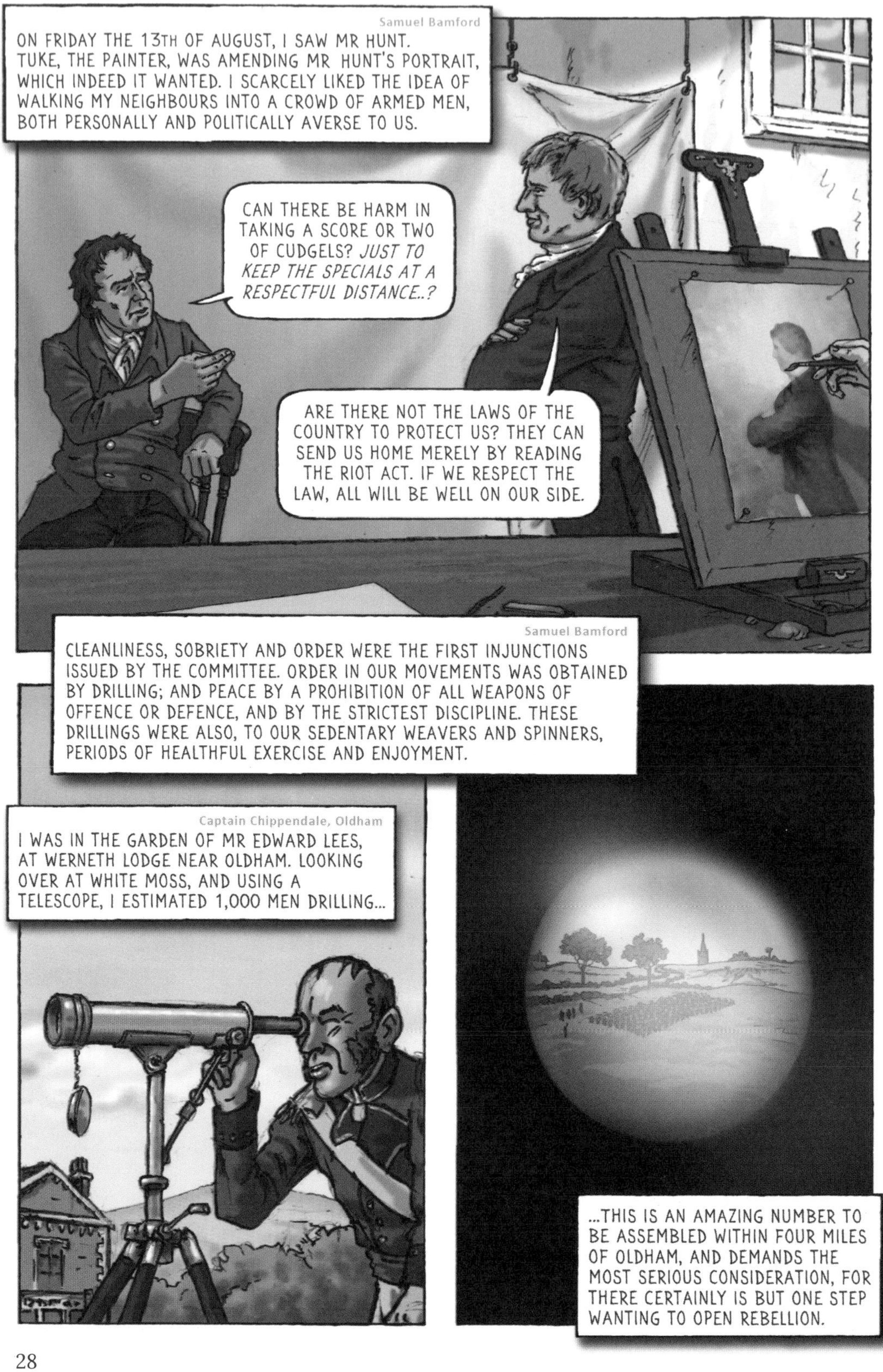
Samuel Bamford
ON FRIDAY THE 13TH OF AUGUST, I SAW MR HUNT. TUKE, THE PAINTER, WAS AMENDING MR HUNT'S PORTRAIT, WHICH INDEED IT WANTED. I SCARCELY LIKED THE IDEA OF WALKING MY NEIGHBOURS INTO A CROWD OF ARMED MEN, BOTH PERSONALLY AND POLITICALLY AVERSE TO US.
CAN THERE BE HARM IN TAKING A SCORE OR TWO OF CUDGELS? *JUST TO KEEP THE SPECIALS AT A RESPECTFUL DISTANCE..?*
ARE THERE NOT THE LAWS OF THE COUNTRY TO PROTECT US? THEY CAN SEND US HOME MERELY BY READING THE RIOT ACT. IF WE RESPECT THE LAW, ALL WILL BE WELL ON OUR SIDE.
Samuel Bamford
CLEANLINESS, SOBRIETY AND ORDER WERE THE FIRST INJUNCTIONS ISSUED BY THE COMMITTEE. ORDER IN OUR MOVEMENTS WAS OBTAINED BY DRILLING; AND PEACE BY A PROHIBITION OF ALL WEAPONS OF OFFENCE OR DEFENCE, AND BY THE STRICTEST DISCIPLINE. THESE DRILLINGS WERE ALSO, TO OUR SEDENTARY WEAVERS AND SPINNERS, PERIODS OF HEALTHFUL EXERCISE AND ENJOYMENT.
Captain Chippendale, Oldham
I WAS IN THE GARDEN OF MR EDWARD LEES, AT WERNETH LODGE NEAR OLDHAM. LOOKING OVER AT WHITE MOSS, AND USING A TELESCOPE, I ESTIMATED 1,000 MEN DRILLING...
...THIS IS AN AMAZING NUMBER TO BE ASSEMBLED WITHIN FOUR MILES OF OLDHAM, AND DEMANDS THE MOST SERIOUS CONSIDERATION, FOR THERE CERTAINLY IS BUT ONE STEP WANTING TO OPEN REBELLION.

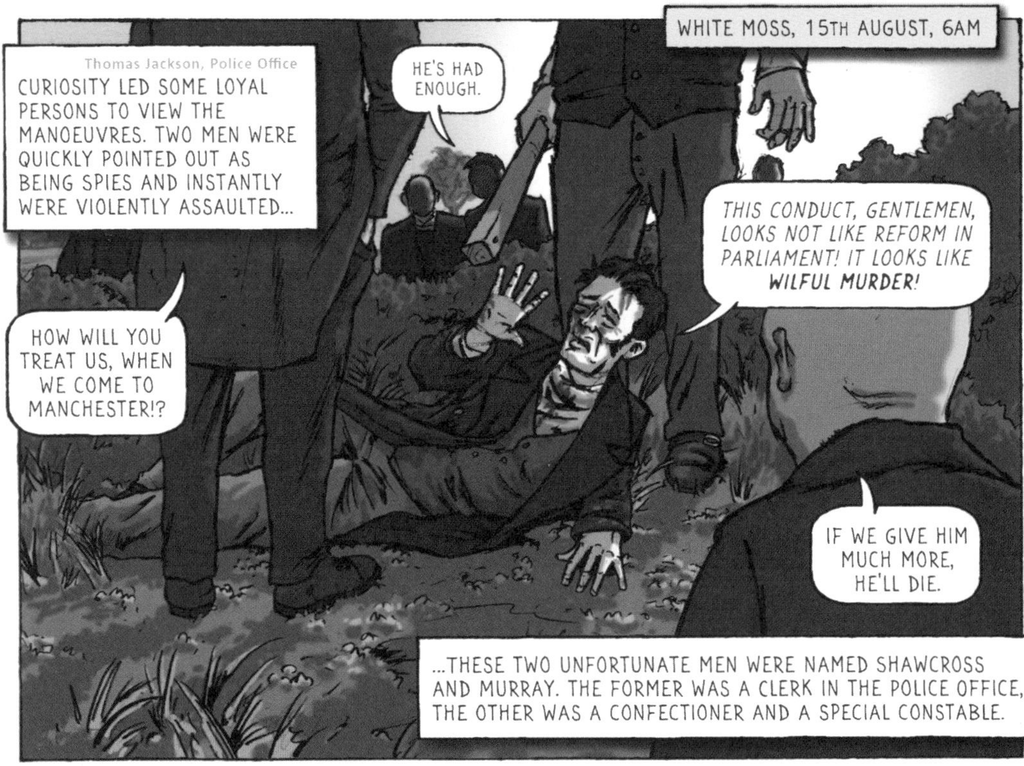
WHITE MOSS, 15TH AUGUST, 6AM
Thomas Jackson, Police Office
CURIOSITY LED SOME LOYAL PERSONS TO VIEW THE MANOEUVRES. TWO MEN WERE QUICKLY POINTED OUT AS BEING SPIES AND INSTANTLY WERE VIOLENTLY ASSAULTED...
HE'S HAD ENOUGH.
HOW WILL YOU TREAT US, WHEN WE COME TO MANCHESTER!?
THIS CONDUCT, GENTLEMEN, LOOKS NOT LIKE REFORM IN PARLIAMENT! IT LOOKS LIKE WILFUL MURDER!
IF WE GIVE HIM MUCH MORE, HE'LL DIE.
...THESE TWO UNFORTUNATE MEN WERE NAMED SHAWCROSS AND MURRAY. THE FORMER WAS A CLERK IN THE POLICE OFFICE, THE OTHER WAS A CONFECTIONER AND A SPECIAL CONSTABLE.

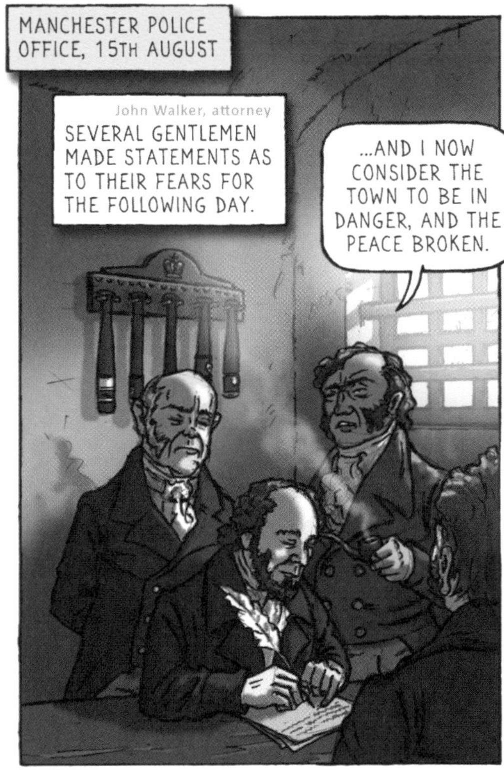
MANCHESTER POLICE OFFICE, 15TH AUGUST
John Walker, attorney
SEVERAL GENTLEMEN MADE STATEMENTS AS TO THEIR FEARS FOR THE FOLLOWING DAY.
...AND I NOW CONSIDER THE TOWN TO BE IN DANGER, AND THE PEACE BROKEN.

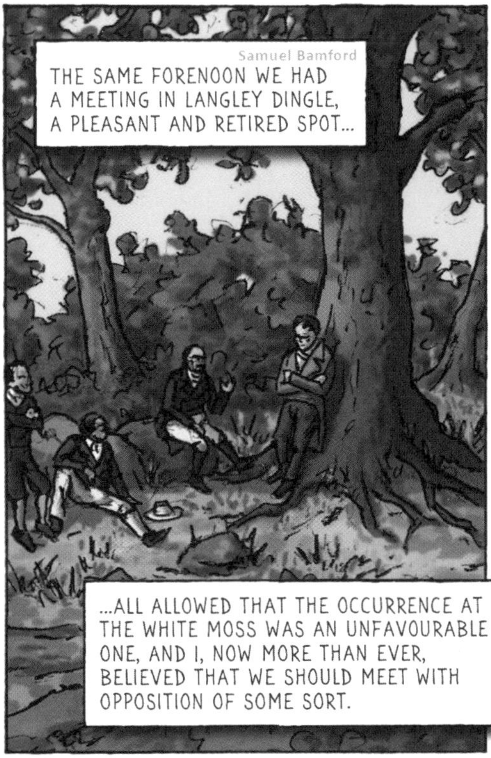
Samuel Bamford
THE SAME FORENOON WE HAD A MEETING IN LANGLEY DINGLE, A PLEASANT AND RETIRED SPOT...
...ALL ALLOWED THAT THE OCCURRENCE AT THE WHITE MOSS WAS AN UNFAVOURABLE ONE, AND I, NOW MORE THAN EVER, BELIEVED THAT WE SHOULD MEET WITH OPPOSITION OF SOME SORT.

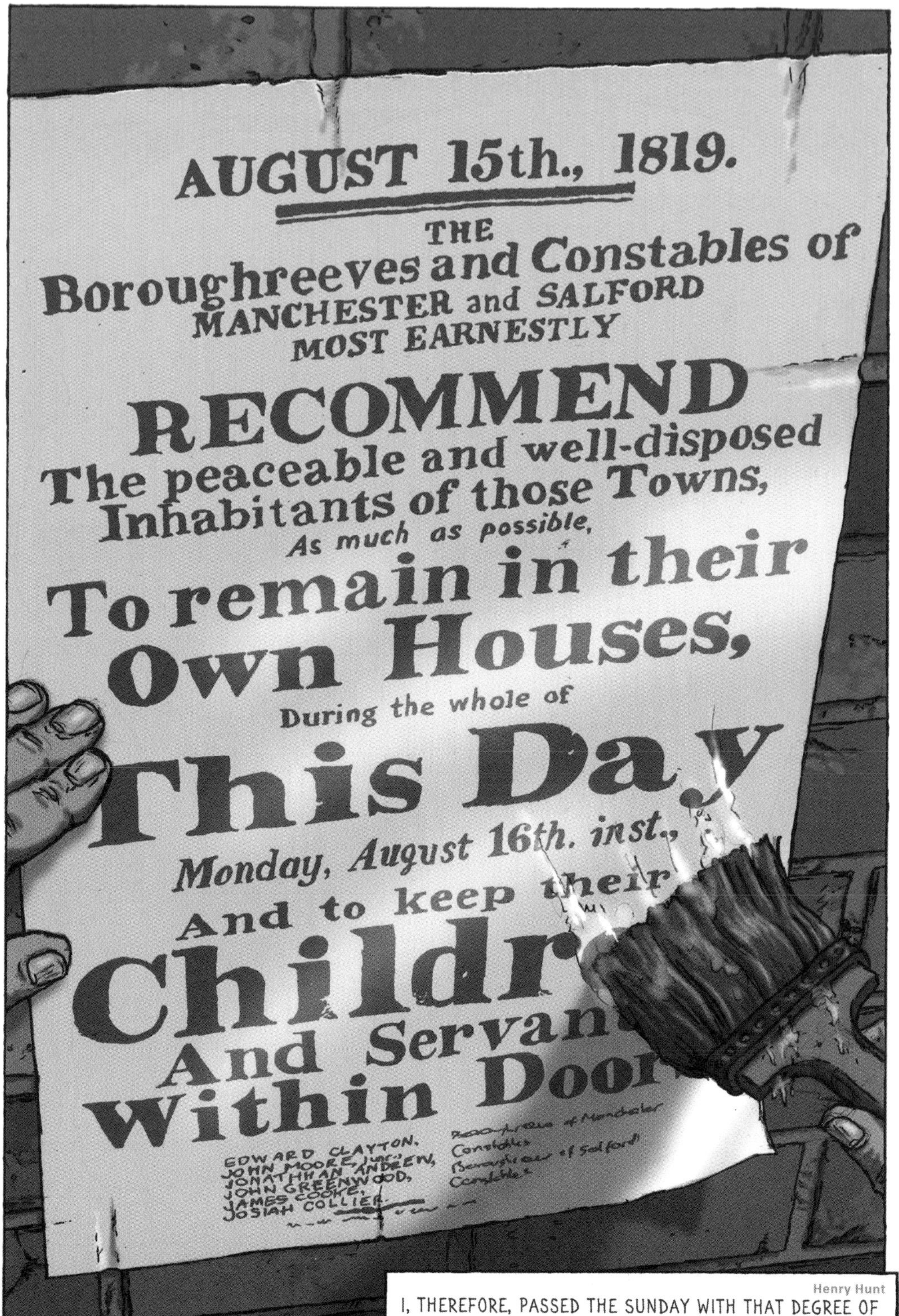

AUGUST 15th., 1819.
THE
Boroughreeves and Constables of
MANCHESTER and SALFORD
MOST EARNESTLY
RECOMMEND
The peaceable and well-disposed
Inhabitants of those Towns,
As much as possible,
To remain in their
Own Houses,
During the whole of
This Day
Monday, August 16th. inst.,
And to keep their
Childr
And Servant
Within Door
EDWARD CLAYTON.
JOHN GREENWOOD,
JAMES COOKE,
JOSIAH COLLIER
Henry Hunt
I, THEREFORE, PASSED THE SUNDAY WITH THAT DEGREE OF ANXIETY WHICH EVERY PERSON OF SENSIBILITY MUST HAVE NATURALLY FELT FOR THE RESULT OF THE COMING DAY.

III

You will not come back as merry as you go.

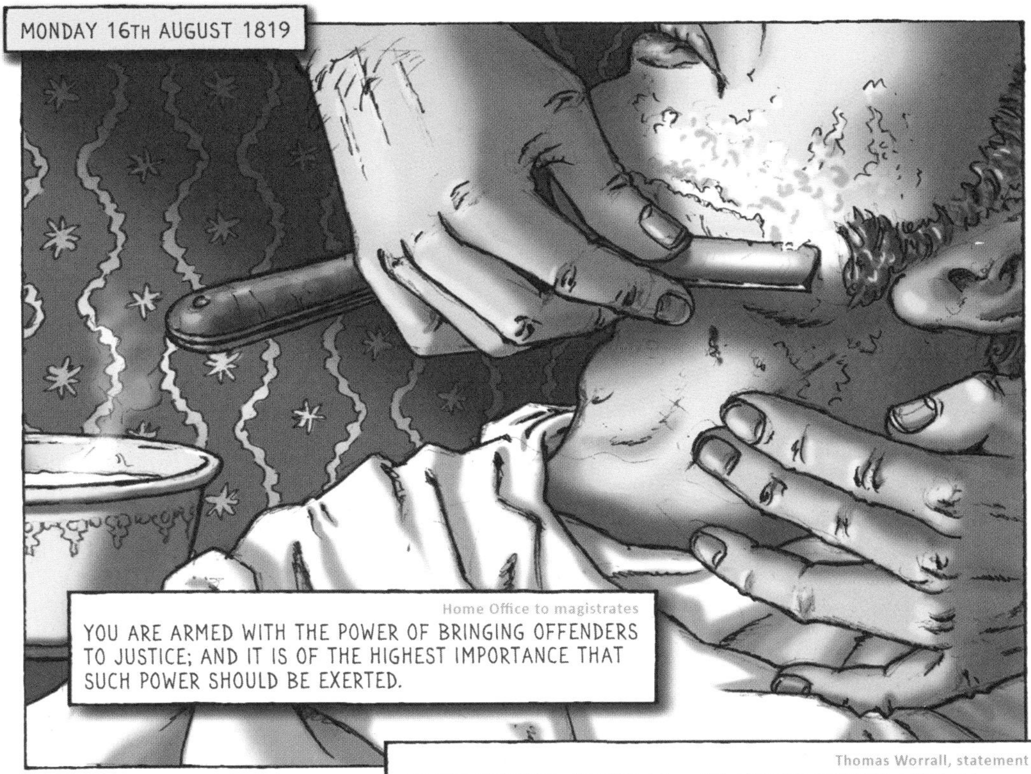
MONDAY 16TH AUGUST 1819
Home Office to magistrates
YOU ARE ARMED WITH THE POWER OF BRINGING OFFENDERS TO JUSTICE; AND IT IS OF THE HIGHEST IMPORTANCE THAT SUCH POWER SHOULD BE EXERTED.

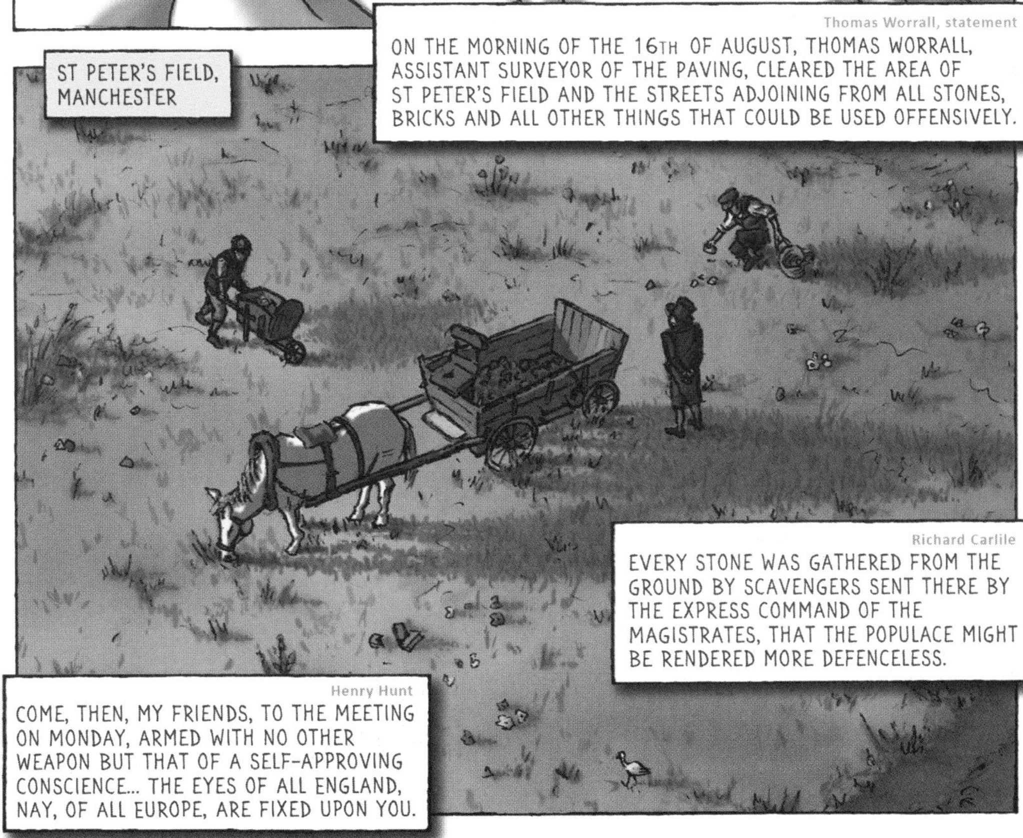
Thomas Worrall, statement
ON THE MORNING OF THE 16TH OF AUGUST, THOMAS WORRALL, ASSISTANT SURVEYOR OF THE PAVING, CLEARED THE AREA OF ST PETER'S FIELD AND THE STREETS ADJOINING FROM ALL STONES, BRICKS AND ALL OTHER THINGS THAT COULD BE USED OFFENSIVELY.
ST PETER'S FIELD, MANCHESTER
Richard Carlile
EVERY STONE WAS GATHERED FROM THE GROUND BY SCAVENGERS SENT THERE BY THE EXPRESS COMMAND OF THE MAGISTRATES, THAT THE POPULACE MIGHT BE RENDERED MORE DEFENCELESS.
Henry Hunt
COME, THEN, MY FRIENDS, TO THE MEETING ON MONDAY, ARMED WITH NO OTHER WEAPON BUT THAT OF A SELF-APPROVING CONSCIENCE... THE EYES OF ALL ENGLAND, NAY, OF ALL EUROPE, ARE FIXED UPON YOU.

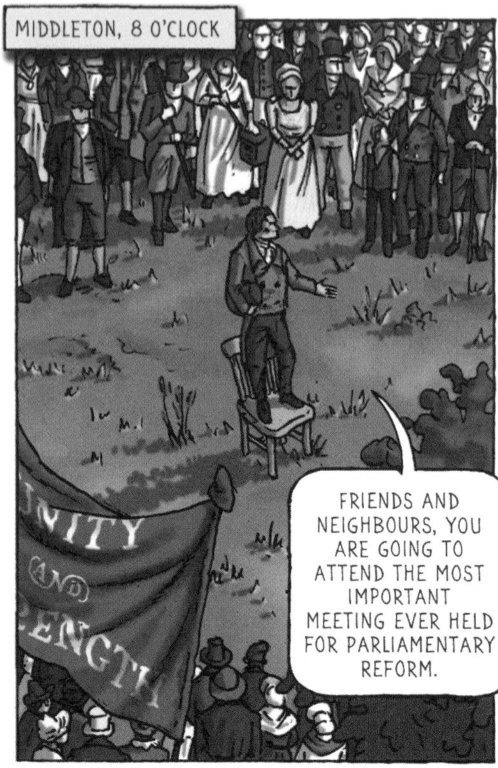
MIDDLETON, 8 O'CLOCK
FRIENDS AND NEIGHBOURS, YOU ARE GOING TO ATTEND THE MOST IMPORTANT MEETING EVER HELD FOR PARLIAMENTARY REFORM.

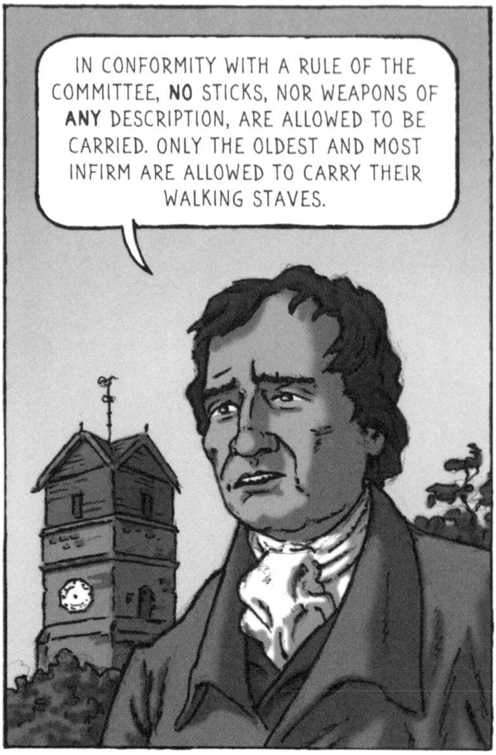
IN CONFORMITY WITH A RULE OF THE COMMITTEE, **NO** STICKS, NOR WEAPONS OF **ANY** DESCRIPTION, ARE ALLOWED TO BE CARRIED. ONLY THE OLDEST AND MOST INFIRM ARE ALLOWED TO CARRY THEIR WALKING STAVES.

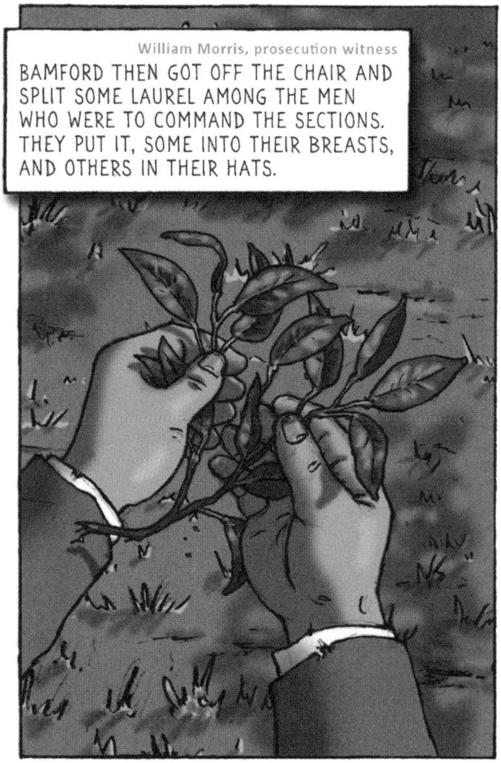
William Morris, prosecution witness
BAMFORD THEN GOT OFF THE CHAIR AND SPLIT SOME LAUREL AMONG THE MEN WHO WERE TO COMMAND THE SECTIONS. THEY PUT IT, SOME INTO THEIR BREASTS, AND OTHERS IN THEIR HATS.

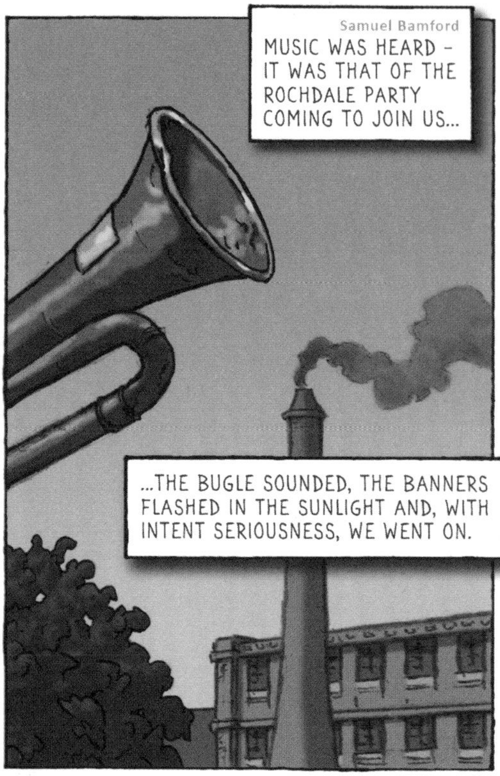
Samuel Bamford
MUSIC WAS HEARD – IT WAS THAT OF THE ROCHDALE PARTY COMING TO JOIN US...
...THE BUGLE SOUNDED, THE BANNERS FLASHED IN THE SUNLIGHT AND, WITH INTENT SERIOUSNESS, WE WENT ON.

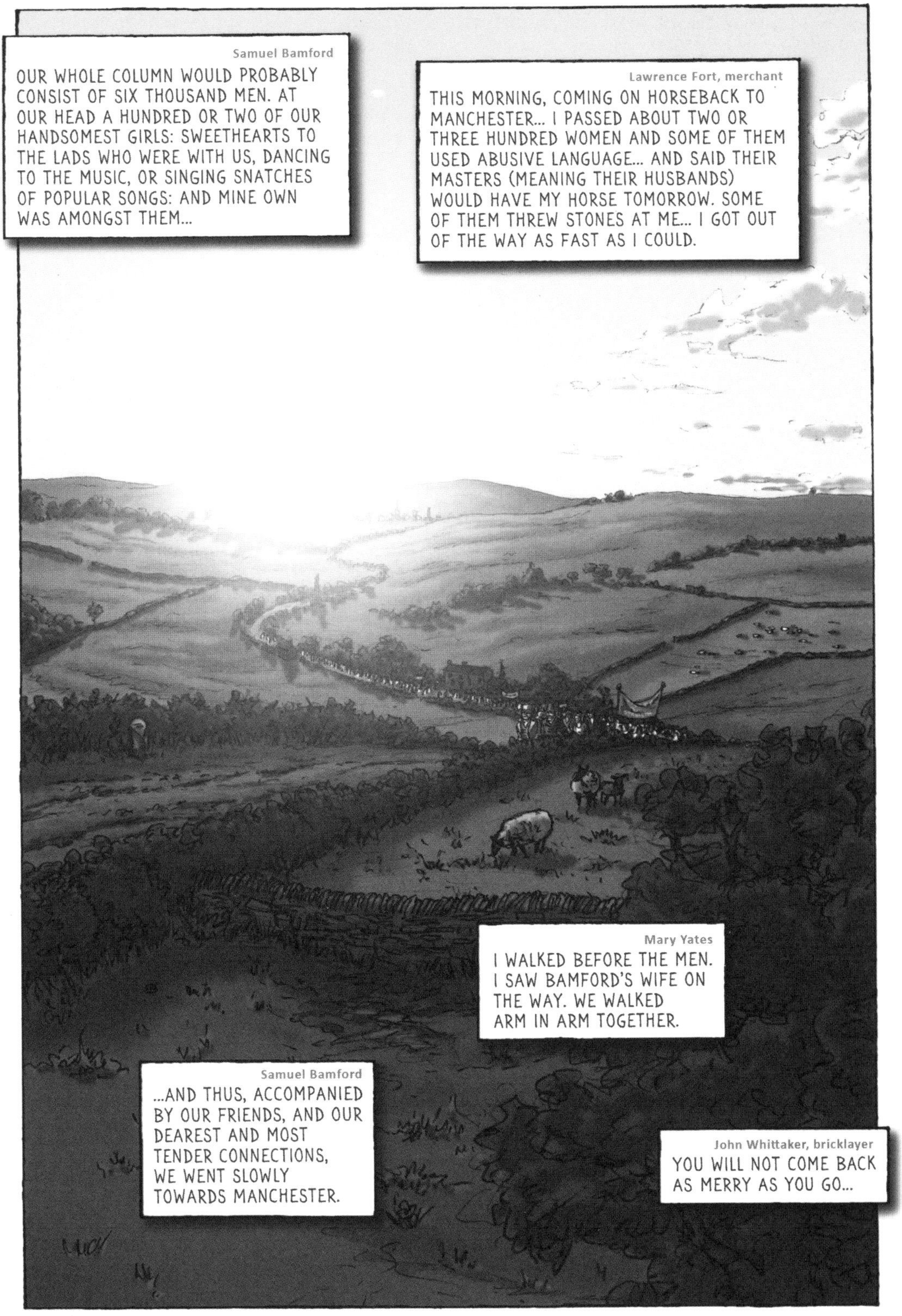
Samuel Bamford
OUR WHOLE COLUMN WOULD PROBABLY CONSIST OF SIX THOUSAND MEN. AT OUR HEAD A HUNDRED OR TWO OF OUR HANDSOMEST GIRLS: SWEETHEARTS TO THE LADS WHO WERE WITH US, DANCING TO THE MUSIC, OR SINGING SNATCHES OF POPULAR SONGS: AND MINE OWN WAS AMONGST THEM...
Lawrence Fort, merchant
THIS MORNING, COMING ON HORSEBACK TO MANCHESTER... I PASSED ABOUT TWO OR THREE HUNDRED WOMEN AND SOME OF THEM USED ABUSIVE LANGUAGE... AND SAID THEIR MASTERS (MEANING THEIR HUSBANDS) WOULD HAVE MY HORSE TOMORROW. SOME OF THEM THREW STONES AT ME... I GOT OUT OF THE WAY AS FAST AS I COULD.
Mary Yates
I WALKED BEFORE THE MEN. I SAW BAMFORD'S WIFE ON THE WAY. WE WALKED ARM IN ARM TOGETHER.
Samuel Bamford
...AND THUS, ACCOMPANIED BY OUR FRIENDS, AND OUR DEAREST AND MOST TENDER CONNECTIONS, WE WENT SLOWLY TOWARDS MANCHESTER.
John Whittaker, bricklayer
YOU WILL NOT COME BACK AS MERRY AS YOU GO...

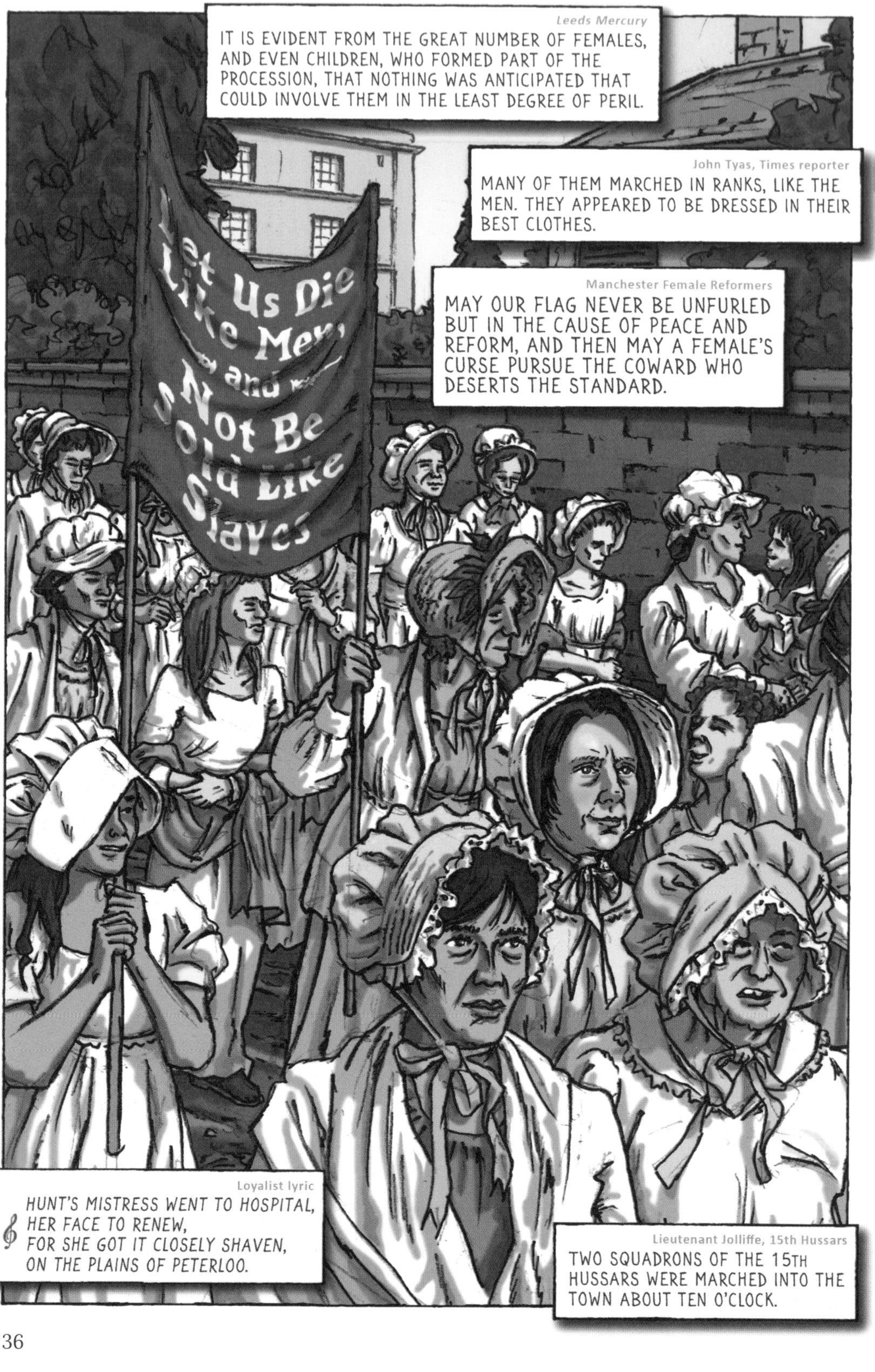
Leeds Mercury
IT IS EVIDENT FROM THE GREAT NUMBER OF FEMALES, AND EVEN CHILDREN, WHO FORMED PART OF THE PROCESSION, THAT NOTHING WAS ANTICIPATED THAT COULD INVOLVE THEM IN THE LEAST DEGREE OF PERIL.
John Tyas, Times reporter
MANY OF THEM MARCHED IN RANKS, LIKE THE MEN. THEY APPEARED TO BE DRESSED IN THEIR BEST CLOTHES.
Let Us Die Like Men, and Not Be Sold Like Slaves
Manchester Female Reformers
MAY OUR FLAG NEVER BE UNFURLED BUT IN THE CAUSE OF PEACE AND REFORM, AND THEN MAY A FEMALE'S CURSE PURSUE THE COWARD WHO DESERTS THE STANDARD.
Loyalist lyric
HUNT'S MISTRESS WENT TO HOSPITAL,
HER FACE TO RENEW,
FOR SHE GOT IT CLOSELY SHAVEN,
ON THE PLAINS OF PETERLOO.
Lieutenant Jolliffe, 15th Hussars
TWO SQUADRONS OF THE 15TH HUSSARS WERE MARCHED INTO THE TOWN ABOUT TEN O'CLOCK.

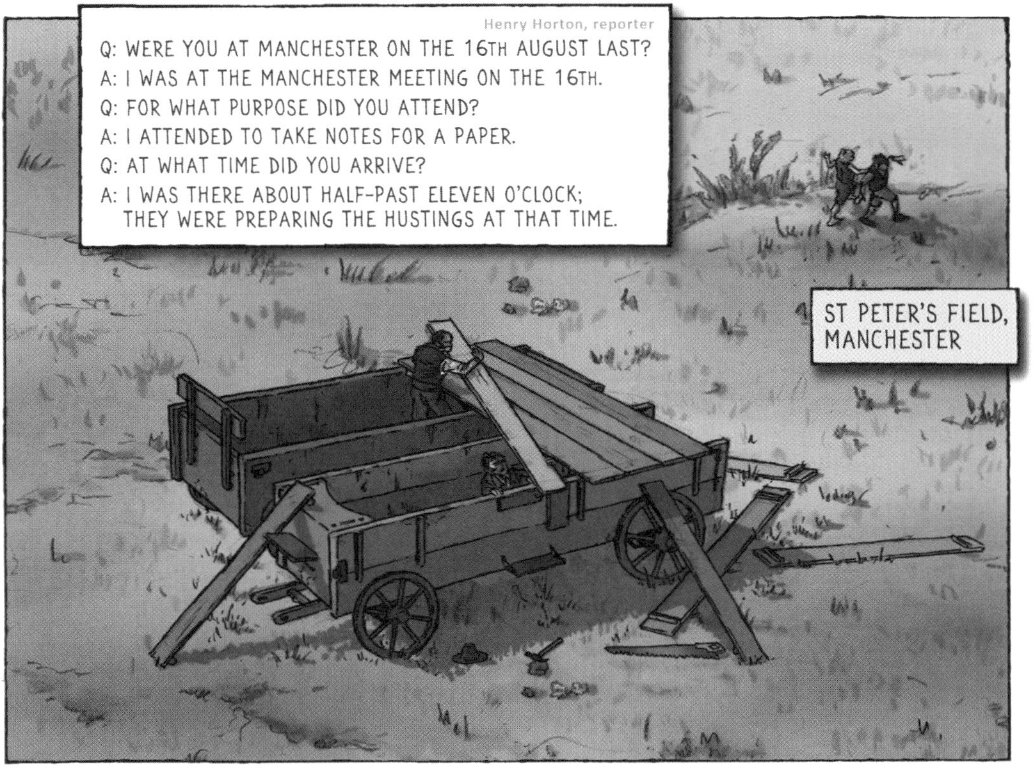
Henry Horton, reporter
Q: WERE YOU AT MANCHESTER ON THE 16TH AUGUST LAST?
A: I WAS AT THE MANCHESTER MEETING ON THE 16TH.
Q: FOR WHAT PURPOSE DID YOU ATTEND?
A: I ATTENDED TO TAKE NOTES FOR A PAPER.
Q: AT WHAT TIME DID YOU ARRIVE?
A: I WAS THERE ABOUT HALF-PAST ELEVEN O'CLOCK; THEY WERE PREPARING THE HUSTINGS AT THAT TIME.
ST PETER'S FIELD, MANCHESTER

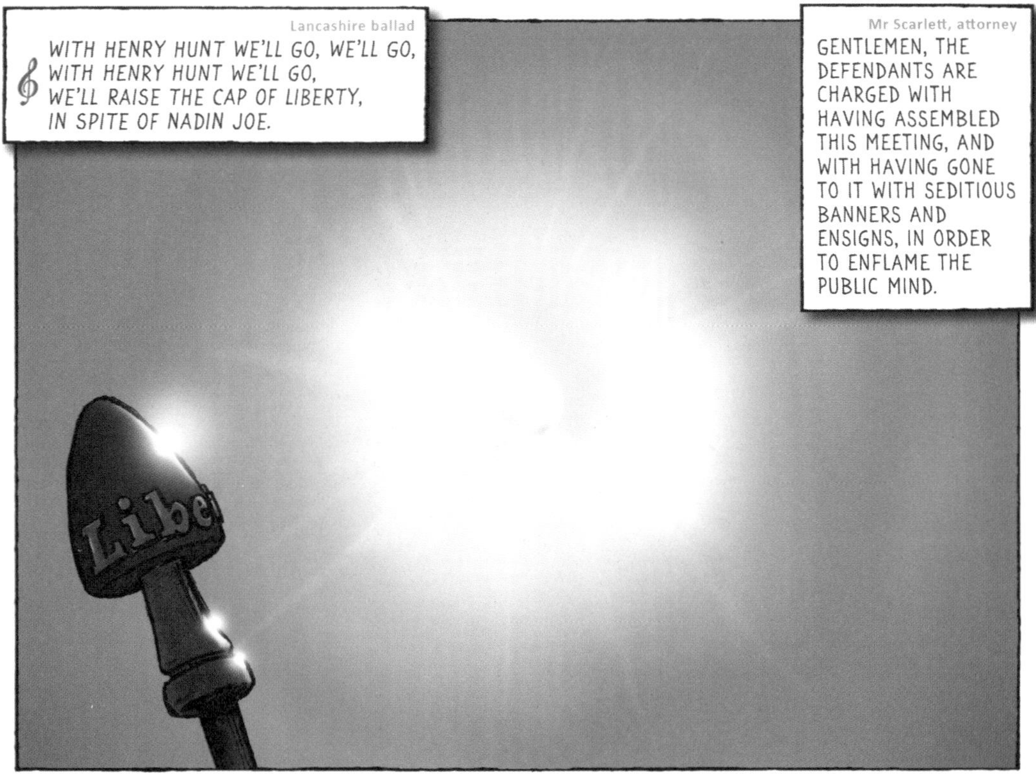
Lancashire ballad
WITH HENRY HUNT WE'LL GO, WE'LL GO,
WITH HENRY HUNT WE'LL GO,
WE'LL RAISE THE CAP OF LIBERTY,
IN SPITE OF NADIN JOE.
Mr Scarlett, attorney
GENTLEMEN, THE DEFENDANTS ARE CHARGED WITH HAVING ASSEMBLED THIS MEETING, AND WITH HAVING GONE TO IT WITH SEDITIOUS BANNERS AND ENSIGNS, IN ORDER TO ENFLAME THE PUBLIC MIND.

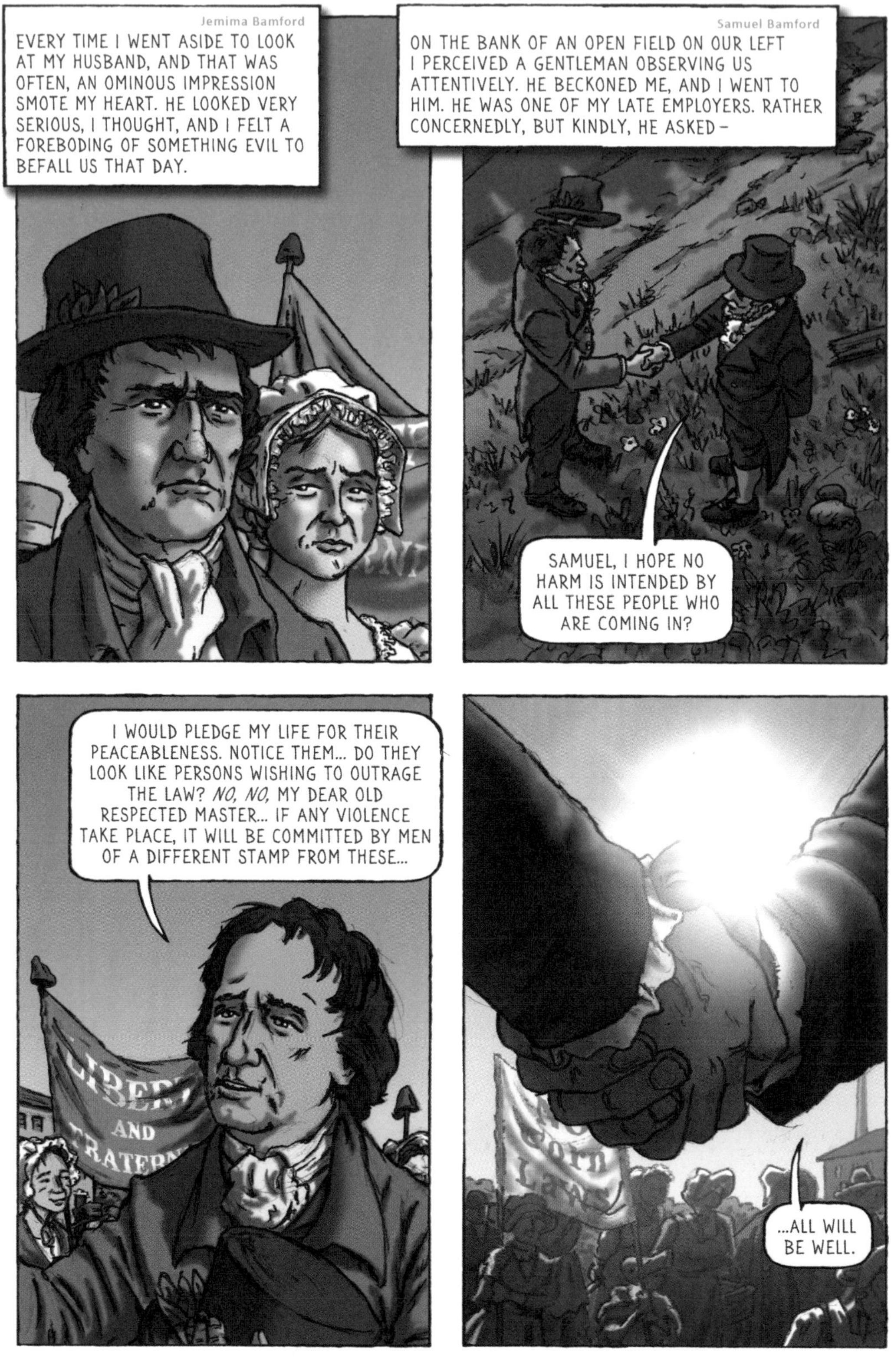
Jemima Bamford
EVERY TIME I WENT ASIDE TO LOOK AT MY HUSBAND, AND THAT WAS OFTEN, AN OMINOUS IMPRESSION SMOTE MY HEART. HE LOOKED VERY SERIOUS, I THOUGHT, AND I FELT A FOREBODING OF SOMETHING EVIL TO BEFALL US THAT DAY.
Samuel Bamford
ON THE BANK OF AN OPEN FIELD ON OUR LEFT I PERCEIVED A GENTLEMAN OBSERVING US ATTENTIVELY. HE BECKONED ME, AND I WENT TO HIM. HE WAS ONE OF MY LATE EMPLOYERS. RATHER CONCERNEDLY, BUT KINDLY, HE ASKED –
SAMUEL, I HOPE NO HARM IS INTENDED BY ALL THESE PEOPLE WHO ARE COMING IN?
I WOULD PLEDGE MY LIFE FOR THEIR PEACEABLENESS. NOTICE THEM... DO THEY LOOK LIKE PERSONS WISHING TO OUTRAGE THE LAW? *NO, NO,* MY DEAR OLD RESPECTED MASTER... IF ANY VIOLENCE TAKE PLACE, IT WILL BE COMMITTED BY MEN OF A DIFFERENT STAMP FROM THESE...
AND
...ALL WILL BE WELL.

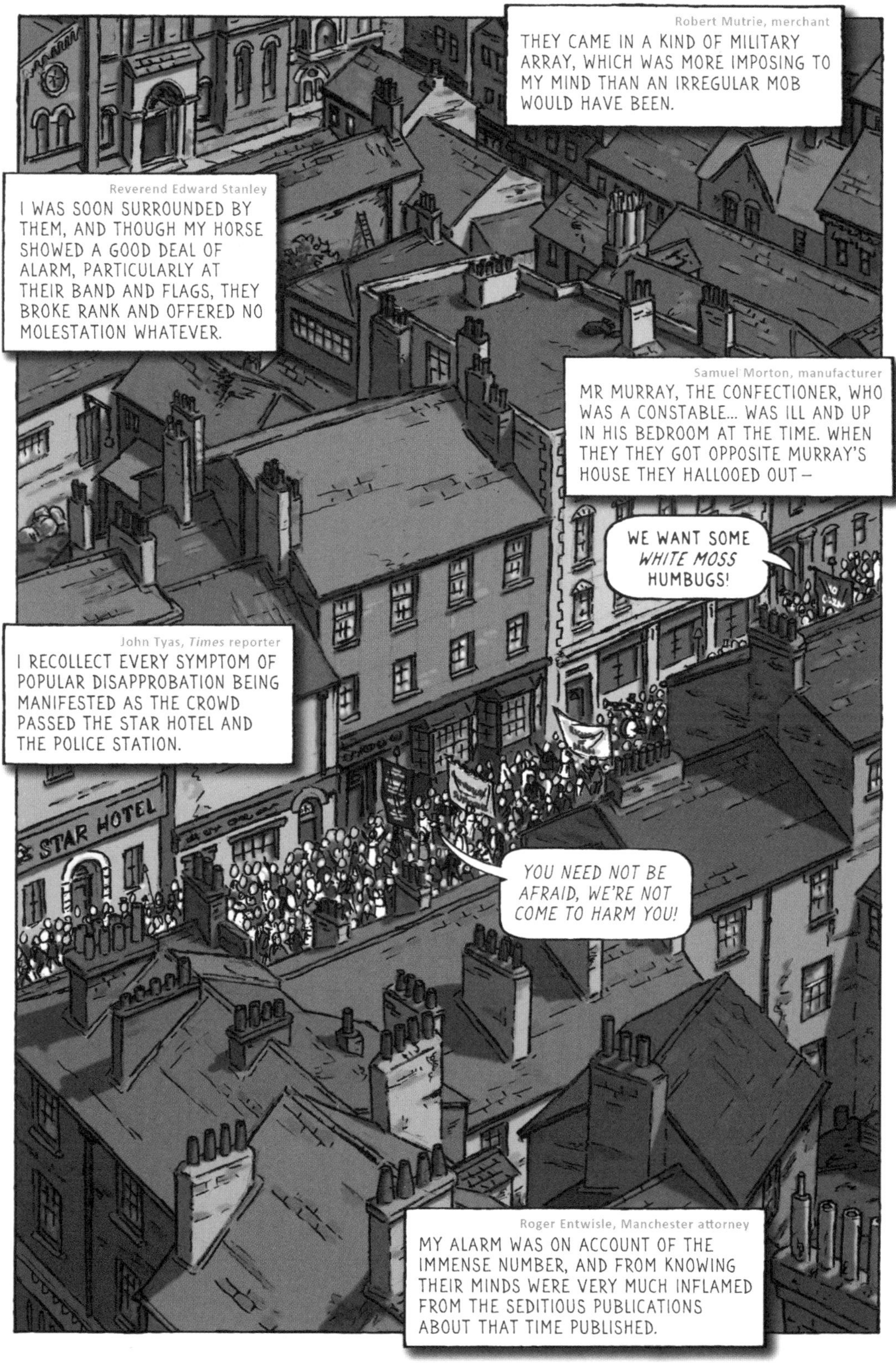
Robert Mutrie, merchant
THEY CAME IN A KIND OF MILITARY ARRAY, WHICH WAS MORE IMPOSING TO MY MIND THAN AN IRREGULAR MOB WOULD HAVE BEEN.
Reverend Edward Stanley
I WAS SOON SURROUNDED BY THEM, AND THOUGH MY HORSE SHOWED A GOOD DEAL OF ALARM, PARTICULARLY AT THEIR BAND AND FLAGS, THEY BROKE RANK AND OFFERED NO MOLESTATION WHATEVER.
Samuel Morton, manufacturer
MR MURRAY, THE CONFECTIONER, WHO WAS A CONSTABLE... WAS ILL AND UP IN HIS BEDROOM AT THE TIME. WHEN THEY THEY GOT OPPOSITE MURRAY'S HOUSE THEY HALLOOED OUT –
WE WANT SOME *WHITE MOSS* HUMBUGS!
John Tyas, *Times* reporter
I RECOLLECT EVERY SYMPTOM OF POPULAR DISAPPROBATION BEING MANIFESTED AS THE CROWD PASSED THE STAR HOTEL AND THE POLICE STATION.
STAR HOTEL
YOU NEED NOT BE AFRAID, WE'RE NOT COME TO HARM YOU!
Roger Entwisle, Manchester attorney
MY ALARM WAS ON ACCOUNT OF THE IMMENSE NUMBER, AND FROM KNOWING THEIR MINDS WERE VERY MUCH INFLAMED FROM THE SEDITIOUS PUBLICATIONS ABOUT THAT TIME PUBLISHED.

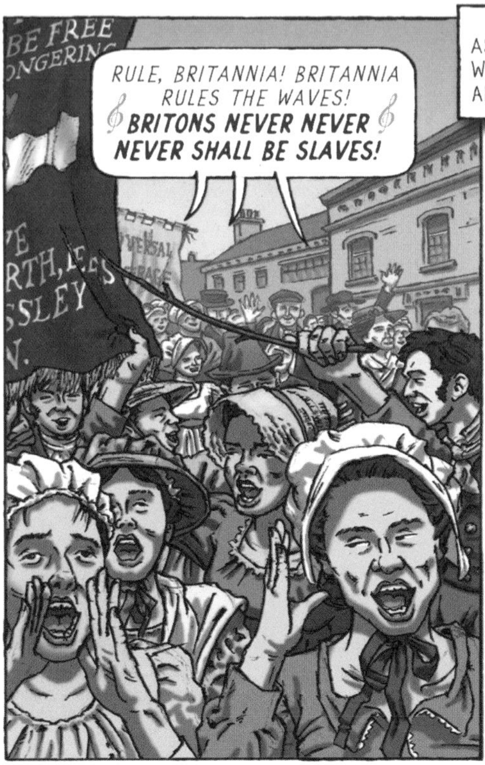
RULE, BRITANNIA! BRITANNIA RULES THE WAVES! BRITONS NEVER NEVER NEVER SHALL BE SLAVES!

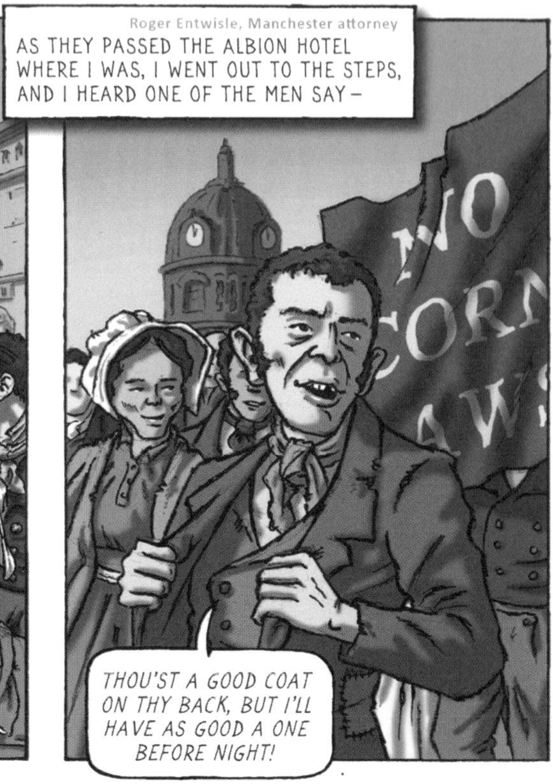
Roger Entwisle, Manchester attorney
AS THEY PASSED THE ALBION HOTEL WHERE I WAS, I WENT OUT TO THE STEPS, AND I HEARD ONE OF THE MEN SAY –
THOU'ST A GOOD COAT ON THY BACK, BUT I'LL HAVE AS GOOD A ONE BEFORE NIGHT!

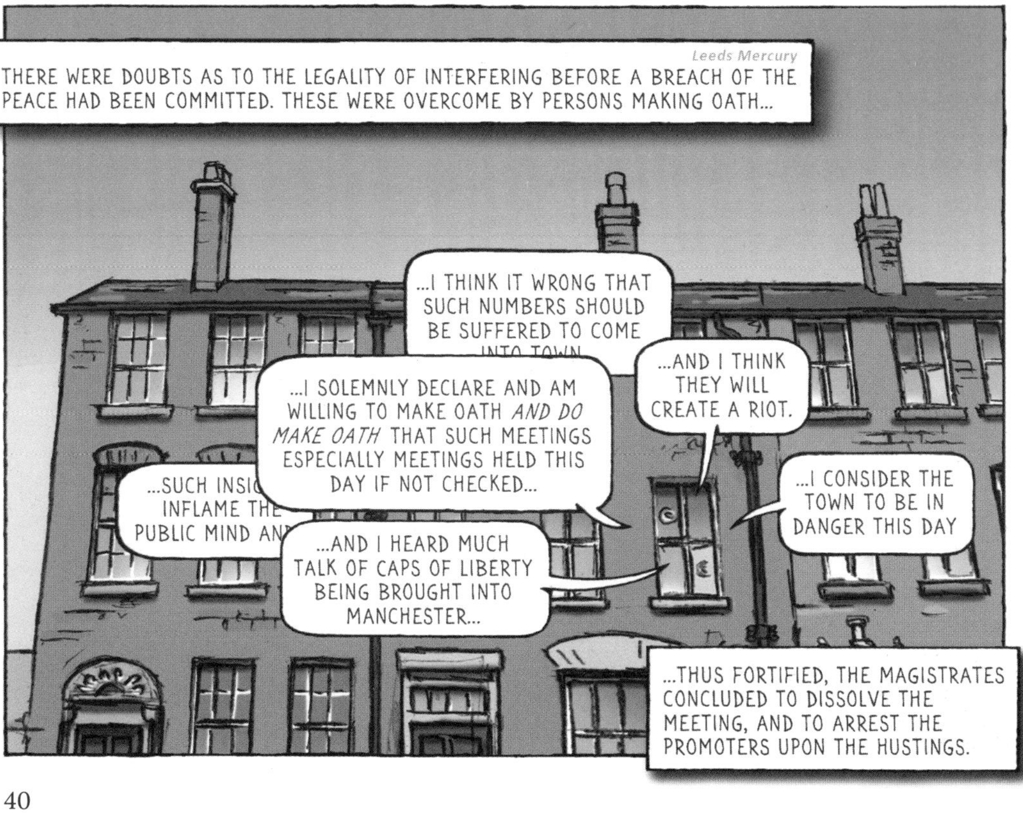
Leeds Mercury
THERE WERE DOUBTS AS TO THE LEGALITY OF INTERFERING BEFORE A BREACH OF THE PEACE HAD BEEN COMMITTED. THESE WERE OVERCOME BY PERSONS MAKING OATH...
...I THINK IT WRONG THAT SUCH NUMBERS SHOULD BE SUFFERED TO COME
...AND I THINK THEY WILL CREATE A RIOT.
...I SOLEMNLY DECLARE AND AM WILLING TO MAKE OATH AND DO MAKE OATH THAT SUCH MEETINGS ESPECIALLY MEETINGS HELD THIS DAY IF NOT CHECKED...
...SUCH INSI
INFLAME THE
PUBLIC MIND AN
...I CONSIDER THE TOWN TO BE IN DANGER THIS DAY
...AND I HEARD MUCH TALK OF CAPS OF LIBERTY BEING BROUGHT INTO MANCHESTER...
...THUS FORTIFIED, THE MAGISTRATES CONCLUDED TO DISSOLVE THE MEETING, AND TO ARREST THE PROMOTERS UPON THE HUSTINGS.

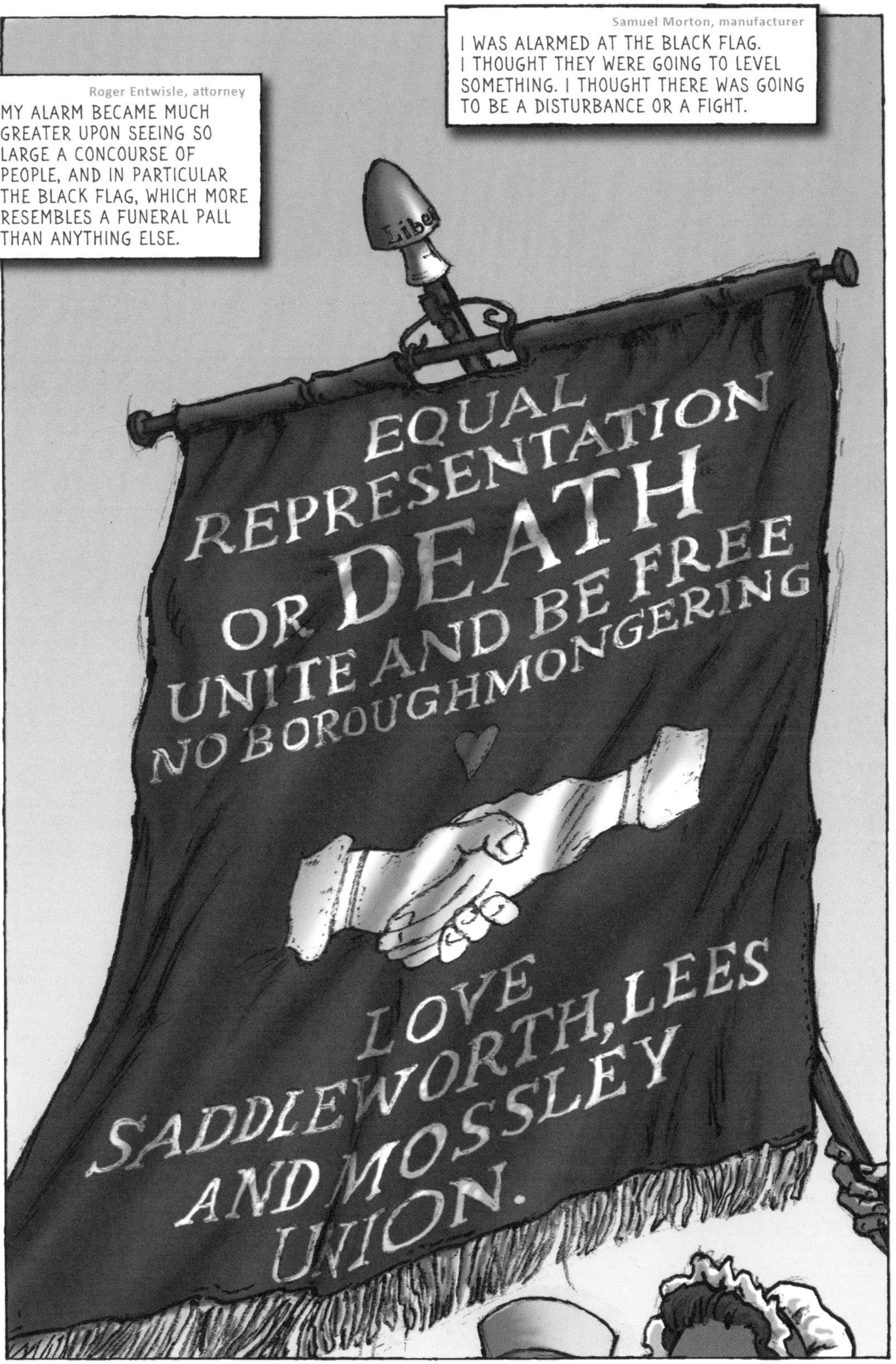
Roger Entwisle, attorney
MY ALARM BECAME MUCH GREATER UPON SEEING SO LARGE A CONCOURSE OF PEOPLE, AND IN PARTICULAR THE BLACK FLAG, WHICH MORE RESEMBLES A FUNERAL PALL THAN ANYTHING ELSE.
Samuel Morton, manufacturer
I WAS ALARMED AT THE BLACK FLAG. I THOUGHT THEY WERE GOING TO LEVEL SOMETHING. I THOUGHT THERE WAS GOING TO BE A DISTURBANCE OR A FIGHT.
EQUAL REPRESENTATION OR DEATH
UNITE AND BE FREE
NO BOROUGHMONGERING
LOVE
SADDLEWORTH, LEES AND MOSSLEY UNION.

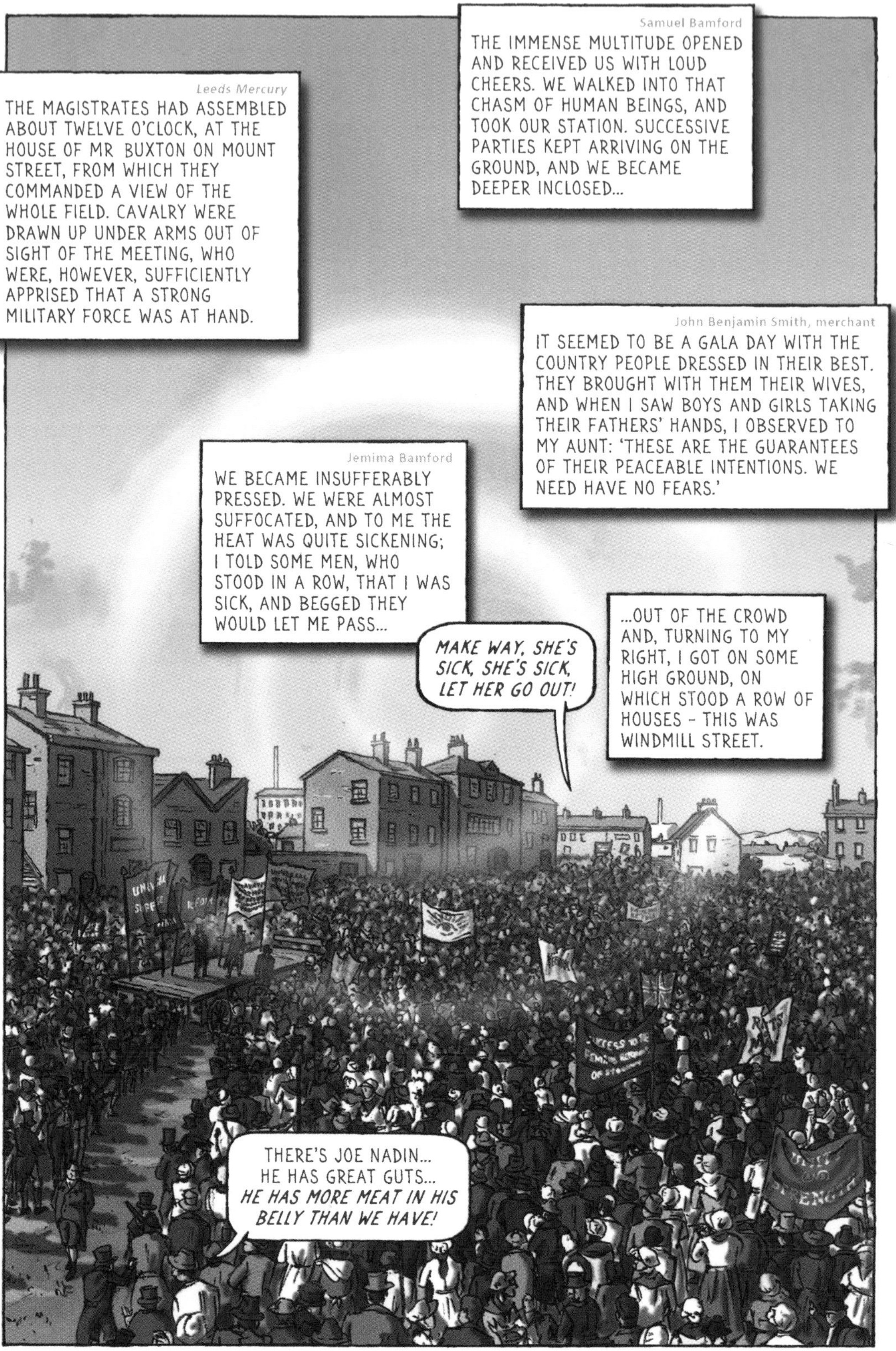
Leeds Mercury
THE MAGISTRATES HAD ASSEMBLED ABOUT TWELVE O'CLOCK, AT THE HOUSE OF MR BUXTON ON MOUNT STREET, FROM WHICH THEY COMMANDED A VIEW OF THE WHOLE FIELD. CAVALRY WERE DRAWN UP UNDER ARMS OUT OF SIGHT OF THE MEETING, WHO WERE, HOWEVER, SUFFICIENTLY APPRISED THAT A STRONG MILITARY FORCE WAS AT HAND.
Samuel Bamford
THE IMMENSE MULTITUDE OPENED AND RECEIVED US WITH LOUD CHEERS. WE WALKED INTO THAT CHASM OF HUMAN BEINGS, AND TOOK OUR STATION. SUCCESSIVE PARTIES KEPT ARRIVING ON THE GROUND, AND WE BECAME DEEPER INCLOSED...
John Benjamin Smith, merchant
IT SEEMED TO BE A GALA DAY WITH THE COUNTRY PEOPLE DRESSED IN THEIR BEST. THEY BROUGHT WITH THEM THEIR WIVES, AND WHEN I SAW BOYS AND GIRLS TAKING THEIR FATHERS' HANDS, I OBSERVED TO MY AUNT: 'THESE ARE THE GUARANTEES OF THEIR PEACEABLE INTENTIONS. WE NEED HAVE NO FEARS.'
Jemima Bamford
WE BECAME INSUFFERABLY PRESSED. WE WERE ALMOST SUFFOCATED, AND TO ME THE HEAT WAS QUITE SICKENING; I TOLD SOME MEN, WHO STOOD IN A ROW, THAT I WAS SICK, AND BEGGED THEY WOULD LET ME PASS...
MAKE WAY, SHE'S SICK, SHE'S SICK, LET HER GO OUT!
...OUT OF THE CROWD AND, TURNING TO MY RIGHT, I GOT ON SOME HIGH GROUND, ON WHICH STOOD A ROW OF HOUSES – THIS WAS WINDMILL STREET.
THERE'S JOE NADIN... HE HAS GREAT GUTS... HE HAS MORE MEAT IN HIS BELLY THAN WE HAVE!

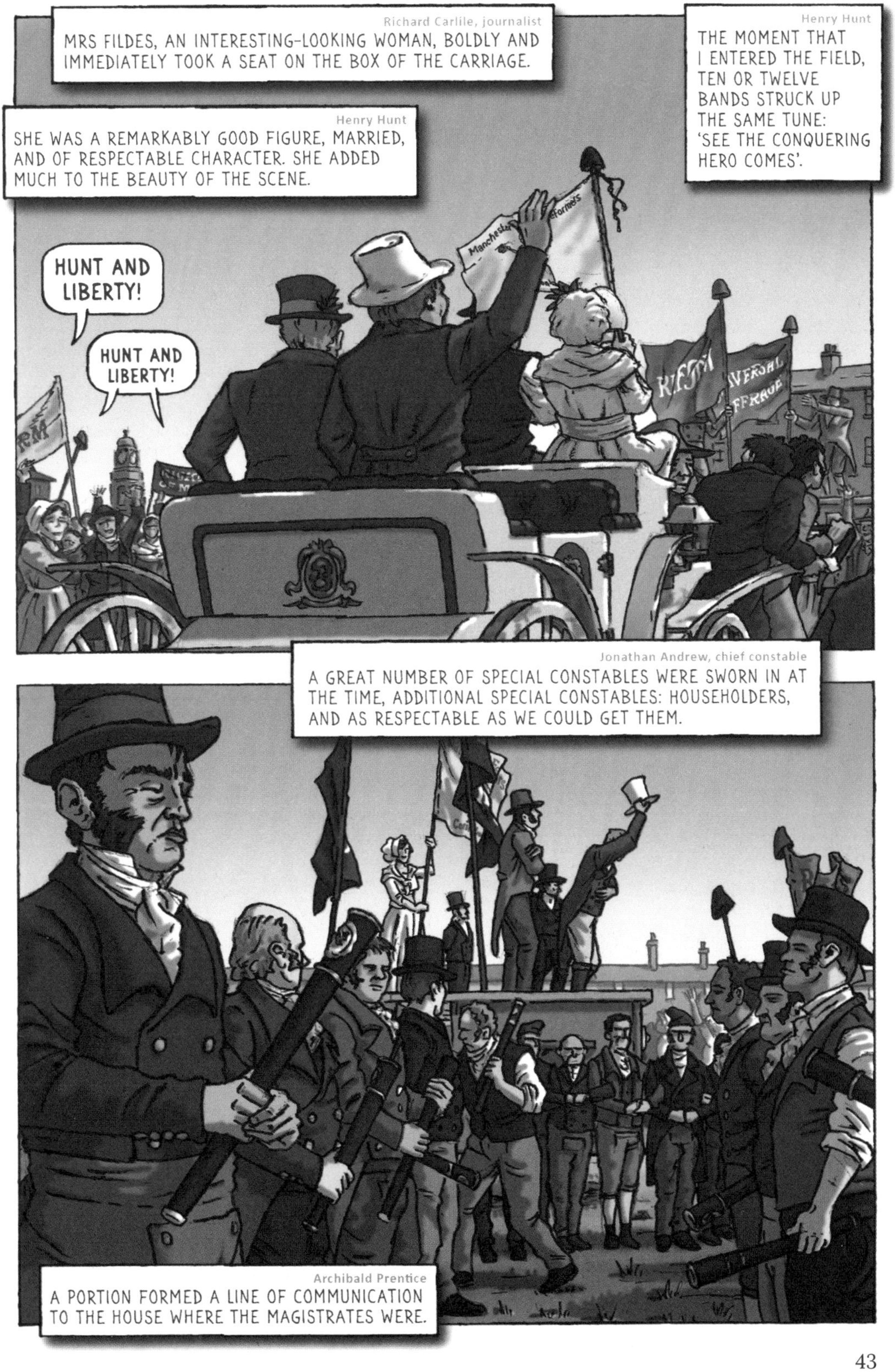
Richard Carlile, journalist
MRS FILDES, AN INTERESTING-LOOKING WOMAN, BOLDLY AND IMMEDIATELY TOOK A SEAT ON THE BOX OF THE CARRIAGE.
Henry Hunt
SHE WAS A REMARKABLY GOOD FIGURE, MARRIED, AND OF RESPECTABLE CHARACTER. SHE ADDED MUCH TO THE BEAUTY OF THE SCENE.
Henry Hunt
THE MOMENT THAT I ENTERED THE FIELD, TEN OR TWELVE BANDS STRUCK UP THE SAME TUNE: 'SEE THE CONQUERING HERO COMES'.
HUNT AND LIBERTY!
HUNT AND LIBERTY!
Jonathan Andrew, chief constable
A GREAT NUMBER OF SPECIAL CONSTABLES WERE SWORN IN AT THE TIME, ADDITIONAL SPECIAL CONSTABLES: HOUSEHOLDERS, AND AS RESPECTABLE AS WE COULD GET THEM.
Archibald Prentice
A PORTION FORMED A LINE OF COMMUNICATION TO THE HOUSE WHERE THE MAGISTRATES WERE.

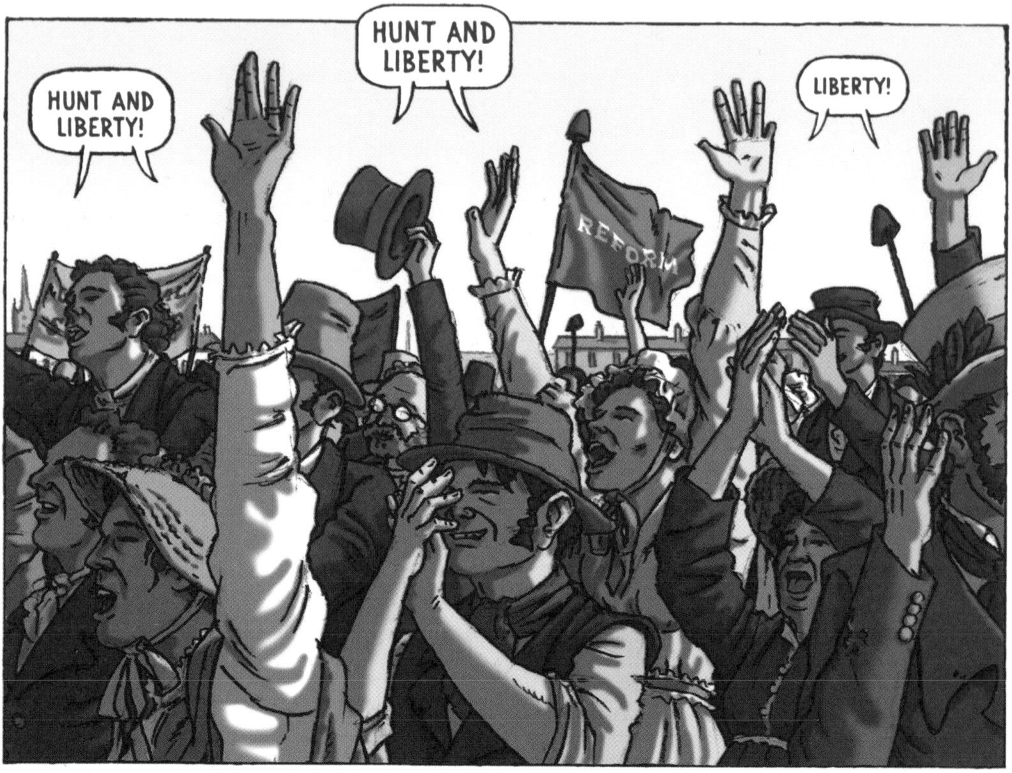
HUNT AND LIBERTY!
HUNT AND LIBERTY!
LIBERTY!
REFORM

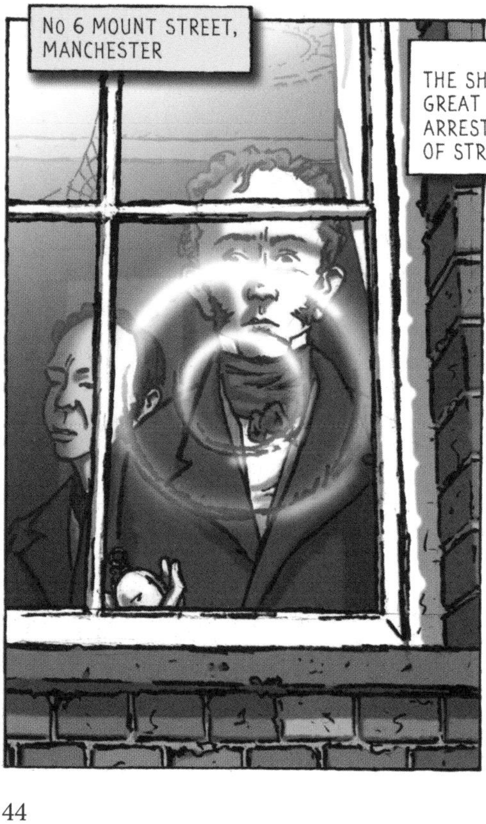
No 6 MOUNT STREET, MANCHESTER

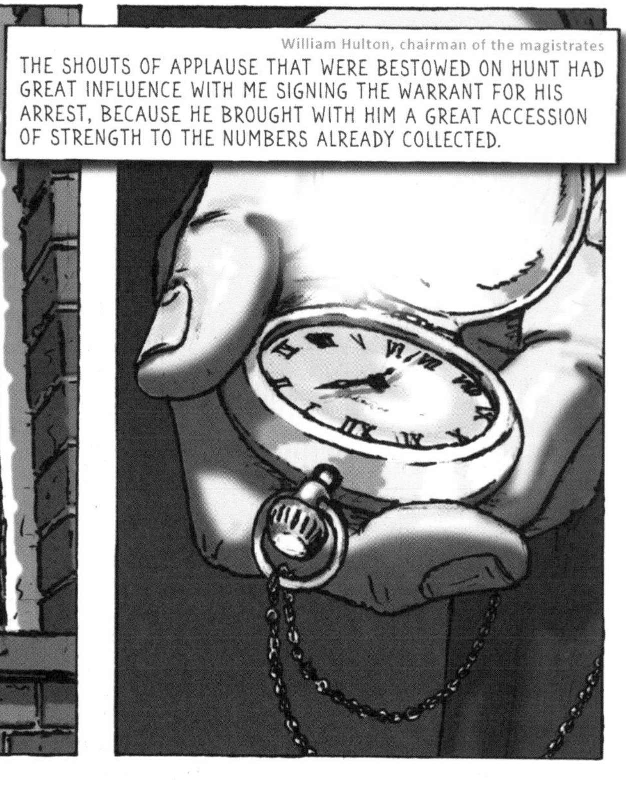
William Hulton, chairman of the magistrates
THE SHOUTS OF APPLAUSE THAT WERE BESTOWED ON HUNT HAD GREAT INFLUENCE WITH ME SIGNING THE WARRANT FOR HIS ARREST, BECAUSE HE BROUGHT WITH HIM A GREAT ACCESSION OF STRENGTH TO THE NUMBERS ALREADY COLLECTED.

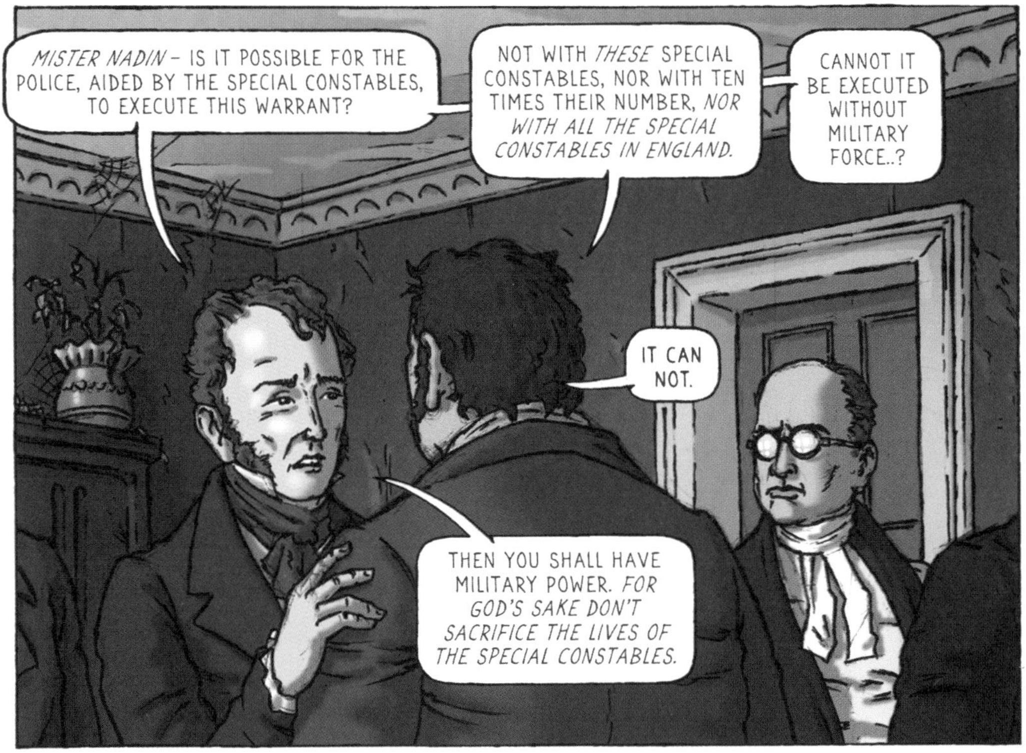
MISTER NADIN – IS IT POSSIBLE FOR THE POLICE, AIDED BY THE SPECIAL CONSTABLES, TO EXECUTE THIS WARRANT?
NOT WITH THESE SPECIAL CONSTABLES, NOR WITH TEN TIMES THEIR NUMBER, NOR WITH ALL THE SPECIAL CONSTABLES IN ENGLAND.
CANNOT IT BE EXECUTED WITHOUT MILITARY FORCE..?
IT CAN NOT.
THEN YOU SHALL HAVE MILITARY POWER. FOR GOD'S SAKE DON'T SACRIFICE THE LIVES OF THE SPECIAL CONSTABLES.

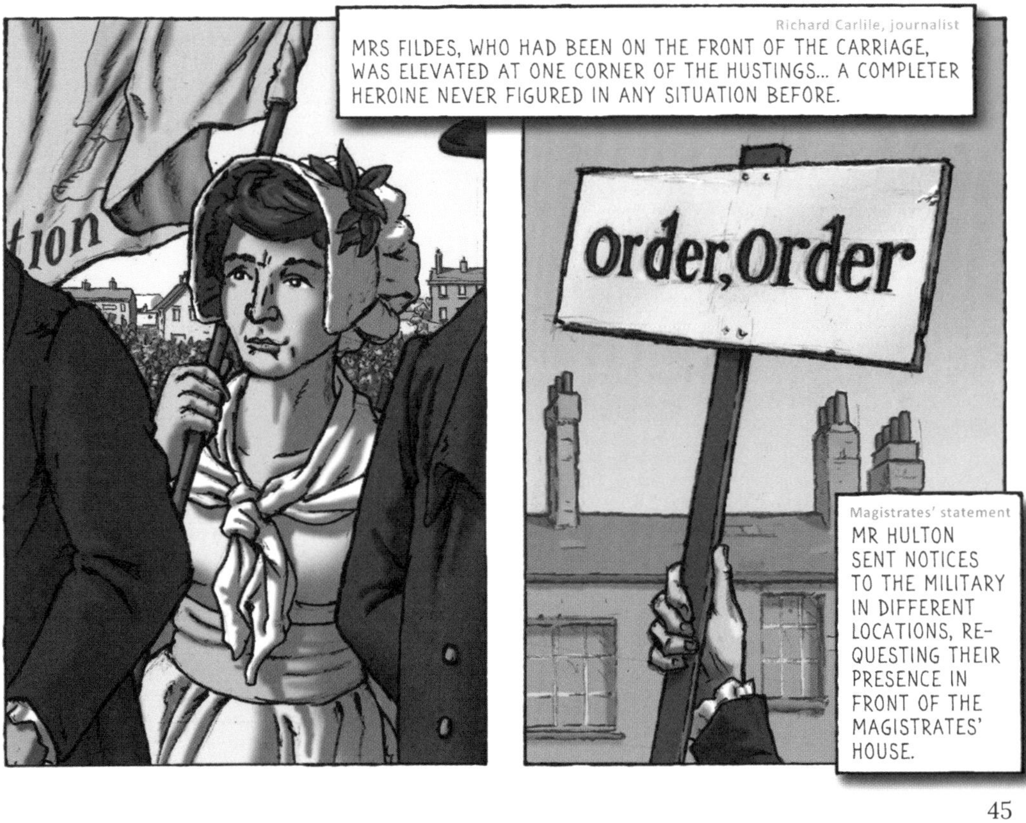
Richard Carlile, journalist
MRS FILDES, WHO HAD BEEN ON THE FRONT OF THE CARRIAGE, WAS ELEVATED AT ONE CORNER OF THE HUSTINGS... A COMPLETER HEROINE NEVER FIGURED IN ANY SITUATION BEFORE.
tion
Order, Order
Magistrates' statement
MR HULTON SENT NOTICES TO THE MILITARY IN DIFFERENT LOCATIONS, REQUESTING THEIR PRESENCE IN FRONT OF THE MAGISTRATES' HOUSE.

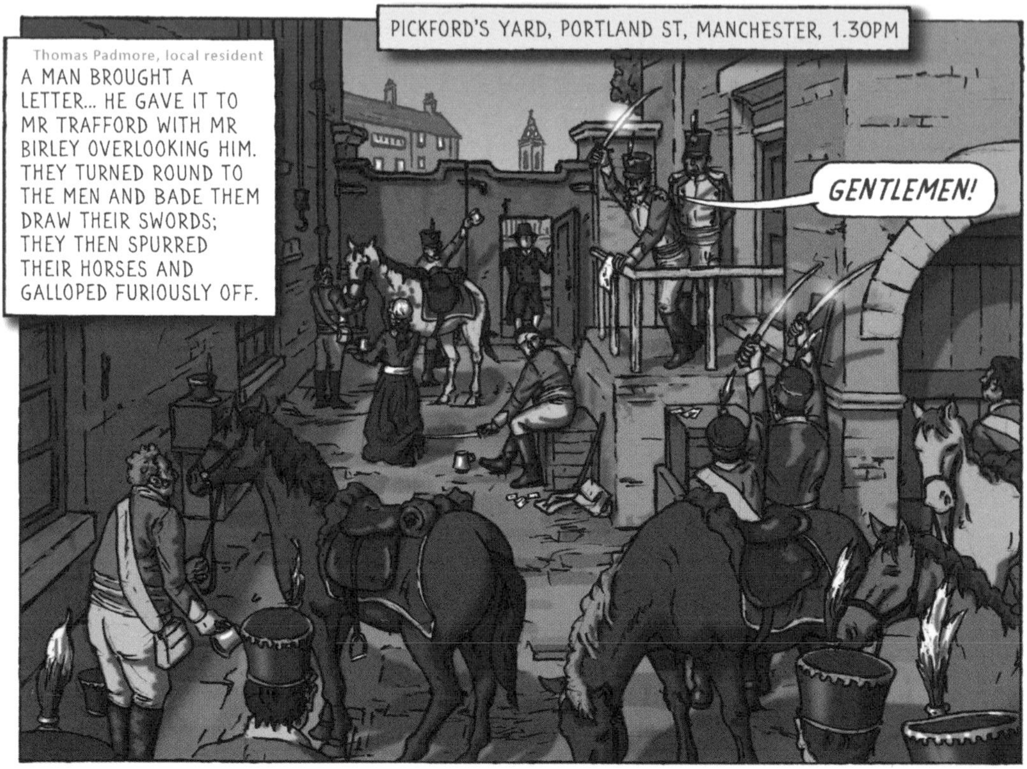
PICKFORD'S YARD, PORTLAND ST, MANCHESTER, 1.30PM
Thomas Padmore, local resident
A MAN BROUGHT A LETTER... HE GAVE IT TO MR TRAFFORD WITH MR BIRLEY OVERLOOKING HIM. THEY TURNED ROUND TO THE MEN AND BADE THEM DRAW THEIR SWORDS; THEY THEN SPURRED THEIR HORSES AND GALLOPED FURIOUSLY OFF.
GENTLEMEN!

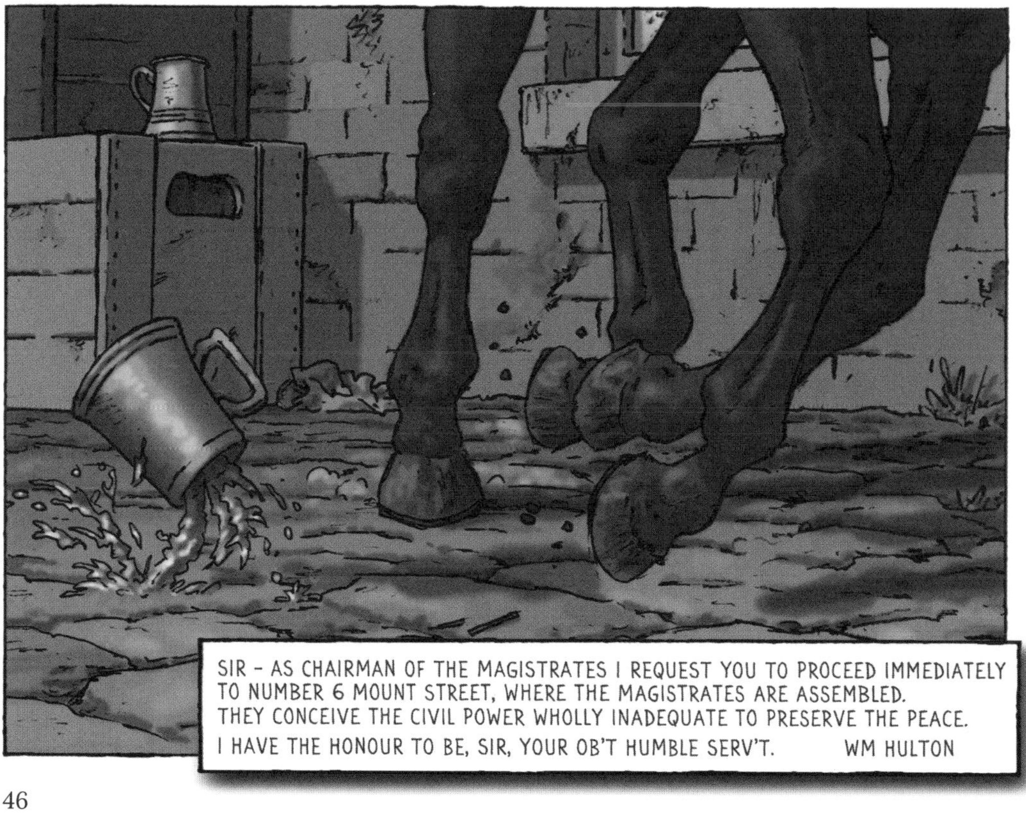
SIR – AS CHAIRMAN OF THE MAGISTRATES I REQUEST YOU TO PROCEED IMMEDIATELY TO NUMBER 6 MOUNT STREET, WHERE THE MAGISTRATES ARE ASSEMBLED.
THEY CONCEIVE THE CIVIL POWER WHOLLY INADEQUATE TO PRESERVE THE PEACE.
I HAVE THE HONOUR TO BE, SIR, YOUR OB'T HUMBLE SERV'T. WM HULTON

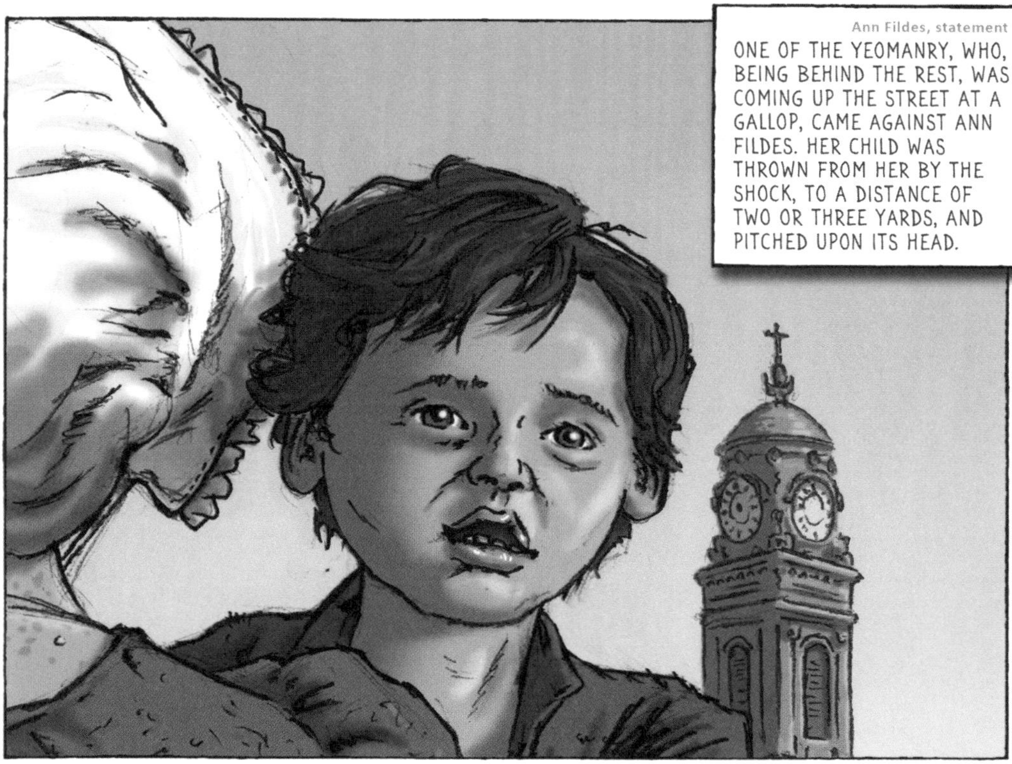
Ann Fildes, statement
ONE OF THE YEOMANRY, WHO, BEING BEHIND THE REST, WAS COMING UP THE STREET AT A GALLOP, CAME AGAINST ANN FILDES. HER CHILD WAS THROWN FROM HER BY THE SHOCK, TO A DISTANCE OF TWO OR THREE YARDS, AND PITCHED UPON ITS HEAD.

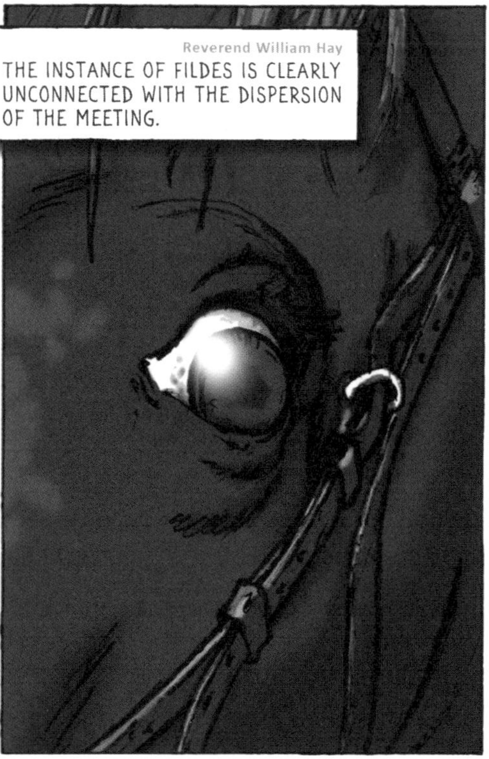
Reverend William Hay
THE INSTANCE OF FILDES IS CLEARLY UNCONNECTED WITH THE DISPERSION OF THE MEETING.

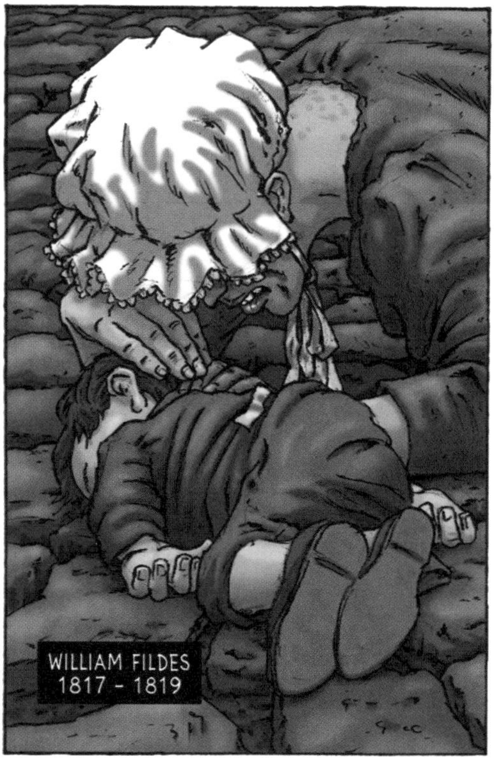
WILLIAM FILDES
1817 - 1819

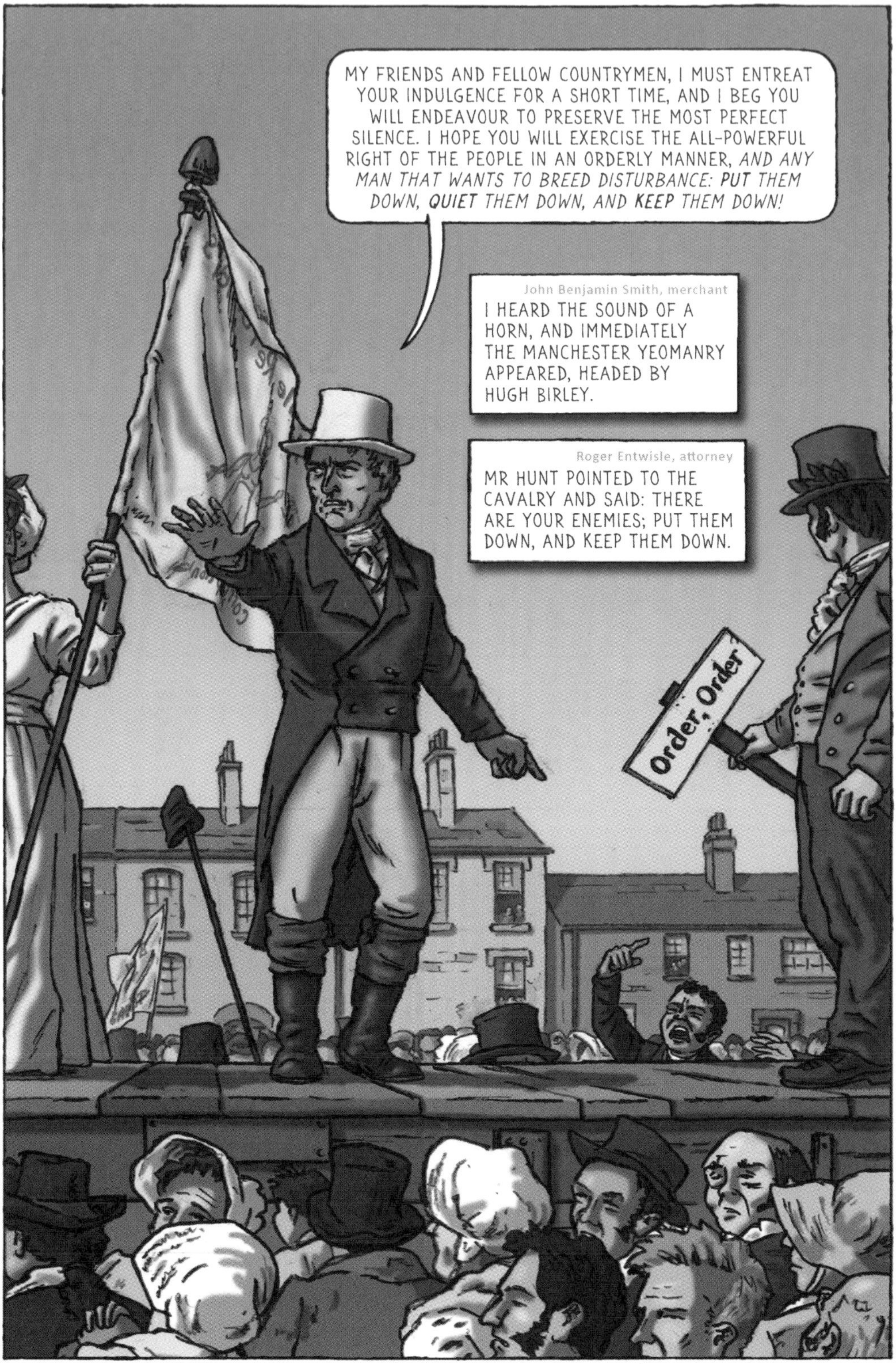
MY FRIENDS AND FELLOW COUNTRYMEN, I MUST ENTREAT YOUR INDULGENCE FOR A SHORT TIME, AND I BEG YOU WILL ENDEAVOUR TO PRESERVE THE MOST PERFECT SILENCE. I HOPE YOU WILL EXERCISE THE ALL-POWERFUL RIGHT OF THE PEOPLE IN AN ORDERLY MANNER, *AND ANY MAN THAT WANTS TO BREED DISTURBANCE:* ***PUT*** *THEM DOWN,* ***QUIET*** *THEM DOWN, AND* ***KEEP*** *THEM DOWN!*
John Benjamin Smith, merchant
I HEARD THE SOUND OF A HORN, AND IMMEDIATELY THE MANCHESTER YEOMANRY APPEARED, HEADED BY HUGH BIRLEY.
Roger Entwisle, attorney
MR HUNT POINTED TO THE CAVALRY AND SAID: THERE ARE YOUR ENEMIES; PUT THEM DOWN, AND KEEP THEM DOWN.
Order, Order

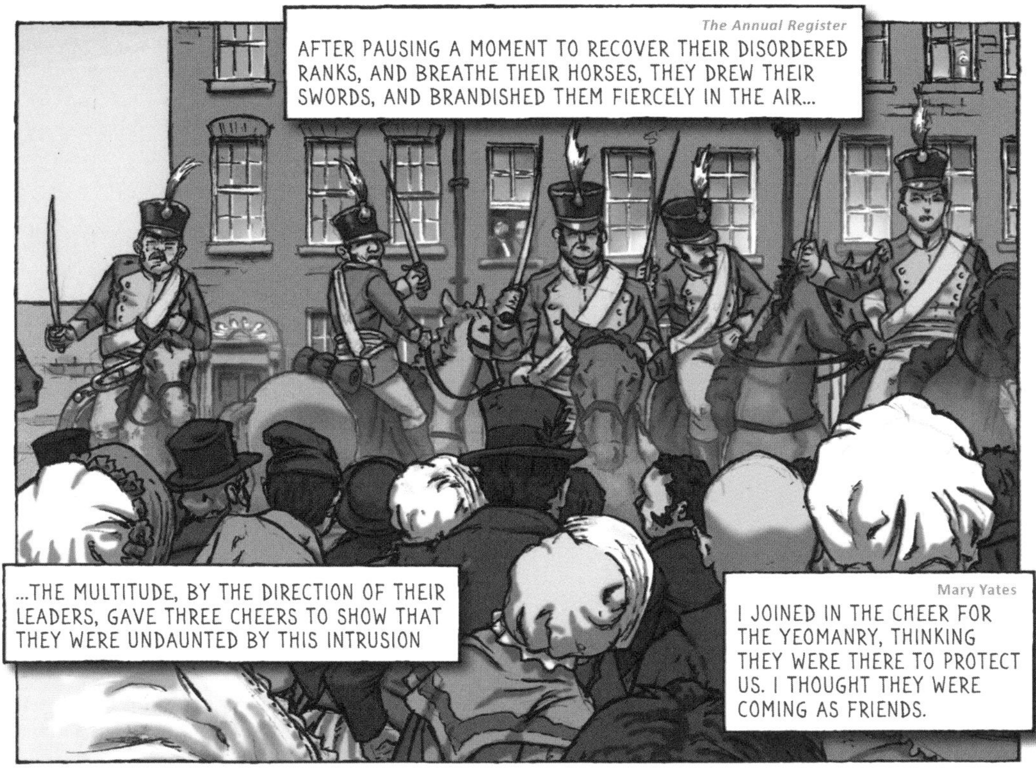
The Annual Register
AFTER PAUSING A MOMENT TO RECOVER THEIR DISORDERED RANKS, AND BREATHE THEIR HORSES, THEY DREW THEIR SWORDS, AND BRANDISHED THEM FIERCELY IN THE AIR...
...THE MULTITUDE, BY THE DIRECTION OF THEIR LEADERS, GAVE THREE CHEERS TO SHOW THAT THEY WERE UNDAUNTED BY THIS INTRUSION
Mary Yates
I JOINED IN THE CHEER FOR THE YEOMANRY, THINKING THEY WERE THERE TO PROTECT US. I THOUGHT THEY WERE COMING AS FRIENDS.

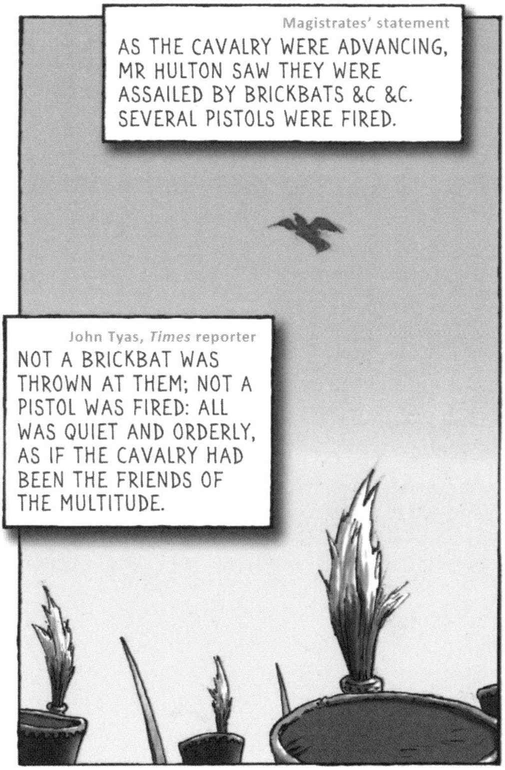
Magistrates' statement
AS THE CAVALRY WERE ADVANCING, MR HULTON SAW THEY WERE ASSAILED BY BRICKBATS &C &C. SEVERAL PISTOLS WERE FIRED.
John Tyas, *Times* reporter
NOT A BRICKBAT WAS THROWN AT THEM; NOT A PISTOL WAS FIRED: ALL WAS QUIET AND ORDERLY, AS IF THE CAVALRY HAD BEEN THE FRIENDS OF THE MULTITUDE.

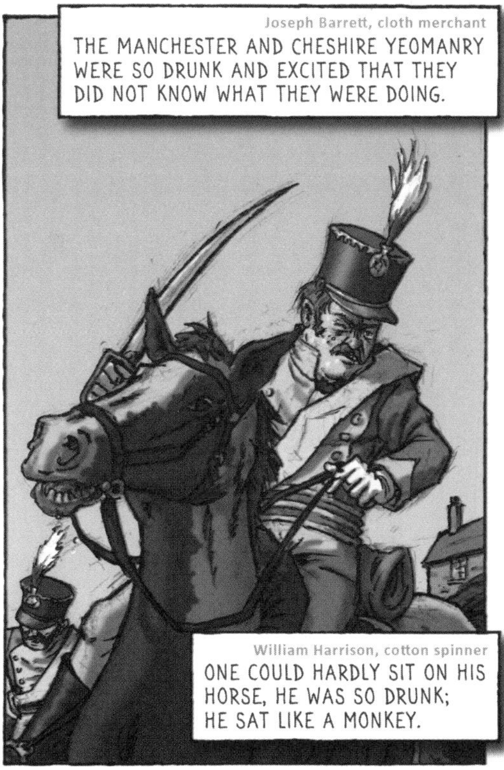
Joseph Barrett, cloth merchant
THE MANCHESTER AND CHESHIRE YEOMANRY WERE SO DRUNK AND EXCITED THAT THEY DID NOT KNOW WHAT THEY WERE DOING.
William Harrison, cotton spinner
ONE COULD HARDLY SIT ON HIS HORSE, HE WAS SO DRUNK; HE SAT LIKE A MONKEY.

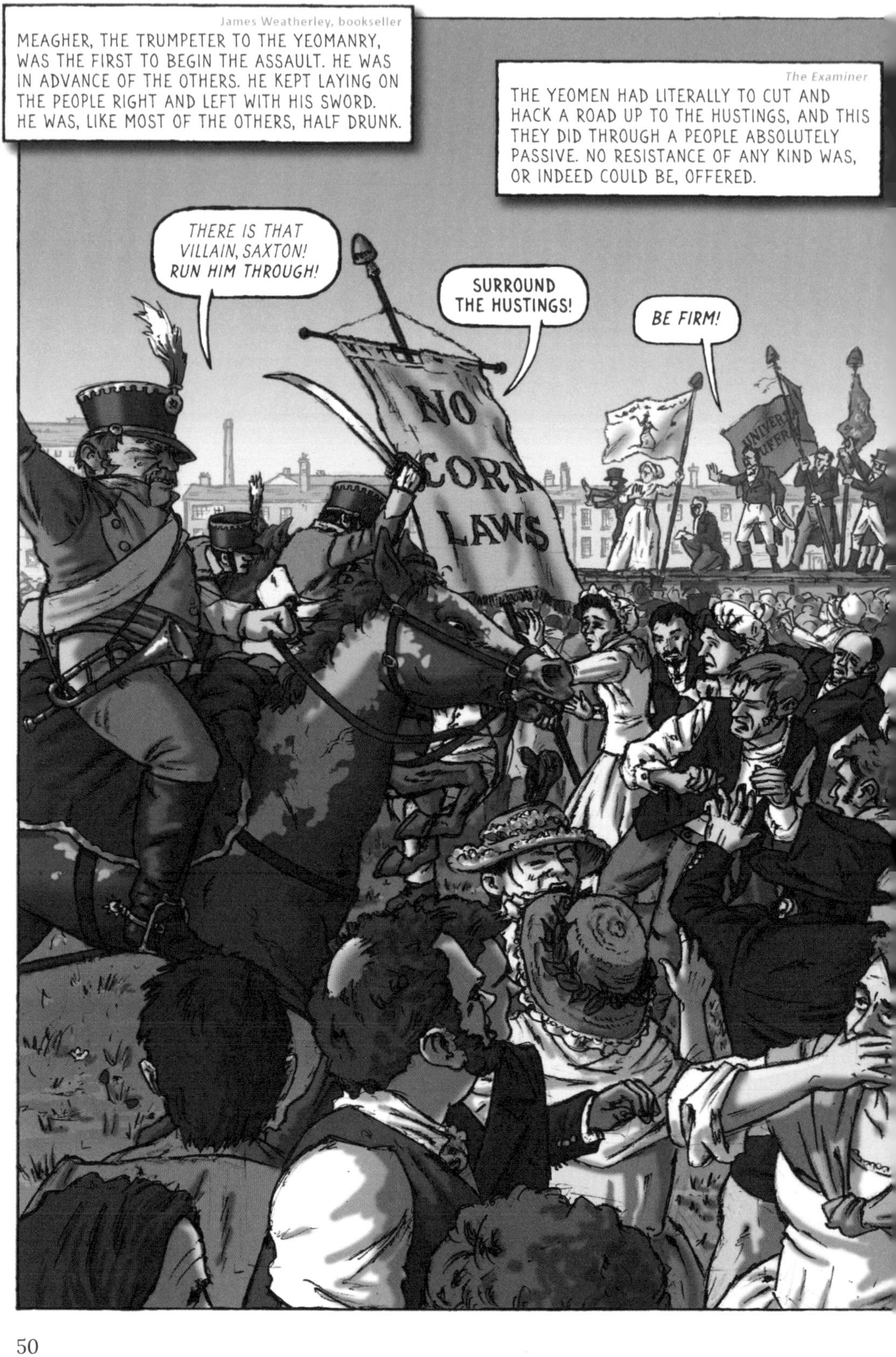
James Weatherley, bookseller
MEAGHER, THE TRUMPETER TO THE YEOMANRY, WAS THE FIRST TO BEGIN THE ASSAULT. HE WAS IN ADVANCE OF THE OTHERS. HE KEPT LAYING ON THE PEOPLE RIGHT AND LEFT WITH HIS SWORD. HE WAS, LIKE MOST OF THE OTHERS, HALF DRUNK.
The Examiner
THE YEOMEN HAD LITERALLY TO CUT AND HACK A ROAD UP TO THE HUSTINGS, AND THIS THEY DID THROUGH A PEOPLE ABSOLUTELY PASSIVE. NO RESISTANCE OF ANY KIND WAS, OR INDEED COULD BE, OFFERED.
THERE IS THAT VILLAIN, SAXTON! RUN HIM THROUGH!
NO CORN LAWS
SURROUND THE HUSTINGS!
BE FIRM!

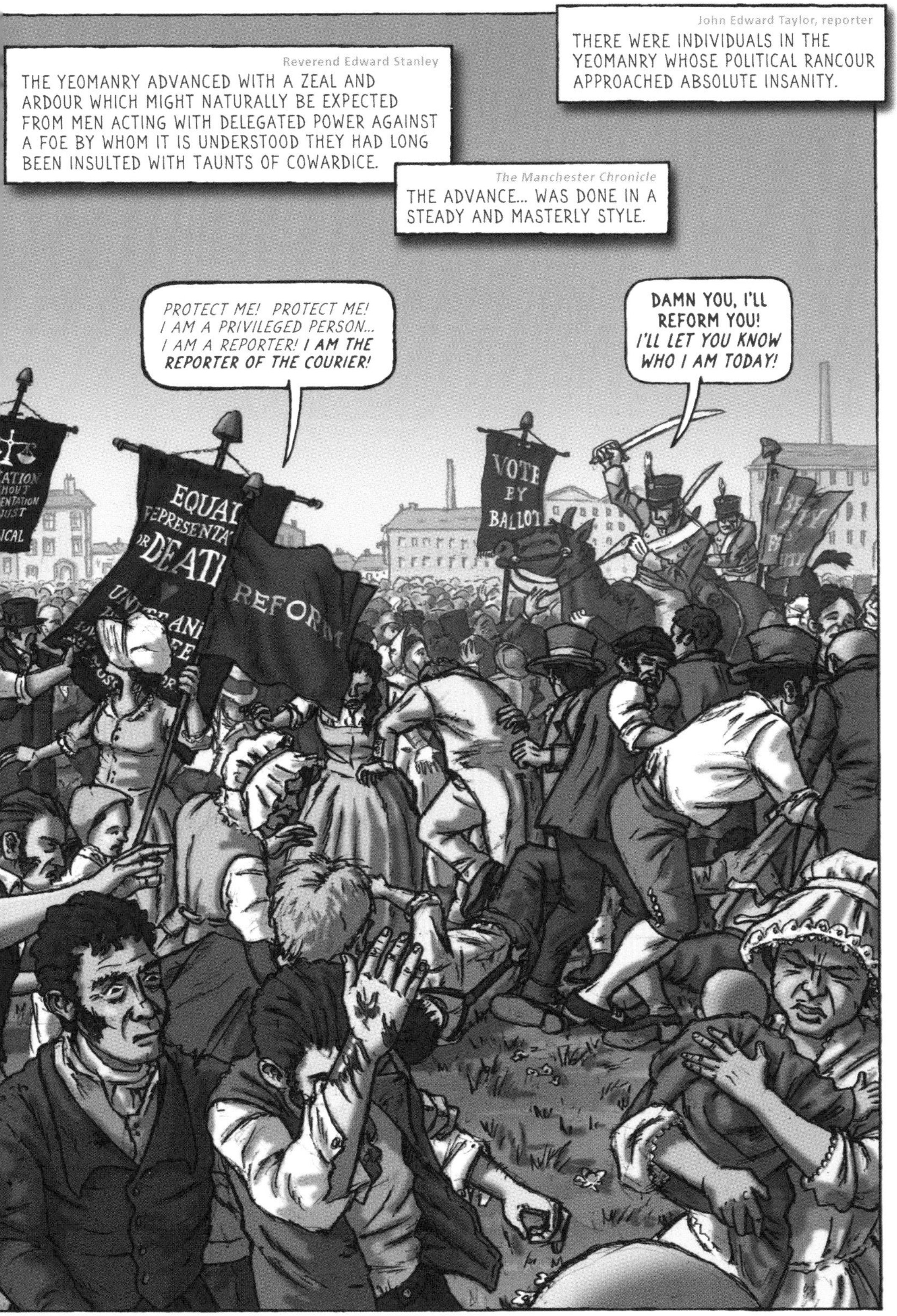
Reverend Edward Stanley
THE YEOMANRY ADVANCED WITH A ZEAL AND ARDOUR WHICH MIGHT NATURALLY BE EXPECTED FROM MEN ACTING WITH DELEGATED POWER AGAINST A FOE BY WHOM IT IS UNDERSTOOD THEY HAD LONG BEEN INSULTED WITH TAUNTS OF COWARDICE.
John Edward Taylor, reporter
THERE WERE INDIVIDUALS IN THE YEOMANRY WHOSE POLITICAL RANCOUR APPROACHED ABSOLUTE INSANITY.
The Manchester Chronicle
THE ADVANCE... WAS DONE IN A STEADY AND MASTERLY STYLE.
PROTECT ME! PROTECT ME! I AM A PRIVILEGED PERSON... I AM A REPORTER! I AM THE REPORTER OF THE COURIER!
DAMN YOU, I'LL REFORM YOU! I'LL LET YOU KNOW WHO I AM TODAY!
REFORM
VOTE BY BALLOT

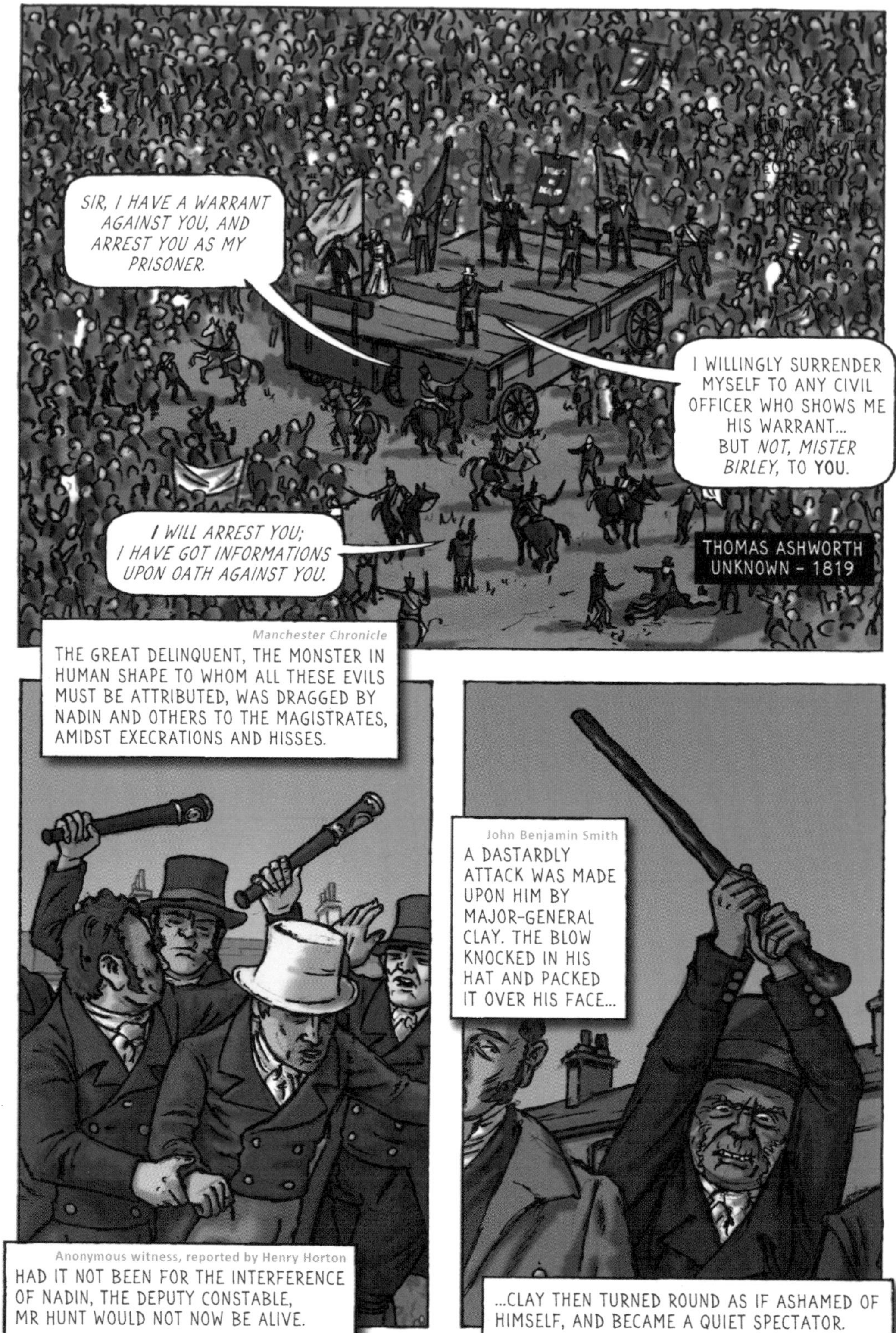

SIR, I HAVE A WARRANT AGAINST YOU, AND ARREST YOU AS MY PRISONER.
I WILLINGLY SURRENDER MYSELF TO ANY CIVIL OFFICER WHO SHOWS ME HIS WARRANT... BUT *NOT, MISTER BIRLEY,* TO **YOU**.
I WILL ARREST YOU; I HAVE GOT INFORMATIONS UPON OATH AGAINST YOU.
THOMAS ASHWORTH UNKNOWN – 1819
Manchester Chronicle
THE GREAT DELINQUENT, THE MONSTER IN HUMAN SHAPE TO WHOM ALL THESE EVILS MUST BE ATTRIBUTED, WAS DRAGGED BY NADIN AND OTHERS TO THE MAGISTRATES, AMIDST EXECRATIONS AND HISSES.
Anonymous witness, reported by Henry Horton
HAD IT NOT BEEN FOR THE INTERFERENCE OF NADIN, THE DEPUTY CONSTABLE, MR HUNT WOULD NOT NOW BE ALIVE.
John Benjamin Smith
A DASTARDLY ATTACK WAS MADE UPON HIM BY MAJOR-GENERAL CLAY. THE BLOW KNOCKED IN HIS HAT AND PACKED IT OVER HIS FACE...
...CLAY THEN TURNED ROUND AS IF ASHAMED OF HIMSELF, AND BECAME A QUIET SPECTATOR.

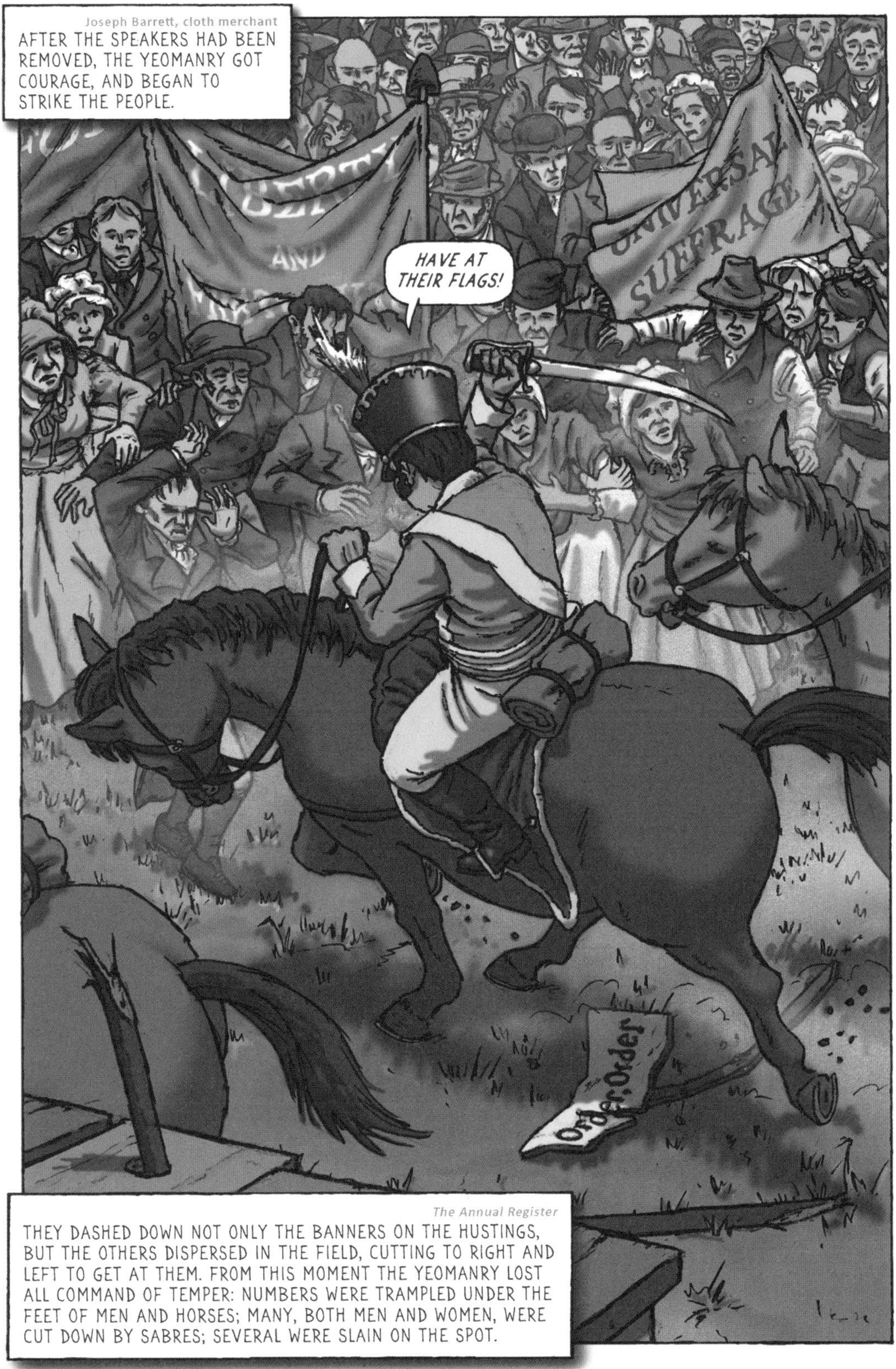
Joseph Barrett, cloth merchant
AFTER THE SPEAKERS HAD BEEN REMOVED, THE YEOMANRY GOT COURAGE, AND BEGAN TO STRIKE THE PEOPLE.
HAVE AT THEIR FLAGS!
UNIVERSAL SUFFRAGE
Order Order
The Annual Register
THEY DASHED DOWN NOT ONLY THE BANNERS ON THE HUSTINGS, BUT THE OTHERS DISPERSED IN THE FIELD, CUTTING TO RIGHT AND LEFT TO GET AT THEM. FROM THIS MOMENT THE YEOMANRY LOST ALL COMMAND OF TEMPER: NUMBERS WERE TRAMPLED UNDER THE FEET OF MEN AND HORSES; MANY, BOTH MEN AND WOMEN, WERE CUT DOWN BY SABRES; SEVERAL WERE SLAIN ON THE SPOT.

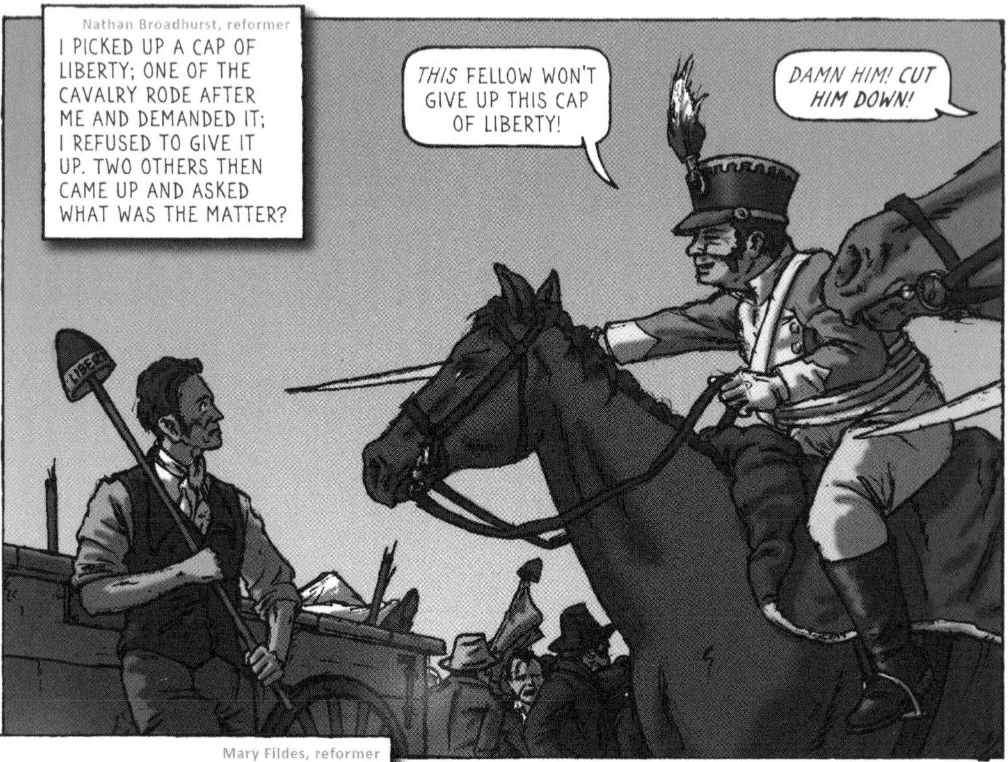
Nathan Broadhurst, reformer
I PICKED UP A CAP OF LIBERTY; ONE OF THE CAVALRY RODE AFTER ME AND DEMANDED IT; I REFUSED TO GIVE IT UP. TWO OTHERS THEN CAME UP AND ASKED WHAT WAS THE MATTER?
THIS FELLOW WON'T GIVE UP THIS CAP OF LIBERTY!
DAMN HIM! CUT HIM DOWN!
LIBERTY

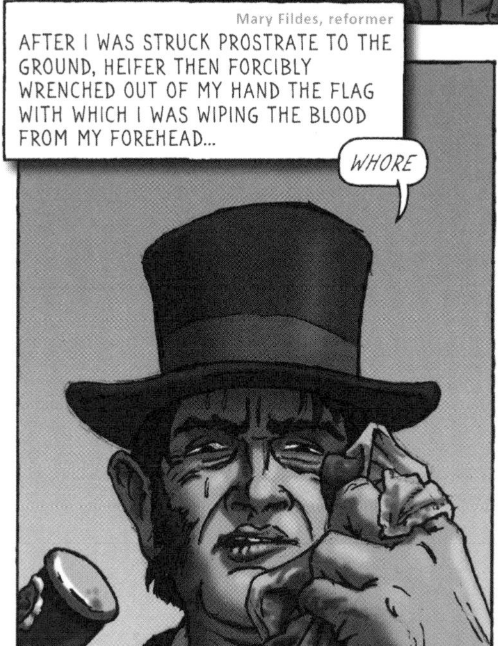
Mary Fildes, reformer
AFTER I WAS STRUCK PROSTRATE TO THE GROUND, HEIFER THEN FORCIBLY WRENCHED OUT OF MY HAND THE FLAG WITH WHICH I WAS WIPING THE BLOOD FROM MY FOREHEAD...
WHORE
HE THEN PUT IT INTO HIS OWN POCKET...

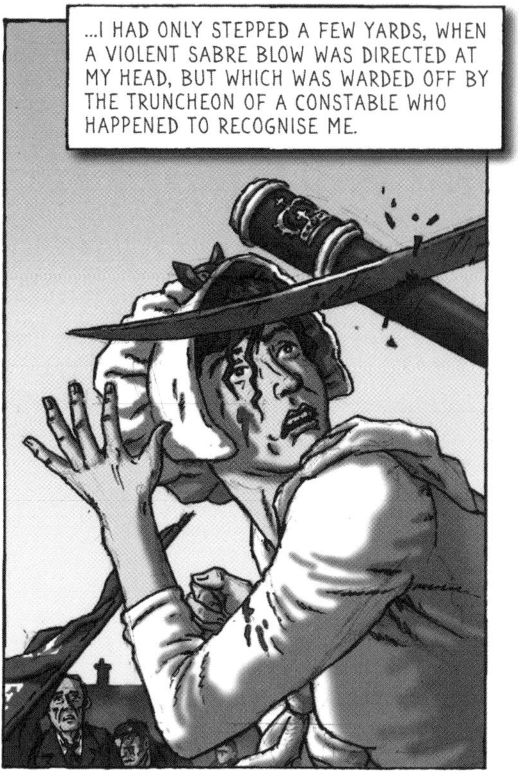
...I HAD ONLY STEPPED A FEW YARDS, WHEN A VIOLENT SABRE BLOW WAS DIRECTED AT MY HEAD, BUT WHICH WAS WARDED OFF BY THE TRUNCHEON OF A CONSTABLE WHO HAPPENED TO RECOGNISE ME.

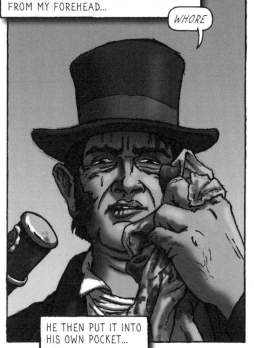

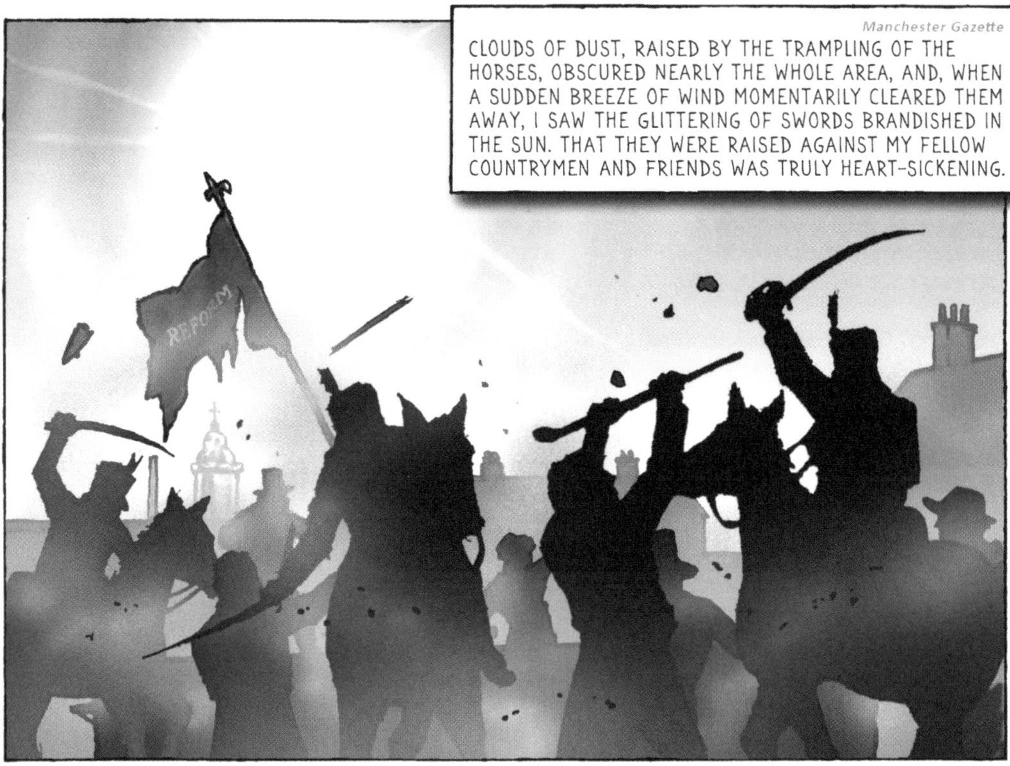
Manchester Gazette
CLOUDS OF DUST, RAISED BY THE TRAMPLING OF THE HORSES, OBSCURED NEARLY THE WHOLE AREA, AND, WHEN A SUDDEN BREEZE OF WIND MOMENTARILY CLEARED THEM AWAY, I SAW THE GLITTERING OF SWORDS BRANDISHED IN THE SUN. THAT THEY WERE RAISED AGAINST MY FELLOW COUNTRYMEN AND FRIENDS WAS TRULY HEART-SICKENING.
REFORM

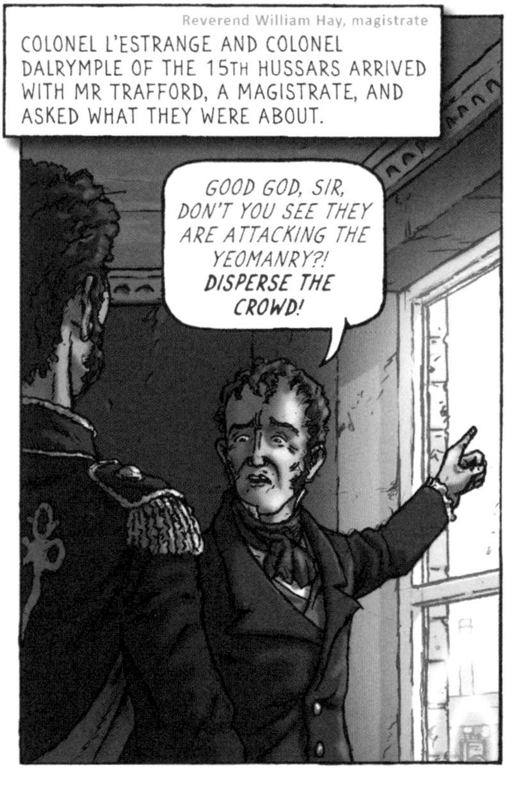
Reverend William Hay, magistrate
COLONEL L'ESTRANGE AND COLONEL DALRYMPLE OF THE 15TH HUSSARS ARRIVED WITH MR TRAFFORD, A MAGISTRATE, AND ASKED WHAT THEY WERE ABOUT.
GOOD GOD, SIR, DON'T YOU SEE THEY ARE ATTACKING THE YEOMANRY?! DISPERSE THE CROWD!

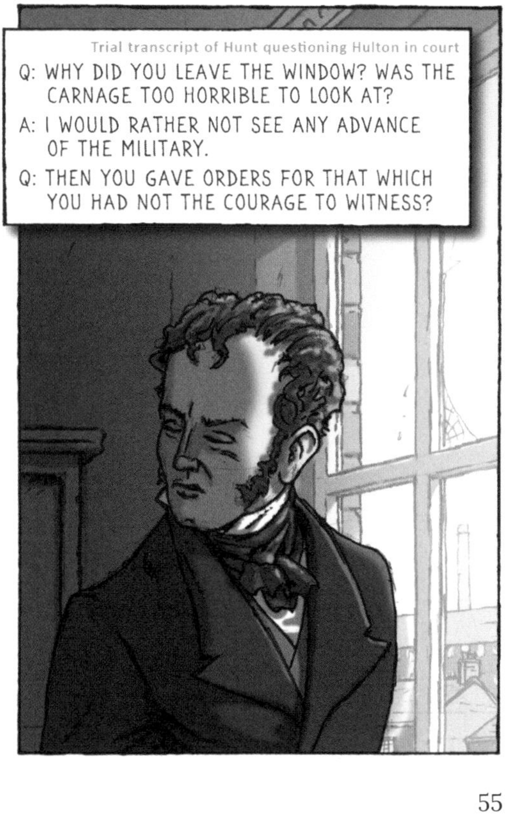
Trial transcript of Hunt questioning Hulton in court
Q: WHY DID YOU LEAVE THE WINDOW? WAS THE CARNAGE TOO HORRIBLE TO LOOK AT?
A: I WOULD RATHER NOT SEE ANY ADVANCE OF THE MILITARY.
Q: THEN YOU GAVE ORDERS FOR THAT WHICH YOU HAD NOT THE COURAGE TO WITNESS?

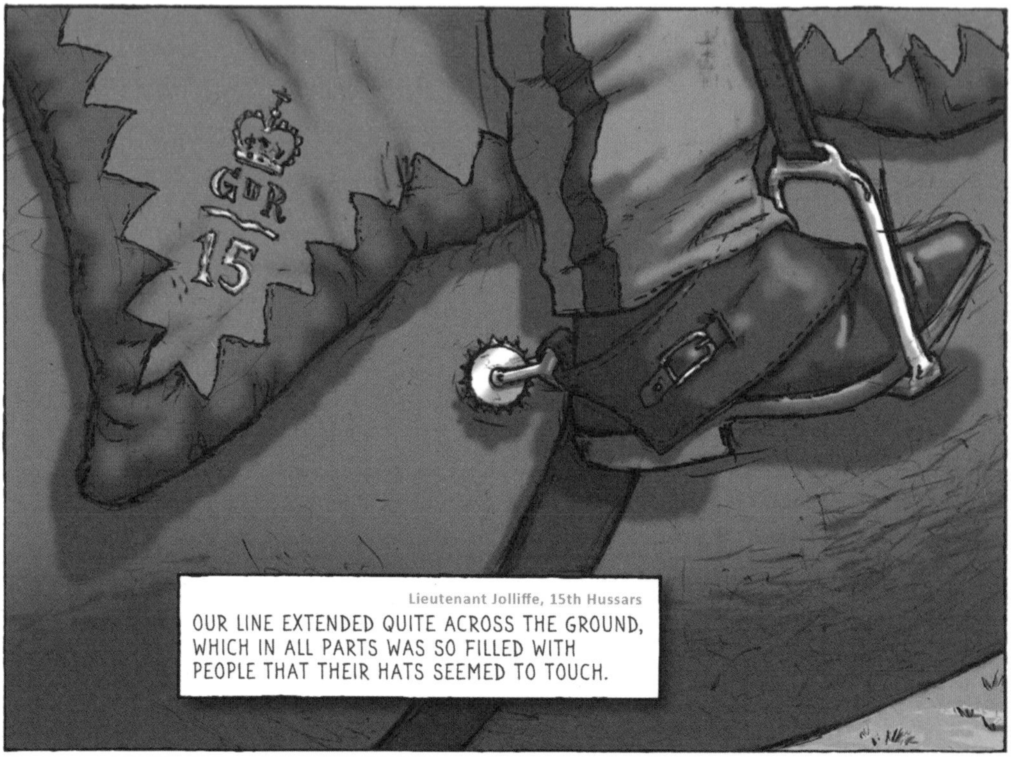
GVR
15
Lieutenant Jolliffe, 15th Hussars
OUR LINE EXTENDED QUITE ACROSS THE GROUND, WHICH IN ALL PARTS WAS SO FILLED WITH PEOPLE THAT THEIR HATS SEEMED TO TOUCH.

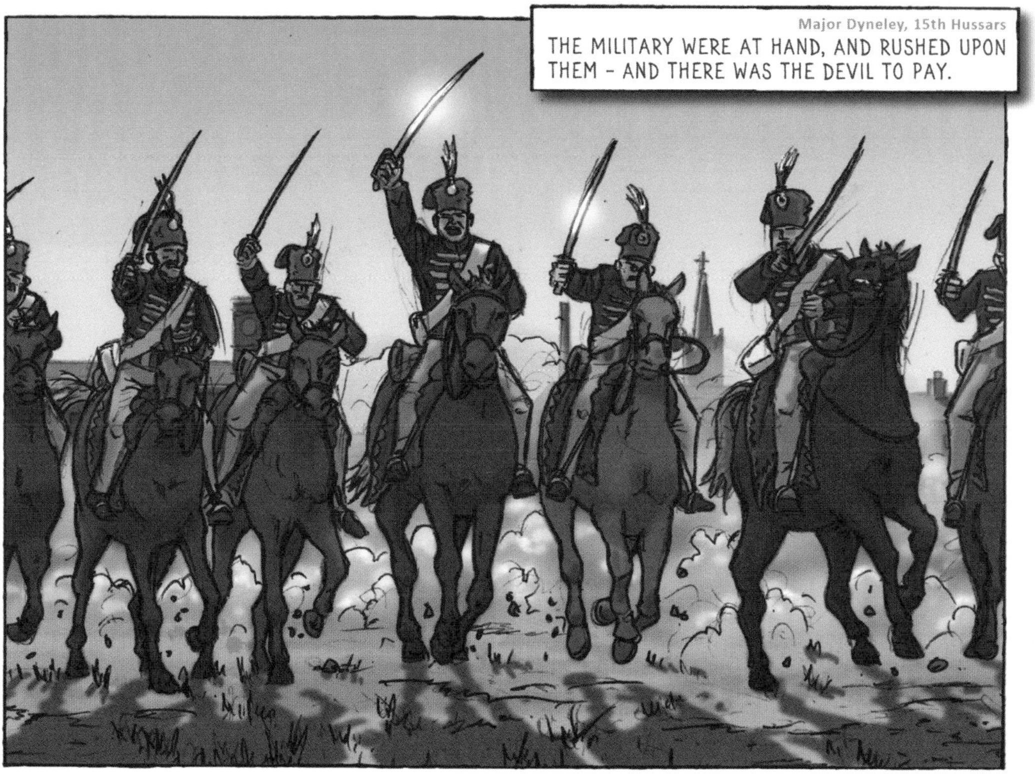
Major Dyneley, 15th Hussars
THE MILITARY WERE AT HAND, AND RUSHED UPON THEM - AND THERE WAS THE DEVIL TO PAY.

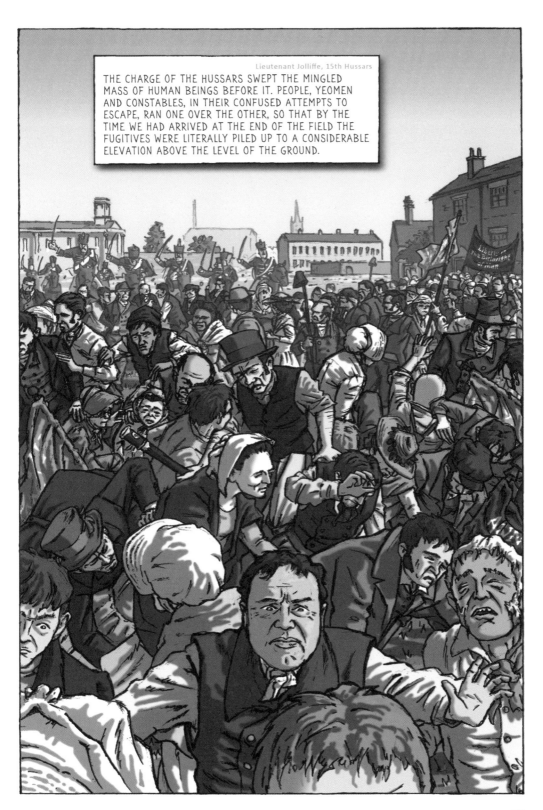

Lieutenant Jolliffe, 15th Hussars

THE CHARGE OF THE HUSSARS SWEPT THE MINGLED MASS OF HUMAN BEINGS BEFORE IT. PEOPLE, YEOMEN AND CONSTABLES, IN THEIR CONFUSED ATTEMPTS TO ESCAPE, RAN ONE OVER THE OTHER, SO THAT BY THE TIME WE HAD ARRIVED AT THE END OF THE FIELD THE FUGITIVES WERE LITERALLY PILED UP TO A CONSIDERABLE ELEVATION ABOVE THE LEVEL OF THE GROUND.

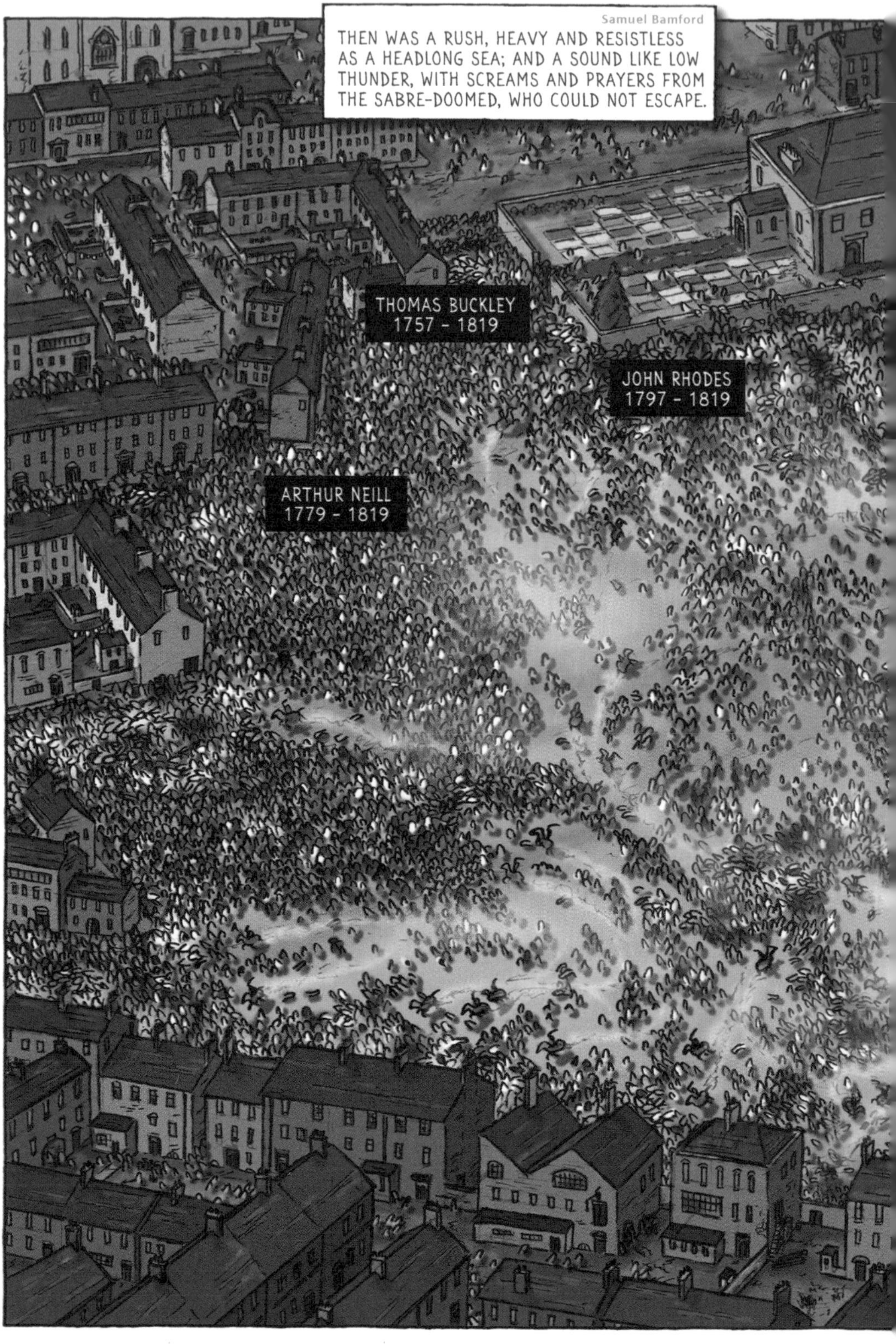
Samuel Bamford
THEN WAS A RUSH, HEAVY AND RESISTLESS AS A HEADLONG SEA; AND A SOUND LIKE LOW THUNDER, WITH SCREAMS AND PRAYERS FROM THE SABRE-DOOMED, WHO COULD NOT ESCAPE.
THOMAS BUCKLEY 1757 - 1819
JOHN RHODES 1797 - 1819
ARTHUR NEILL 1779 - 1819

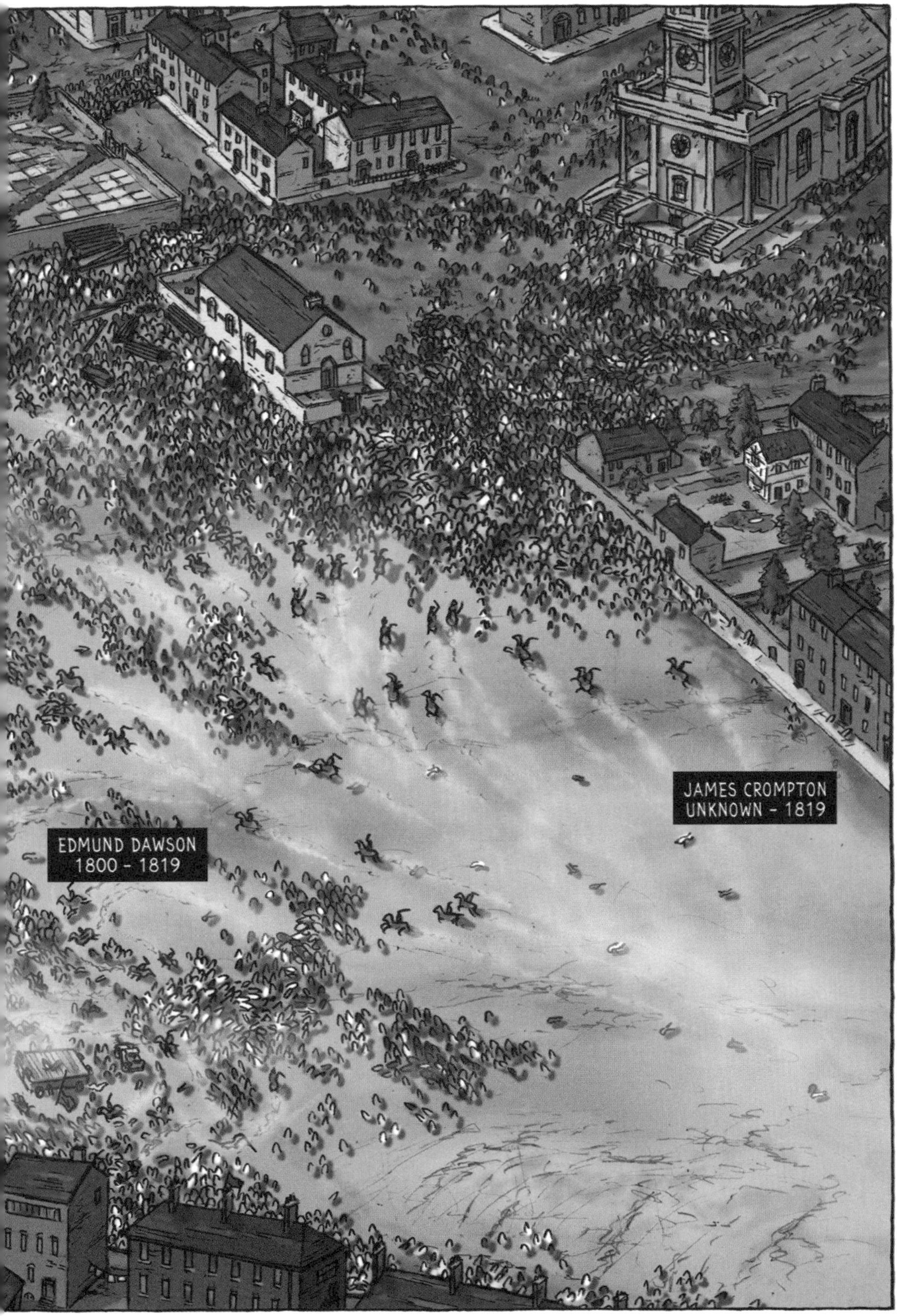

JAMES CROMPTON
UNKNOWN - 1819
EDMUND DAWSON
1800 - 1819

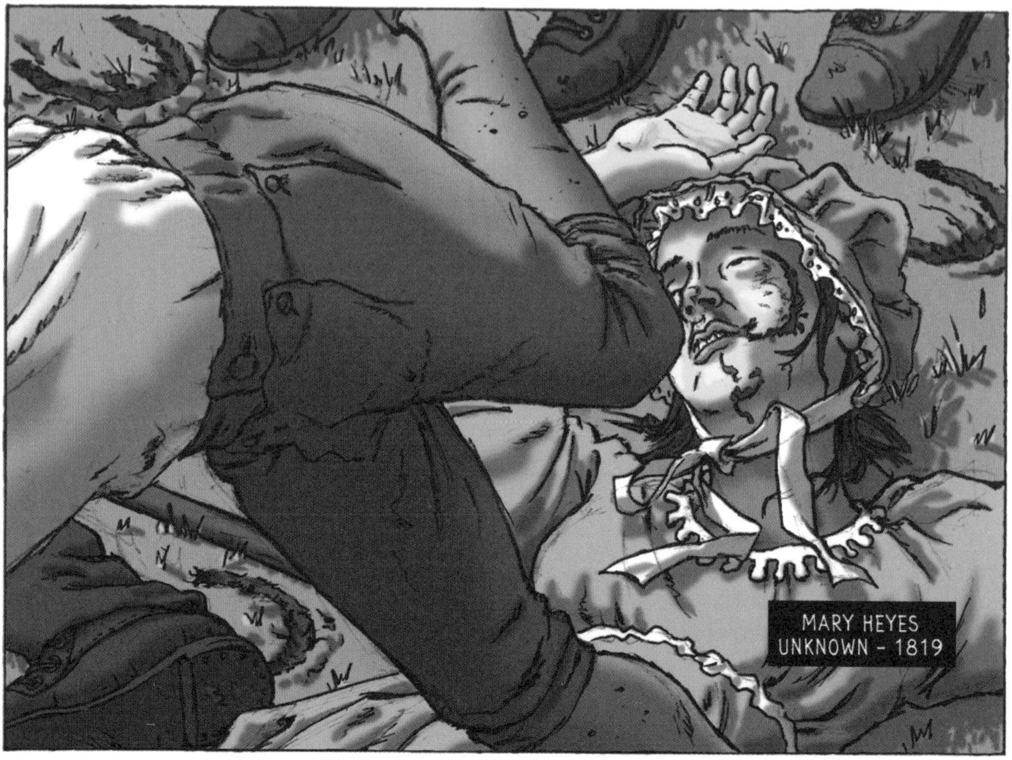
MARY HEYES
UNKNOWN - 1819

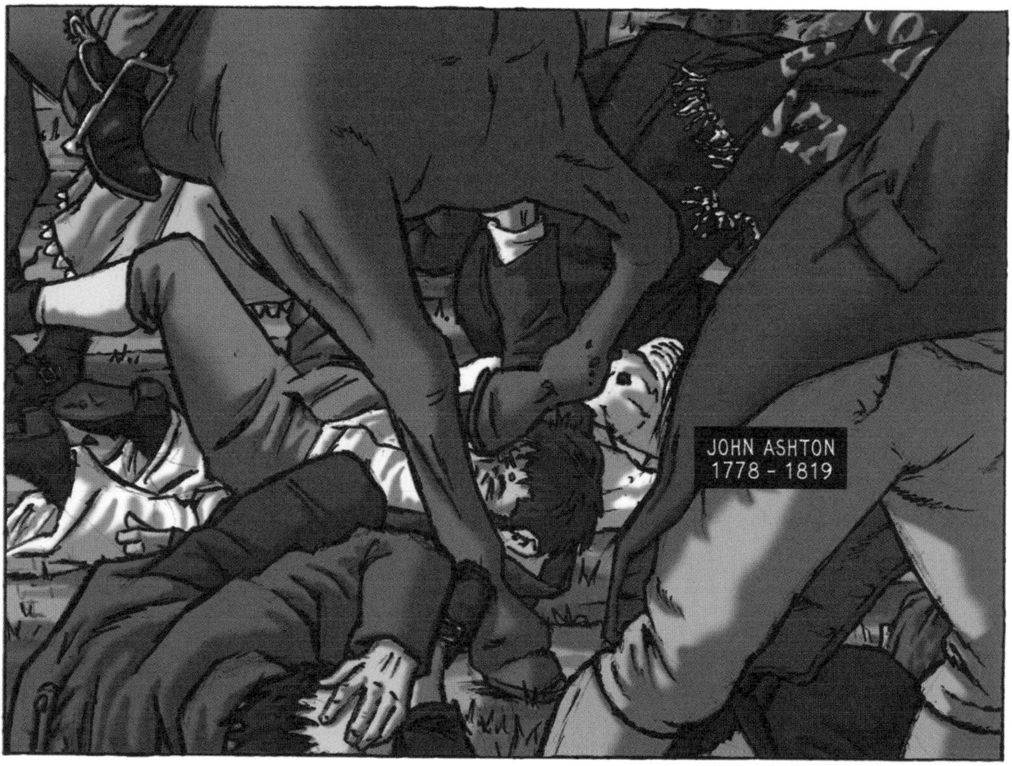
JOHN ASHTON
1778 - 1819

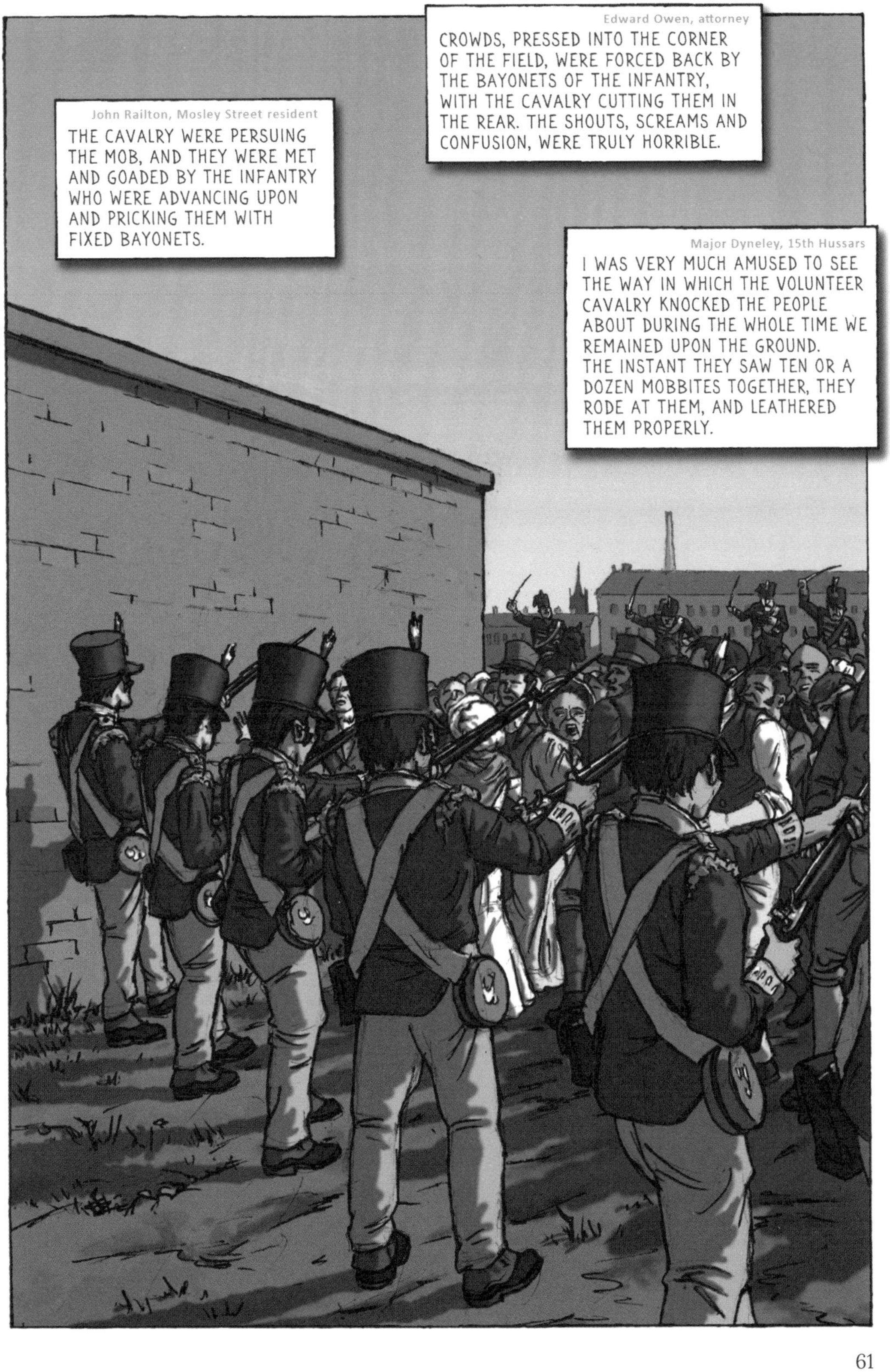
John Railton, Mosley Street resident
THE CAVALRY WERE PERSUING THE MOB, AND THEY WERE MET AND GOADED BY THE INFANTRY WHO WERE ADVANCING UPON AND PRICKING THEM WITH FIXED BAYONETS.
Edward Owen, attorney
CROWDS, PRESSED INTO THE CORNER OF THE FIELD, WERE FORCED BACK BY THE BAYONETS OF THE INFANTRY, WITH THE CAVALRY CUTTING THEM IN THE REAR. THE SHOUTS, SCREAMS AND CONFUSION, WERE TRULY HORRIBLE.
Major Dyneley, 15th Hussars
I WAS VERY MUCH AMUSED TO SEE THE WAY IN WHICH THE VOLUNTEER CAVALRY KNOCKED THE PEOPLE ABOUT DURING THE WHOLE TIME WE REMAINED UPON THE GROUND. THE INSTANT THEY SAW TEN OR A DOZEN MOBBITES TOGETHER, THEY RODE AT THEM, AND LEATHERED THEM PROPERLY.

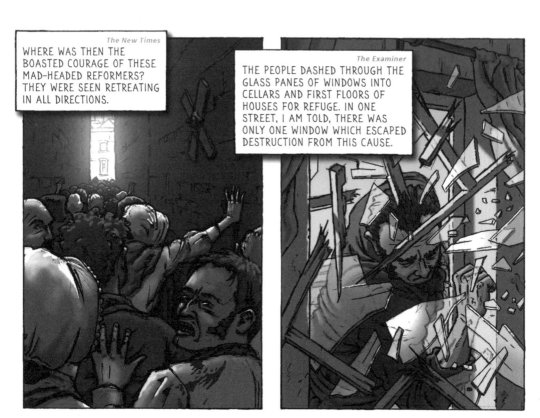

The New Times
WHERE WAS THEN THE BOASTED COURAGE OF THESE MAD-HEADED REFORMERS? THEY WERE SEEN RETREATING IN ALL DIRECTIONS.

The Examiner
THE PEOPLE DASHED THROUGH THE GLASS PANES OF WINDOWS INTO CELLARS AND FIRST FLOORS OF HOUSES FOR REFUGE. IN ONE STREET, I AM TOLD, THERE WAS ONLY ONE WINDOW WHICH ESCAPED DESTRUCTION FROM THIS CAUSE.

Joseph Brierley, hatter
I WAS FORCED AGAINST AN IRON RAILING OF A NEARBY CELLAR WHICH GAVE WAY; A LOT OF PEOPLE FELL ON TOP OF ME.

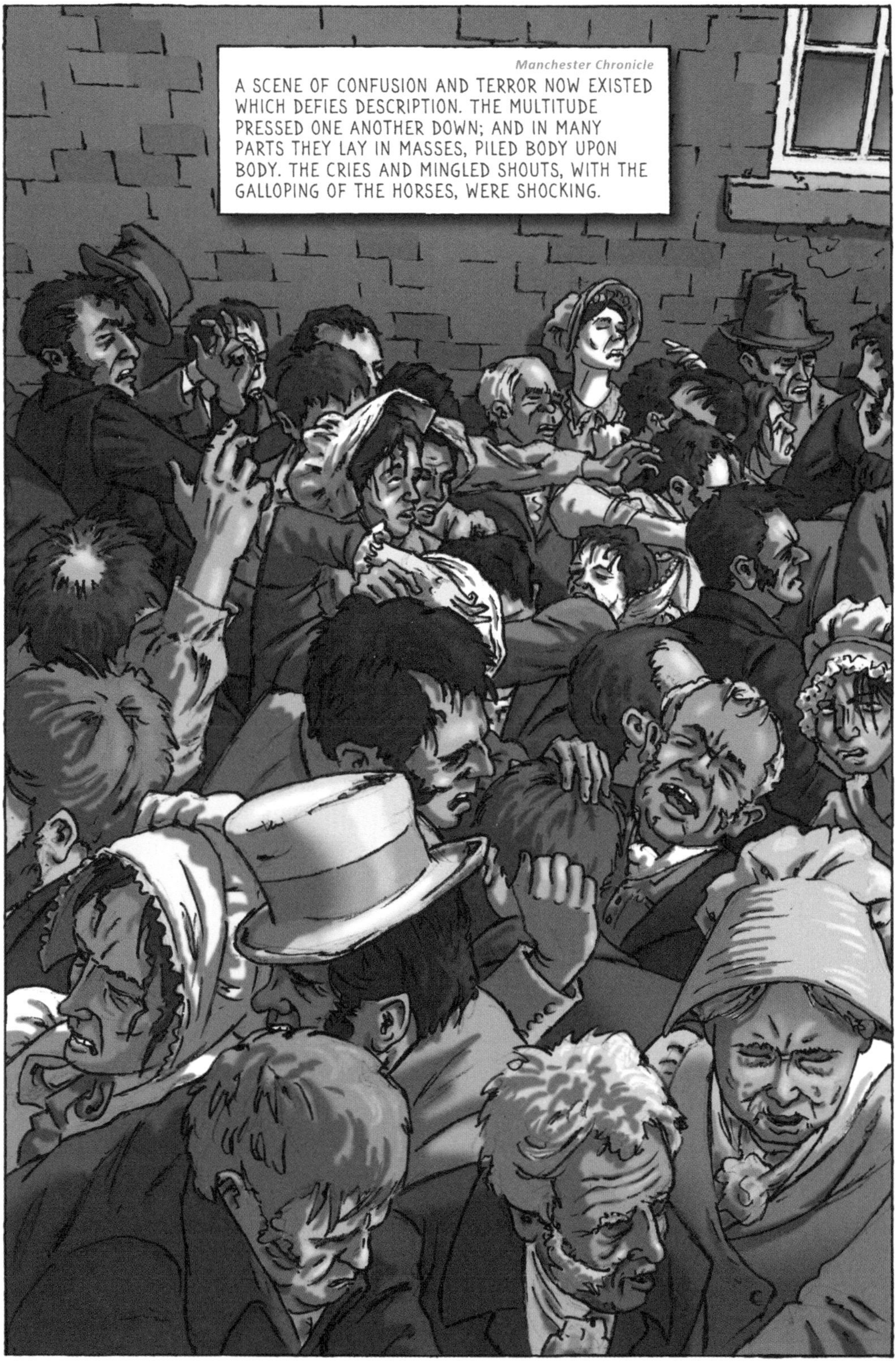
Manchester Chronicle
A SCENE OF CONFUSION AND TERROR NOW EXISTED WHICH DEFIES DESCRIPTION. THE MULTITUDE PRESSED ONE ANOTHER DOWN; AND IN MANY PARTS THEY LAY IN MASSES, PILED BODY UPON BODY. THE CRIES AND MINGLED SHOUTS, WITH THE GALLOPING OF THE HORSES, WERE SHOCKING.

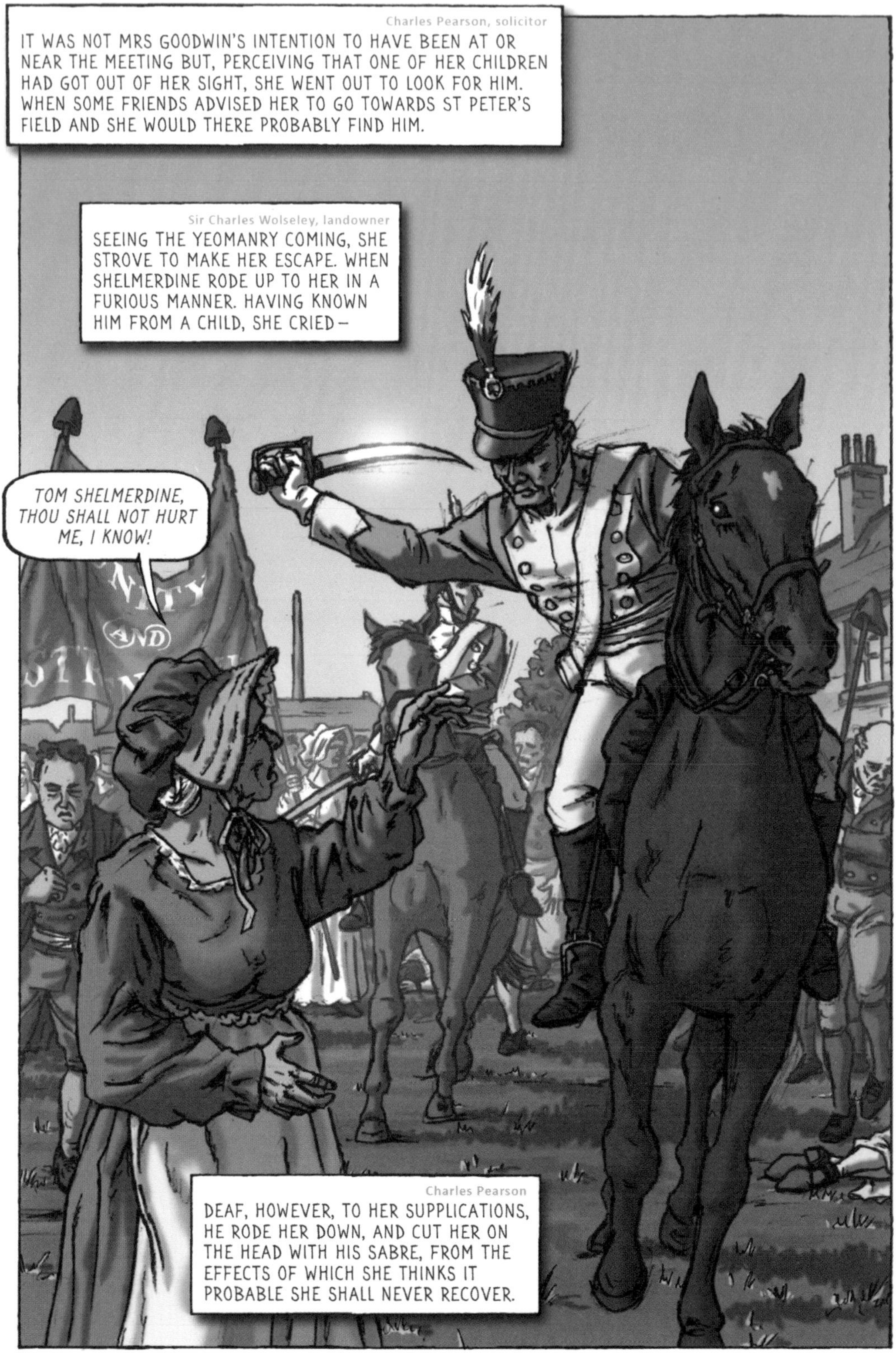
Charles Pearson, solicitor
IT WAS NOT MRS GOODWIN'S INTENTION TO HAVE BEEN AT OR NEAR THE MEETING BUT, PERCEIVING THAT ONE OF HER CHILDREN HAD GOT OUT OF HER SIGHT, SHE WENT OUT TO LOOK FOR HIM. WHEN SOME FRIENDS ADVISED HER TO GO TOWARDS ST PETER'S FIELD AND SHE WOULD THERE PROBABLY FIND HIM.
Sir Charles Wolseley, landowner
SEEING THE YEOMANRY COMING, SHE STROVE TO MAKE HER ESCAPE. WHEN SHELMERDINE RODE UP TO HER IN A FURIOUS MANNER. HAVING KNOWN HIM FROM A CHILD, SHE CRIED—
TOM SHELMERDINE, THOU SHALL NOT HURT ME, I KNOW!
Charles Pearson
DEAF, HOWEVER, TO HER SUPPLICATIONS, HE RODE HER DOWN, AND CUT HER ON THE HEAD WITH HIS SABRE, FROM THE EFFECTS OF WHICH SHE THINKS IT PROBABLE SHE SHALL NEVER RECOVER.

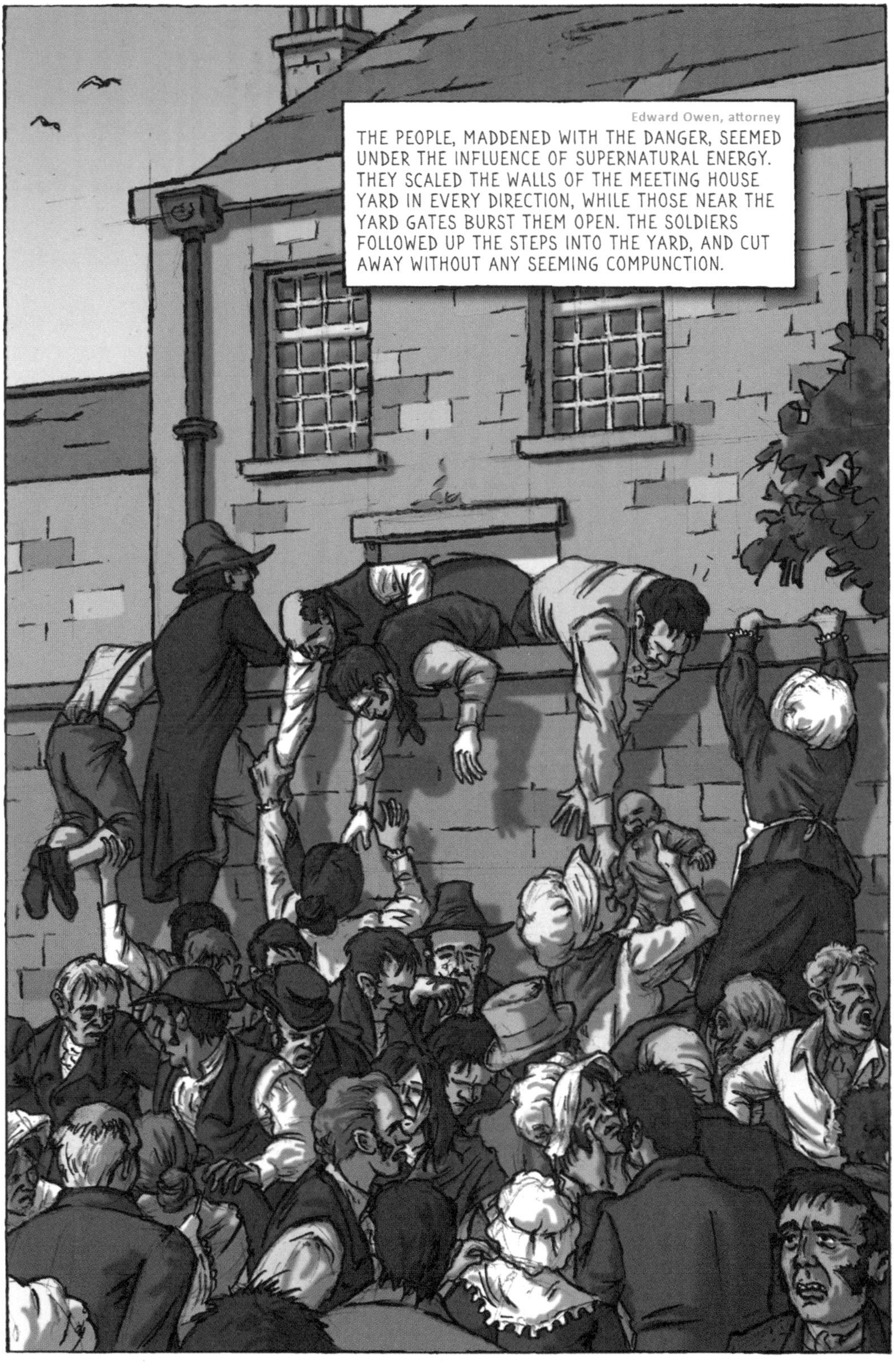
Edward Owen, attorney
THE PEOPLE, MADDENED WITH THE DANGER, SEEMED UNDER THE INFLUENCE OF SUPERNATURAL ENERGY. THEY SCALED THE WALLS OF THE MEETING HOUSE YARD IN EVERY DIRECTION, WHILE THOSE NEAR THE YARD GATES BURST THEM OPEN. THE SOLDIERS FOLLOWED UP THE STEPS INTO THE YARD, AND CUT AWAY WITHOUT ANY SEEMING COMPUNCTION.

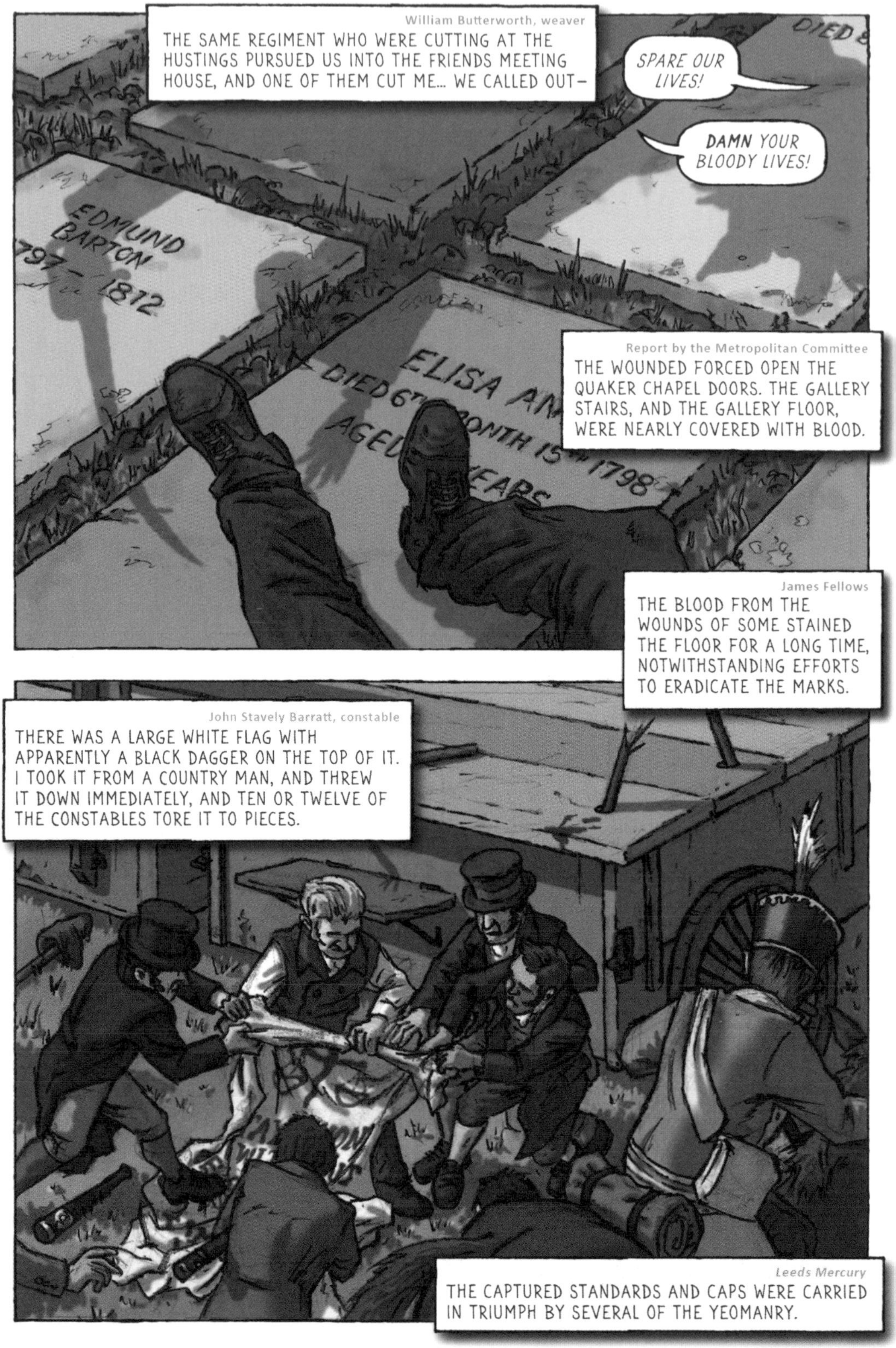
William Butterworth, weaver
THE SAME REGIMENT WHO WERE CUTTING AT THE HUSTINGS PURSUED US INTO THE FRIENDS MEETING HOUSE, AND ONE OF THEM CUT ME... WE CALLED OUT–
SPARE OUR LIVES!
DAMN YOUR BLOODY LIVES!
EDMUND BARTON
Report by the Metropolitan Committee
THE WOUNDED FORCED OPEN THE QUAKER CHAPEL DOORS. THE GALLERY STAIRS, AND THE GALLERY FLOOR, WERE NEARLY COVERED WITH BLOOD.
James Fellows
THE BLOOD FROM THE WOUNDS OF SOME STAINED THE FLOOR FOR A LONG TIME, NOTWITHSTANDING EFFORTS TO ERADICATE THE MARKS.
John Stavely Barratt, constable
THERE WAS A LARGE WHITE FLAG WITH APPARENTLY A BLACK DAGGER ON THE TOP OF IT. I TOOK IT FROM A COUNTRY MAN, AND THREW IT DOWN IMMEDIATELY, AND TEN OR TWELVE OF THE CONSTABLES TORE IT TO PIECES.
Leeds Mercury
THE CAPTURED STANDARDS AND CAPS WERE CARRIED IN TRIUMPH BY SEVERAL OF THE YEOMANRY.

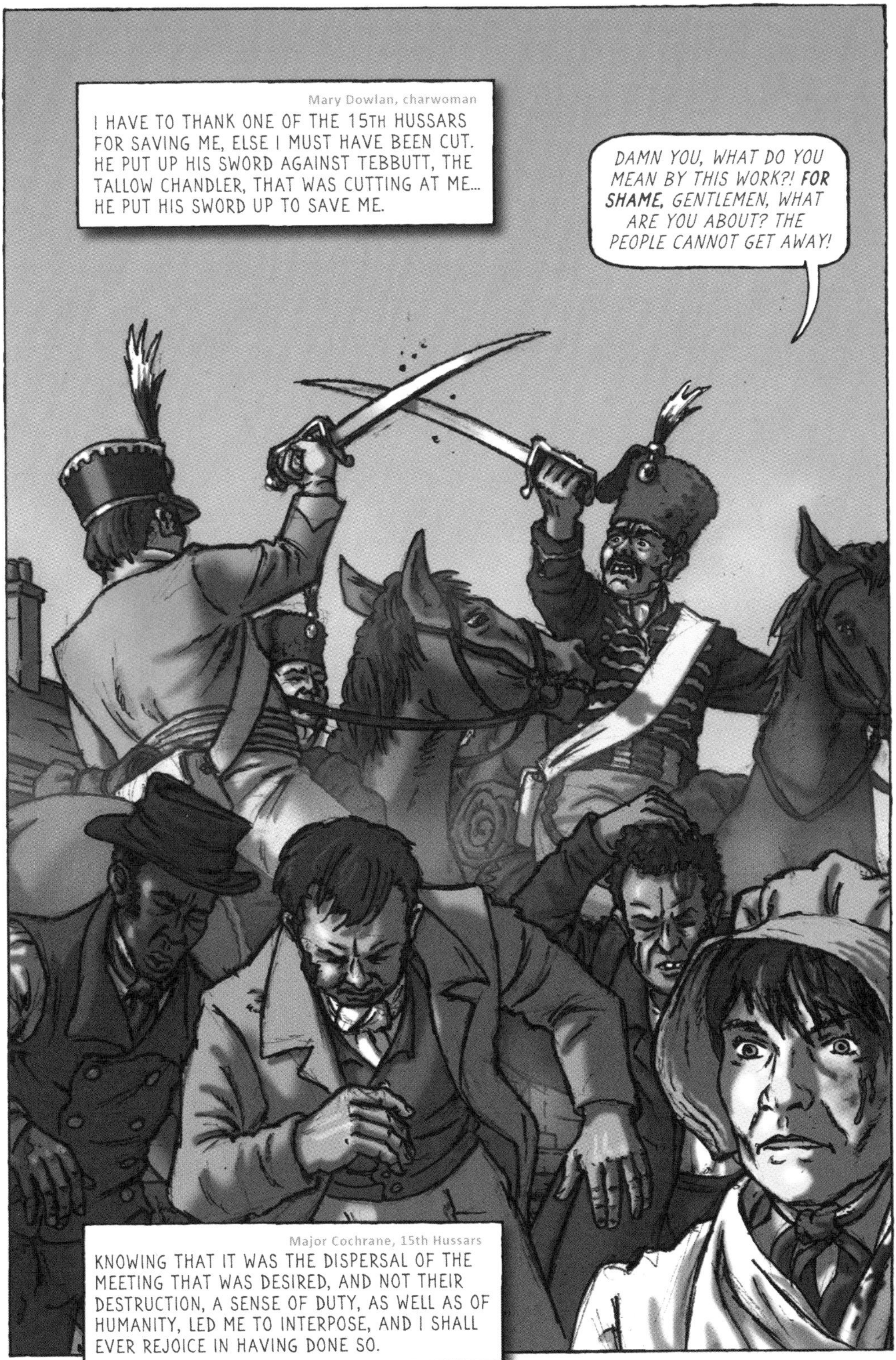
Mary Dowlan, charwoman
I HAVE TO THANK ONE OF THE 15TH HUSSARS FOR SAVING ME, ELSE I MUST HAVE BEEN CUT. HE PUT UP HIS SWORD AGAINST TEBBUTT, THE TALLOW CHANDLER, THAT WAS CUTTING AT ME... HE PUT HIS SWORD UP TO SAVE ME.
DAMN YOU, WHAT DO YOU MEAN BY THIS WORK?! FOR SHAME, GENTLEMEN, WHAT ARE YOU ABOUT? THE PEOPLE CANNOT GET AWAY!
Major Cochrane, 15th Hussars
KNOWING THAT IT WAS THE DISPERSAL OF THE MEETING THAT WAS DESIRED, AND NOT THEIR DESTRUCTION, A SENSE OF DUTY, AS WELL AS OF HUMANITY, LED ME TO INTERPOSE, AND I SHALL EVER REJOICE IN HAVING DONE SO.

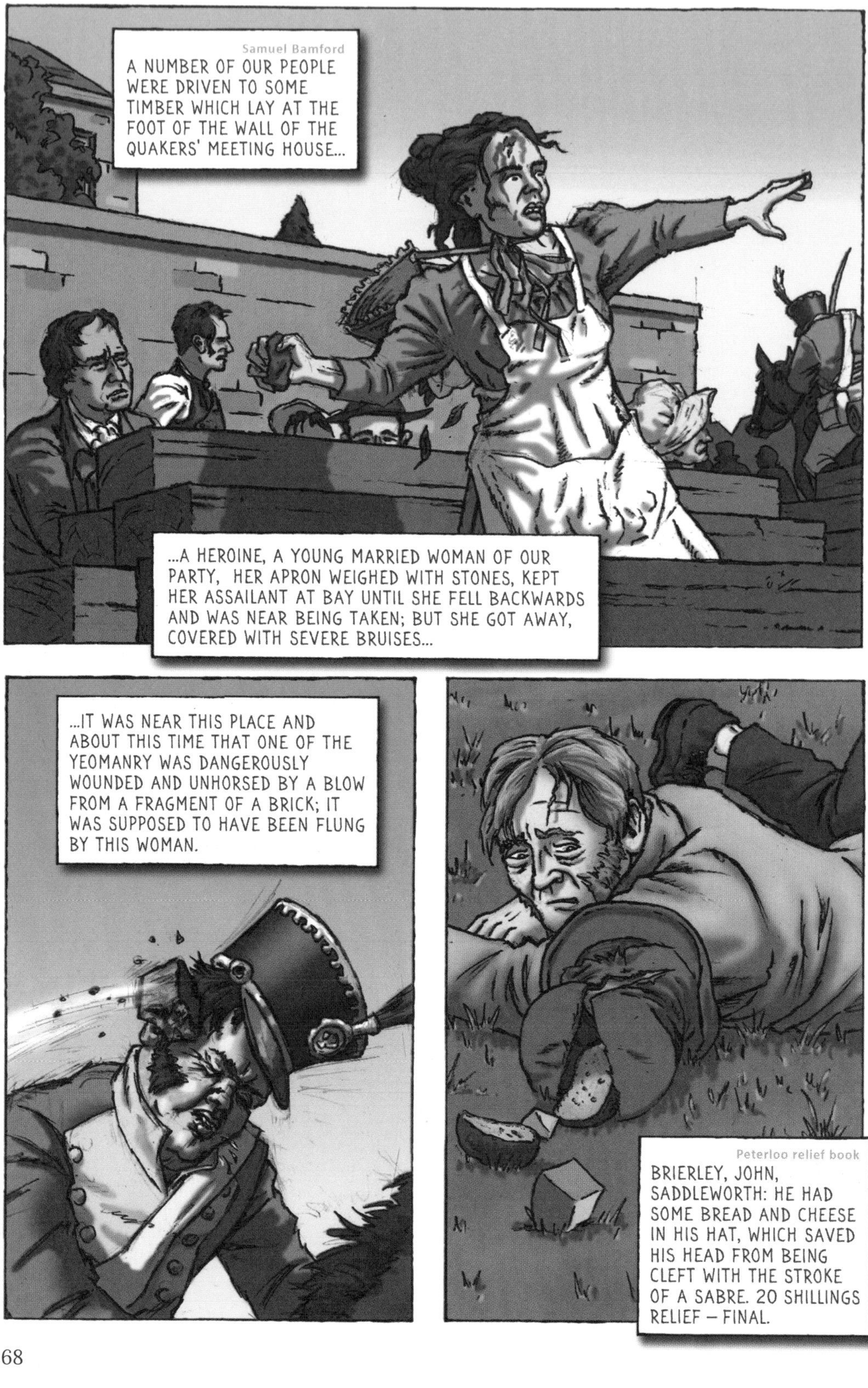
Samuel Bamford
A NUMBER OF OUR PEOPLE WERE DRIVEN TO SOME TIMBER WHICH LAY AT THE FOOT OF THE WALL OF THE QUAKERS' MEETING HOUSE...
...A HEROINE, A YOUNG MARRIED WOMAN OF OUR PARTY, HER APRON WEIGHED WITH STONES, KEPT HER ASSAILANT AT BAY UNTIL SHE FELL BACKWARDS AND WAS NEAR BEING TAKEN; BUT SHE GOT AWAY, COVERED WITH SEVERE BRUISES...
...IT WAS NEAR THIS PLACE AND ABOUT THIS TIME THAT ONE OF THE YEOMANRY WAS DANGEROUSLY WOUNDED AND UNHORSED BY A BLOW FROM A FRAGMENT OF A BRICK; IT WAS SUPPOSED TO HAVE BEEN FLUNG BY THIS WOMAN.
Peterloo relief book
BRIERLEY, JOHN, SADDLEWORTH: HE HAD SOME BREAD AND CHEESE IN HIS HAT, WHICH SAVED HIS HEAD FROM BEING CLEFT WITH THE STROKE OF A SABRE. 20 SHILLINGS RELIEF – FINAL.

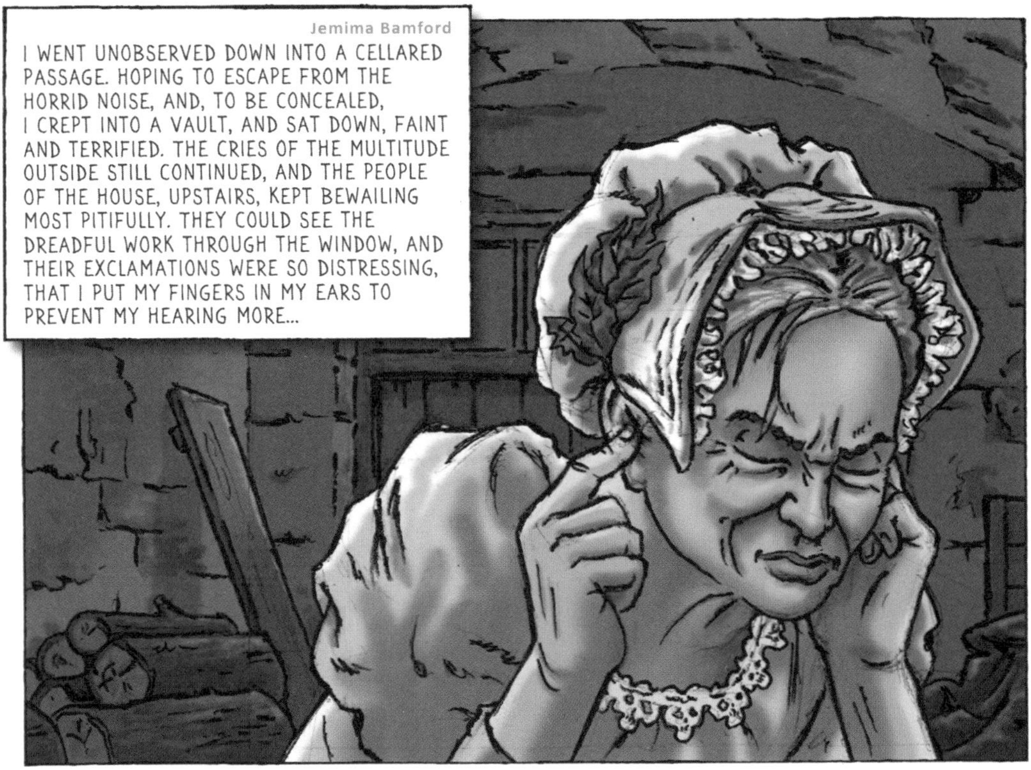
Jemima Bamford
I WENT UNOBSERVED DOWN INTO A CELLARED PASSAGE. HOPING TO ESCAPE FROM THE HORRID NOISE, AND, TO BE CONCEALED, I CREPT INTO A VAULT, AND SAT DOWN, FAINT AND TERRIFIED. THE CRIES OF THE MULTITUDE OUTSIDE STILL CONTINUED, AND THE PEOPLE OF THE HOUSE, UPSTAIRS, KEPT BEWAILING MOST PITIFULLY. THEY COULD SEE THE DREADFUL WORK THROUGH THE WINDOW, AND THEIR EXCLAMATIONS WERE SO DISTRESSING, THAT I PUT MY FINGERS IN MY EARS TO PREVENT MY HEARING MORE...

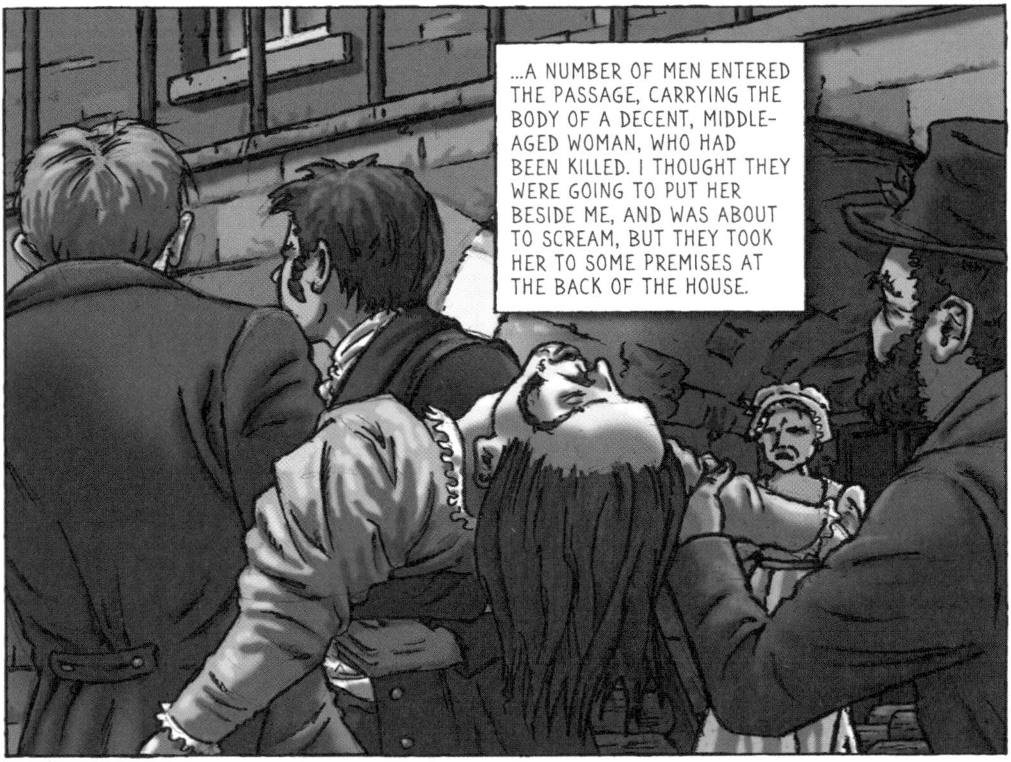
...A NUMBER OF MEN ENTERED THE PASSAGE, CARRYING THE BODY OF A DECENT, MIDDLE-AGED WOMAN, WHO HAD BEEN KILLED. I THOUGHT THEY WERE GOING TO PUT HER BESIDE ME, AND WAS ABOUT TO SCREAM, BUT THEY TOOK HER TO SOME PREMISES AT THE BACK OF THE HOUSE.

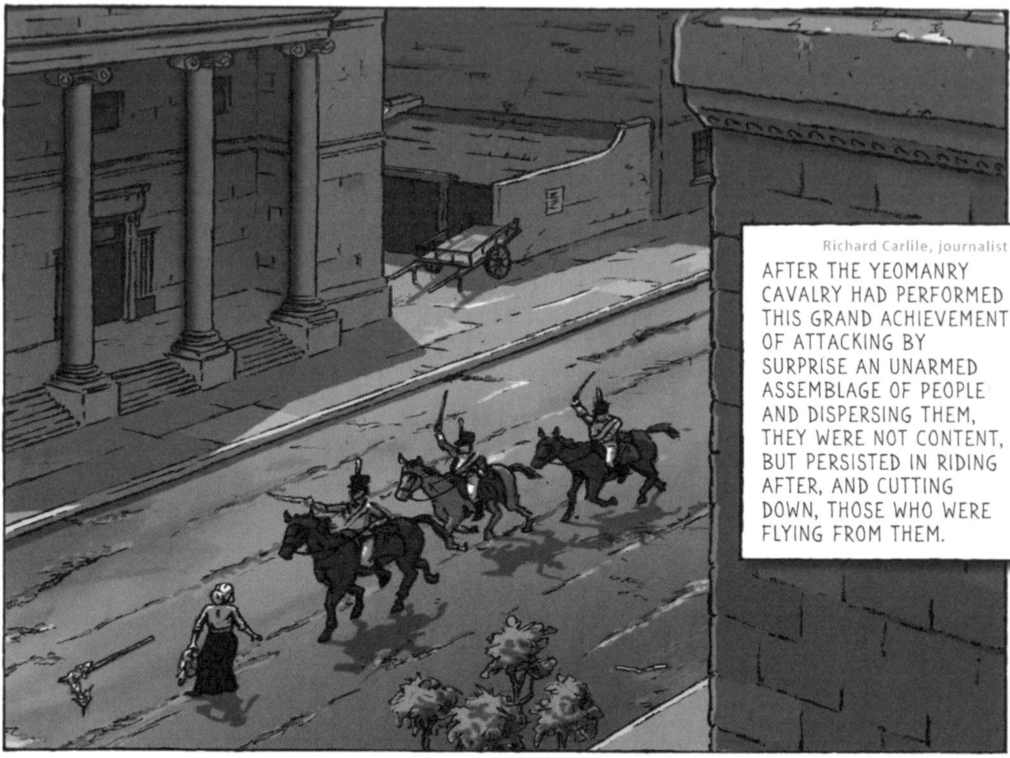
Richard Carlile, journalist
AFTER THE YEOMANRY CAVALRY HAD PERFORMED THIS GRAND ACHIEVEMENT OF ATTACKING BY SURPRISE AN UNARMED ASSEMBLAGE OF PEOPLE AND DISPERSING THEM, THEY WERE NOT CONTENT, BUT PERSISTED IN RIDING AFTER, AND CUTTING DOWN, THOSE WHO WERE FLYING FROM THEM.

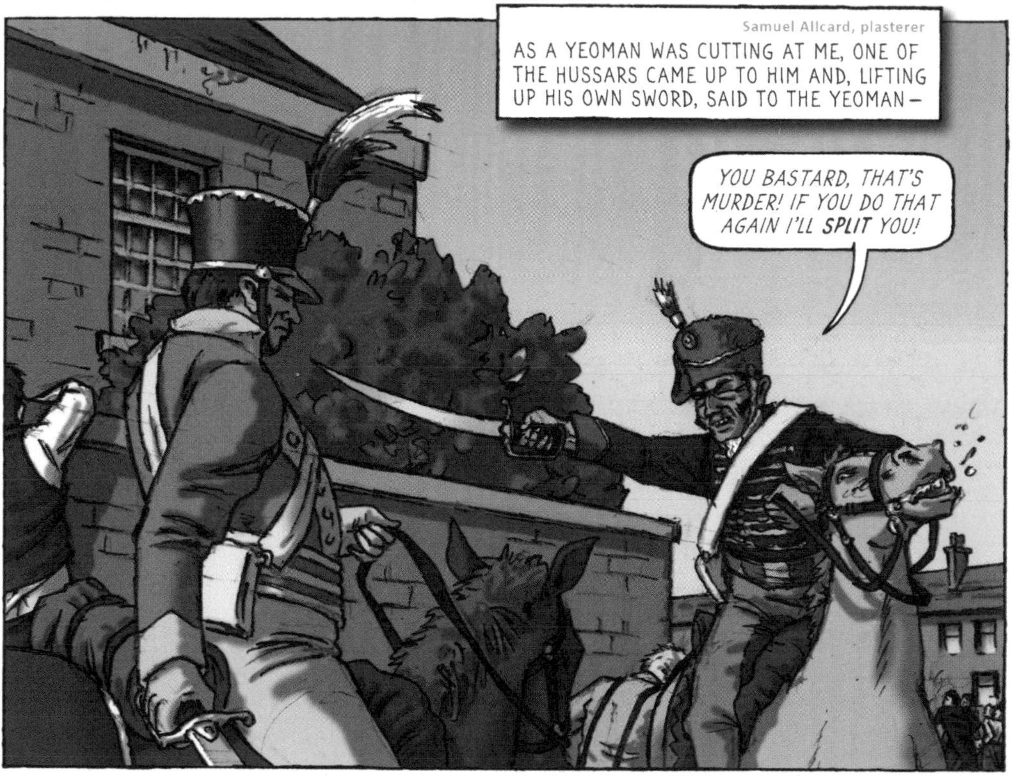
Samuel Allcard, plasterer
AS A YEOMAN WAS CUTTING AT ME, ONE OF THE HUSSARS CAME UP TO HIM AND, LIFTING UP HIS OWN SWORD, SAID TO THE YEOMAN –
YOU BASTARD, THAT'S MURDER! IF YOU DO THAT AGAIN I'LL **SPLIT** YOU!

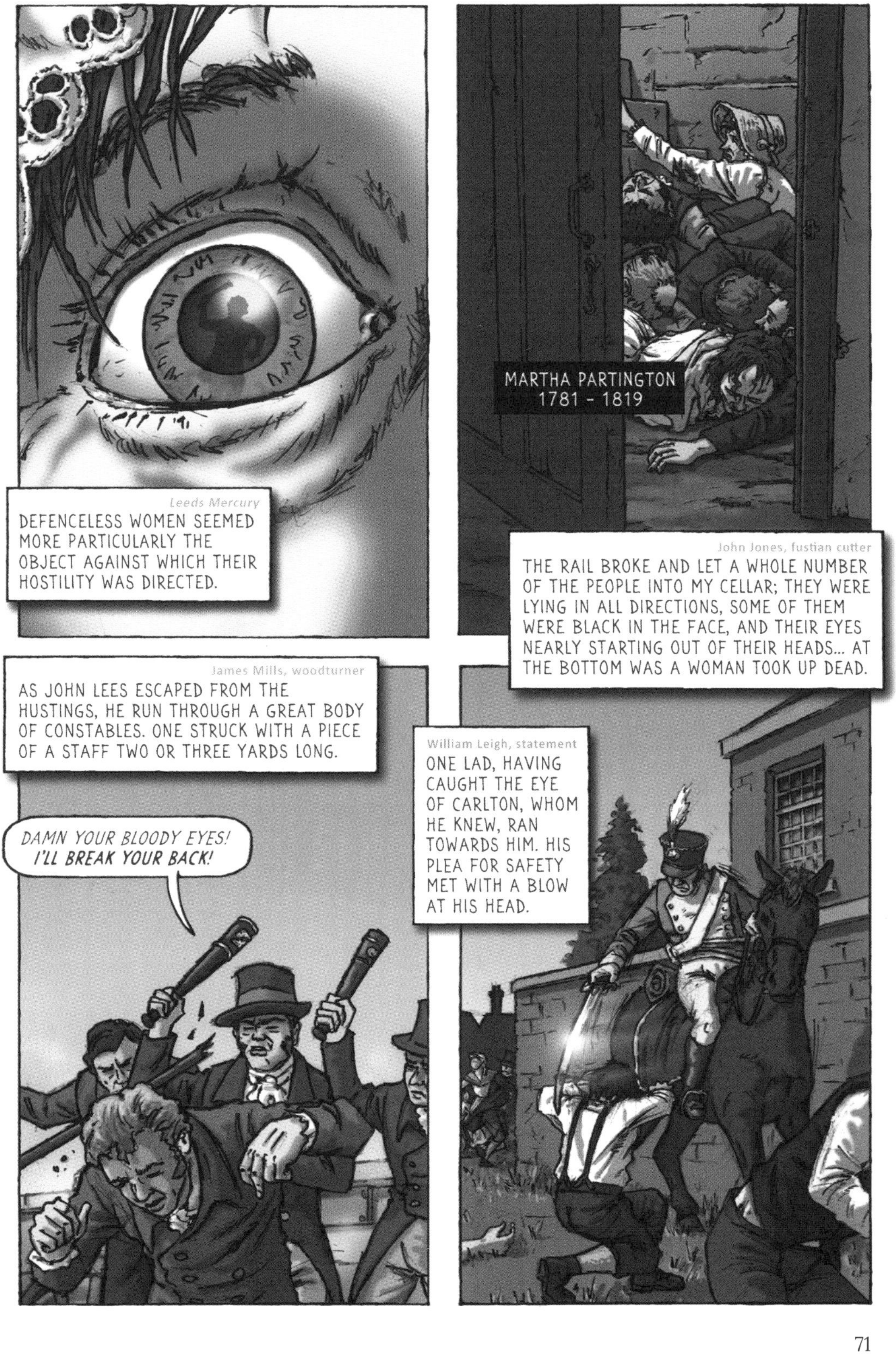
Leeds Mercury
DEFENCELESS WOMEN SEEMED MORE PARTICULARLY THE OBJECT AGAINST WHICH THEIR HOSTILITY WAS DIRECTED.
MARTHA PARTINGTON 1781 - 1819
John Jones, fustian cutter
THE RAIL BROKE AND LET A WHOLE NUMBER OF THE PEOPLE INTO MY CELLAR; THEY WERE LYING IN ALL DIRECTIONS, SOME OF THEM WERE BLACK IN THE FACE, AND THEIR EYES NEARLY STARTING OUT OF THEIR HEADS... AT THE BOTTOM WAS A WOMAN TOOK UP DEAD.
James Mills, woodturner
AS JOHN LEES ESCAPED FROM THE HUSTINGS, HE RUN THROUGH A GREAT BODY OF CONSTABLES. ONE STRUCK WITH A PIECE OF A STAFF TWO OR THREE YARDS LONG.
DAMN YOUR BLOODY EYES! I'LL BREAK YOUR BACK!
William Leigh, statement
ONE LAD, HAVING CAUGHT THE EYE OF CARLTON, WHOM HE KNEW, RAN TOWARDS HIM. HIS PLEA FOR SAFETY MET WITH A BLOW AT HIS HEAD.

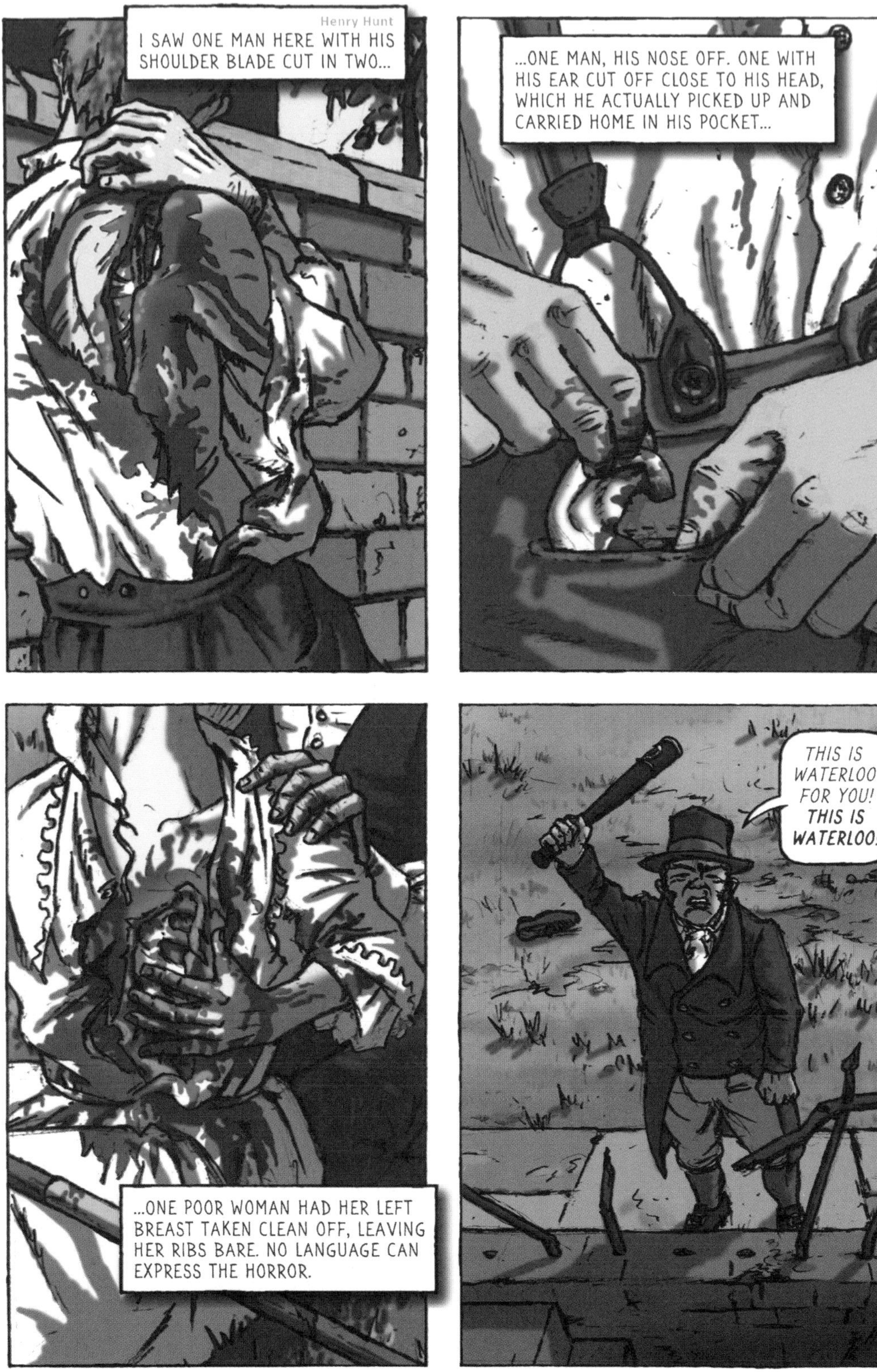
Henry Hunt
I SAW ONE MAN HERE WITH HIS SHOULDER BLADE CUT IN TWO...
...ONE MAN, HIS NOSE OFF. ONE WITH HIS EAR CUT OFF CLOSE TO HIS HEAD, WHICH HE ACTUALLY PICKED UP AND CARRIED HOME IN HIS POCKET...
...ONE POOR WOMAN HAD HER LEFT BREAST TAKEN CLEAN OFF, LEAVING HER RIBS BARE. NO LANGUAGE CAN EXPRESS THE HORROR.
THIS IS WATERLOO FOR YOU! THIS IS WATERLOO!

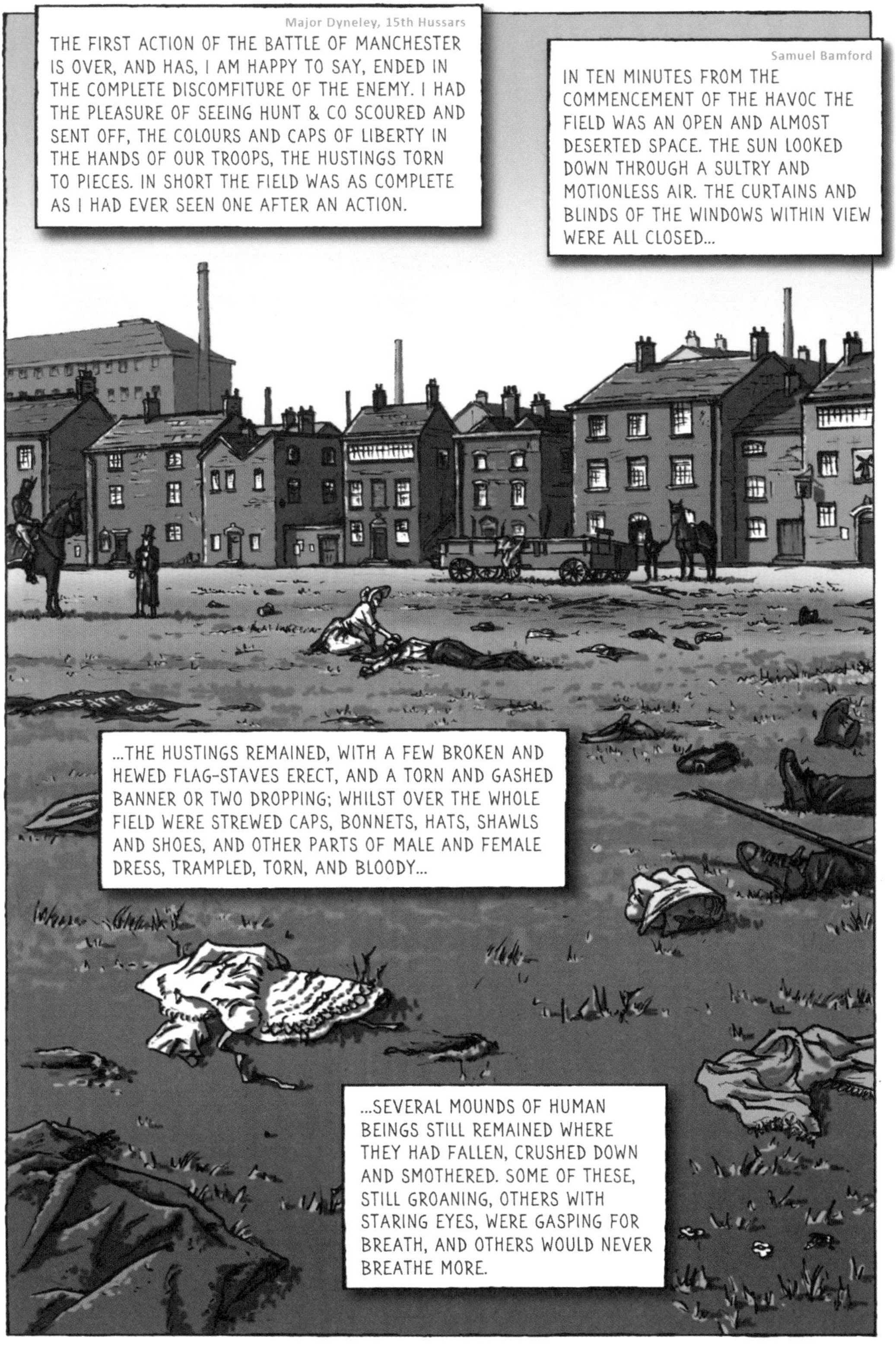
Major Dyneley, 15th Hussars
THE FIRST ACTION OF THE BATTLE OF MANCHESTER IS OVER, AND HAS, I AM HAPPY TO SAY, ENDED IN THE COMPLETE DISCOMFITURE OF THE ENEMY. I HAD THE PLEASURE OF SEEING HUNT & CO SCOURED AND SENT OFF, THE COLOURS AND CAPS OF LIBERTY IN THE HANDS OF OUR TROOPS, THE HUSTINGS TORN TO PIECES. IN SHORT THE FIELD WAS AS COMPLETE AS I HAD EVER SEEN ONE AFTER AN ACTION.
Samuel Bamford
IN TEN MINUTES FROM THE COMMENCEMENT OF THE HAVOC THE FIELD WAS AN OPEN AND ALMOST DESERTED SPACE. THE SUN LOOKED DOWN THROUGH A SULTRY AND MOTIONLESS AIR. THE CURTAINS AND BLINDS OF THE WINDOWS WITHIN VIEW WERE ALL CLOSED...
...THE HUSTINGS REMAINED, WITH A FEW BROKEN AND HEWED FLAG-STAVES ERECT, AND A TORN AND GASHED BANNER OR TWO DROPPING; WHILST OVER THE WHOLE FIELD WERE STREWED CAPS, BONNETS, HATS, SHAWLS AND SHOES, AND OTHER PARTS OF MALE AND FEMALE DRESS, TRAMPLED, TORN, AND BLOODY...
...SEVERAL MOUNDS OF HUMAN BEINGS STILL REMAINED WHERE THEY HAD FALLEN, CRUSHED DOWN AND SMOTHERED. SOME OF THESE, STILL GROANING, OTHERS WITH STARING EYES, WERE GASPING FOR BREATH, AND OTHERS WOULD NEVER BREATHE MORE.

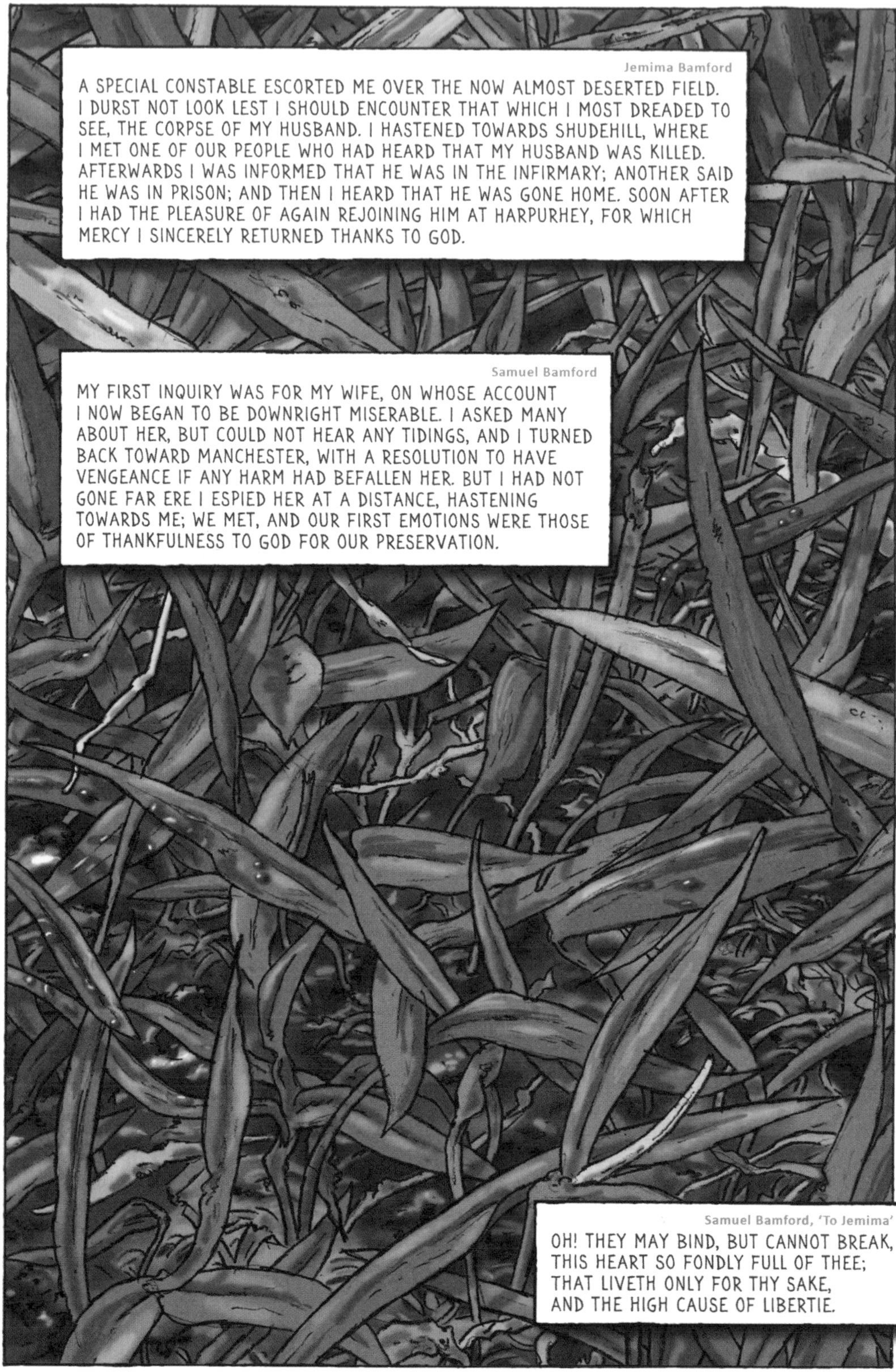
Jemima Bamford
A SPECIAL CONSTABLE ESCORTED ME OVER THE NOW ALMOST DESERTED FIELD. I DURST NOT LOOK LEST I SHOULD ENCOUNTER THAT WHICH I MOST DREADED TO SEE, THE CORPSE OF MY HUSBAND. I HASTENED TOWARDS SHUDEHILL, WHERE I MET ONE OF OUR PEOPLE WHO HAD HEARD THAT MY HUSBAND WAS KILLED. AFTERWARDS I WAS INFORMED THAT HE WAS IN THE INFIRMARY; ANOTHER SAID HE WAS IN PRISON; AND THEN I HEARD THAT HE WAS GONE HOME. SOON AFTER I HAD THE PLEASURE OF AGAIN REJOINING HIM AT HARPURHEY, FOR WHICH MERCY I SINCERELY RETURNED THANKS TO GOD.
Samuel Bamford
MY FIRST INQUIRY WAS FOR MY WIFE, ON WHOSE ACCOUNT I NOW BEGAN TO BE DOWNRIGHT MISERABLE. I ASKED MANY ABOUT HER, BUT COULD NOT HEAR ANY TIDINGS, AND I TURNED BACK TOWARD MANCHESTER, WITH A RESOLUTION TO HAVE VENGEANCE IF ANY HARM HAD BEFALLEN HER. BUT I HAD NOT GONE FAR ERE I ESPIED HER AT A DISTANCE, HASTENING TOWARDS ME; WE MET, AND OUR FIRST EMOTIONS WERE THOSE OF THANKFULNESS TO GOD FOR OUR PRESERVATION.
Samuel Bamford, 'To Jemima'
OH! THEY MAY BIND, BUT CANNOT BREAK,
THIS HEART SO FONDLY FULL OF THEE;
THAT LIVETH ONLY FOR THY SAKE,
AND THE HIGH CAUSE OF LIBERTIE.

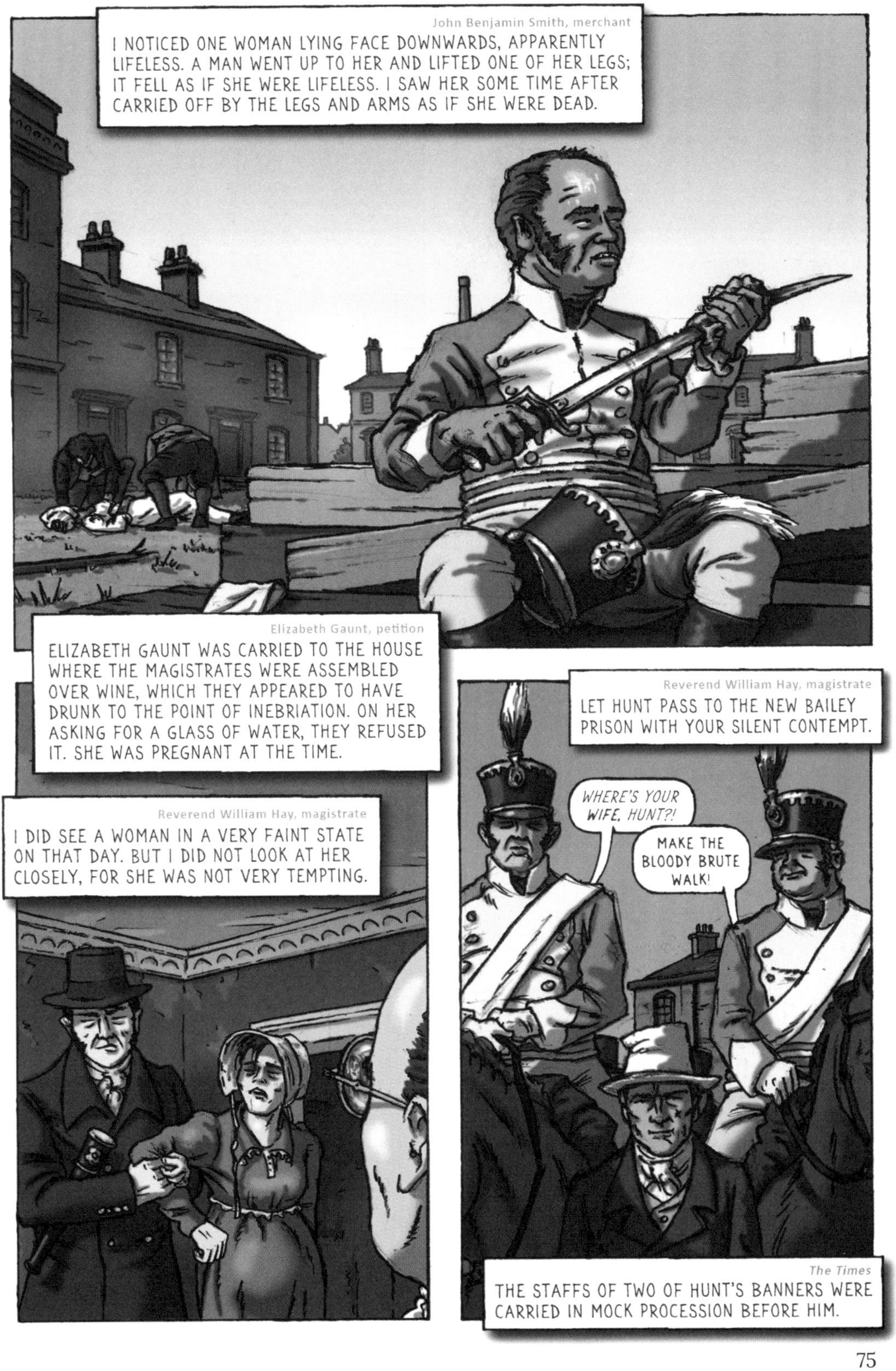
John Benjamin Smith, merchant
I NOTICED ONE WOMAN LYING FACE DOWNWARDS, APPARENTLY LIFELESS. A MAN WENT UP TO HER AND LIFTED ONE OF HER LEGS; IT FELL AS IF SHE WERE LIFELESS. I SAW HER SOME TIME AFTER CARRIED OFF BY THE LEGS AND ARMS AS IF SHE WERE DEAD.
Elizabeth Gaunt, petition
ELIZABETH GAUNT WAS CARRIED TO THE HOUSE WHERE THE MAGISTRATES WERE ASSEMBLED OVER WINE, WHICH THEY APPEARED TO HAVE DRUNK TO THE POINT OF INEBRIATION. ON HER ASKING FOR A GLASS OF WATER, THEY REFUSED IT. SHE WAS PREGNANT AT THE TIME.
Reverend William Hay, magistrate
I DID SEE A WOMAN IN A VERY FAINT STATE ON THAT DAY. BUT I DID NOT LOOK AT HER CLOSELY, FOR SHE WAS NOT VERY TEMPTING.
Reverend William Hay, magistrate
LET HUNT PASS TO THE NEW BAILEY PRISON WITH YOUR SILENT CONTEMPT.
WHERE'S YOUR WIFE, HUNT?!
MAKE THE BLOODY BRUTE WALK!
The Times
THE STAFFS OF TWO OF HUNT'S BANNERS WERE CARRIED IN MOCK PROCESSION BEFORE HIM.

Joseph Barrett, cloth merchant

ONE OF THE CATHEDRAL MINISTERS, HIGH IN OFFICE, KEPT WALKING ABOUT IN THE FIELD, AND SEEMED HIGHLY PLEASED WITH THE SCENE, FOR HE STRUTTED ABOUT LIKE A COCK THAT HAD BEATEN HIS OPPONENT.

Frederick Buckley

A WOUNDED YEOMAN CAVALRY-MAN WAS CARRIED ALONG MOSLEY STREET ON A DOOR.

Liverpool Mercury

SIX COACHES, THREE CARTS AND THREE LITTERS, LOADED WITH THE WOUNDED, PROCEEDED TO THE INFIRMARY. AMONG THE WOUNDED WERE SEVERAL GIRLS DRESSED IN WHITE.

Reverend Charles Ethelston, magistrate

NOTHING, I THINK, COULD BE MORE COMPLETE THAN THE MANNER IN WHICH THE BUSINESS HAS BEEN ACCOMPLISHED.

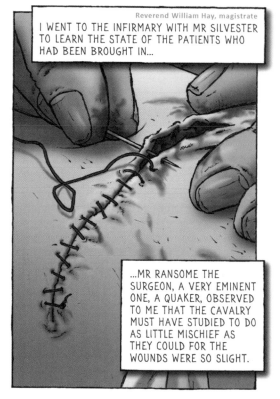

Reverend William Hay, magistrate

I WENT TO THE INFIRMARY WITH MR SILVESTER TO LEARN THE STATE OF THE PATIENTS WHO HAD BEEN BROUGHT IN...

...MR RANSOME THE SURGEON, A VERY EMINENT ONE, A QUAKER, OBSERVED TO ME THAT THE CAVALRY MUST HAVE STUDIED TO DO AS LITTLE MISCHIEF AS THEY COULD FOR THE WOUNDS WERE SO SLIGHT.

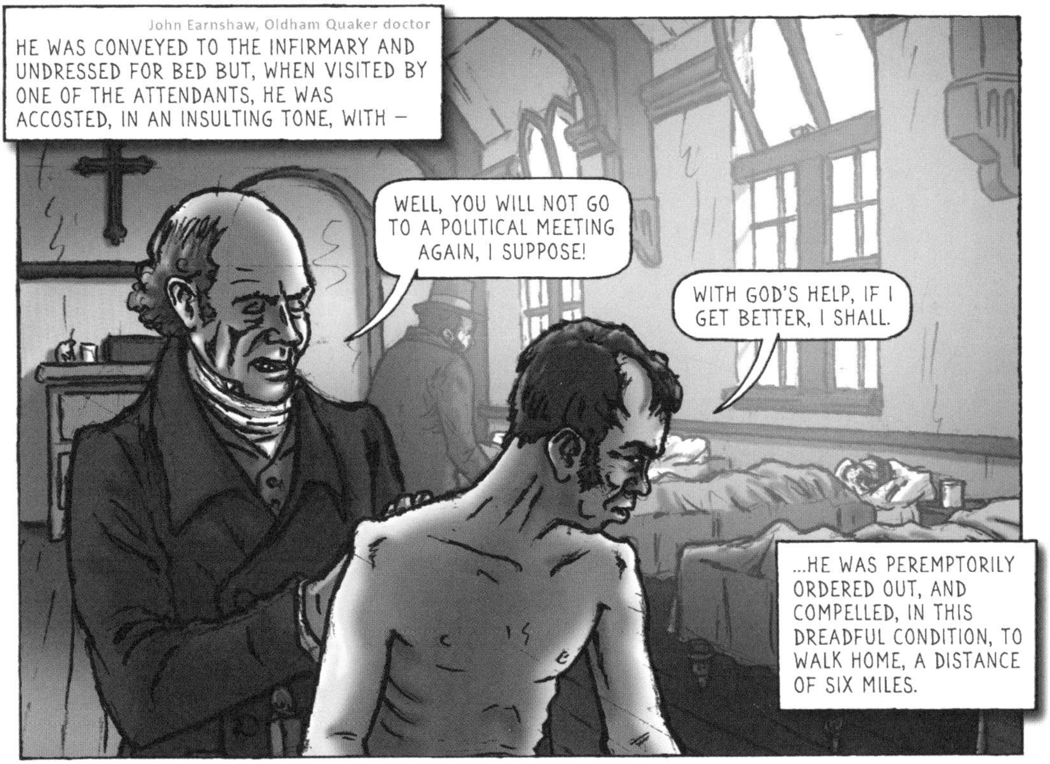
John Earnshaw, Oldham Quaker doctor
HE WAS CONVEYED TO THE INFIRMARY AND UNDRESSED FOR BED BUT, WHEN VISITED BY ONE OF THE ATTENDANTS, HE WAS ACCOSTED, IN AN INSULTING TONE, WITH –
WELL, YOU WILL NOT GO TO A POLITICAL MEETING AGAIN, I SUPPOSE!
WITH GOD'S HELP, IF I GET BETTER, I SHALL.
...HE WAS PEREMPTORILY ORDERED OUT, AND COMPELLED, IN THIS DREADFUL CONDITION, TO WALK HOME, A DISTANCE OF SIX MILES.

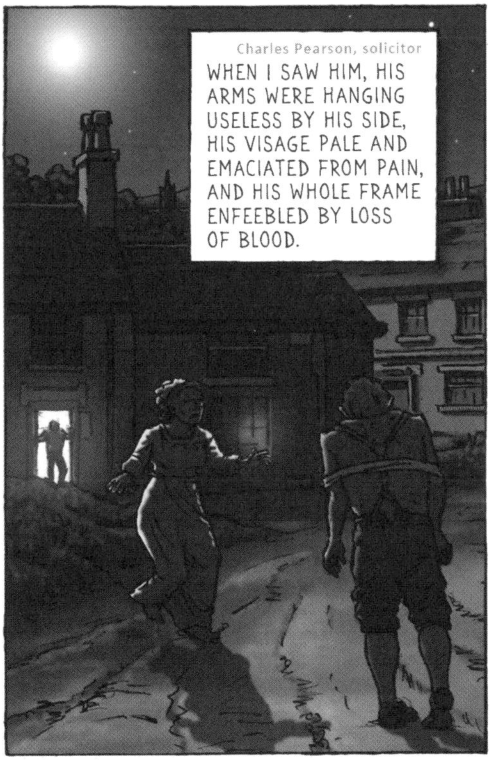
Charles Pearson, solicitor
WHEN I SAW HIM, HIS ARMS WERE HANGING USELESS BY HIS SIDE, HIS VISAGE PALE AND EMACIATED FROM PAIN, AND HIS WHOLE FRAME ENFEEBLED BY LOSS OF BLOOD.

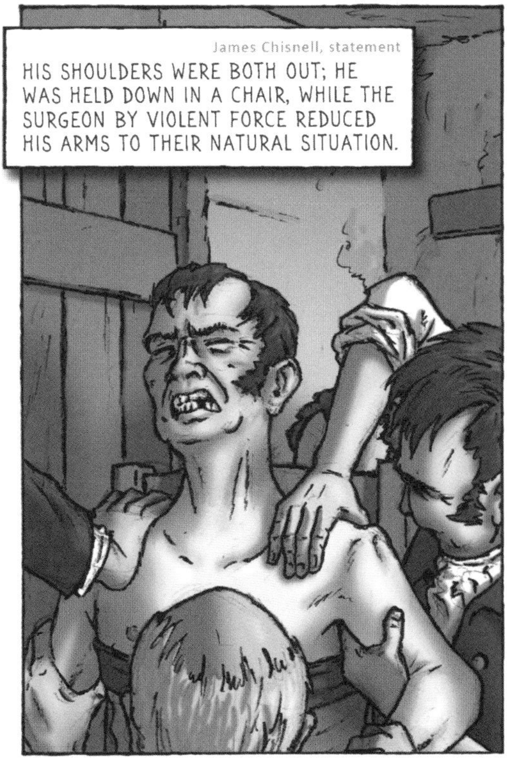
James Chisnell, statement
HIS SHOULDERS WERE BOTH OUT; HE WAS HELD DOWN IN A CHAIR, WHILE THE SURGEON BY VIOLENT FORCE REDUCED HIS ARMS TO THEIR NATURAL SITUATION.

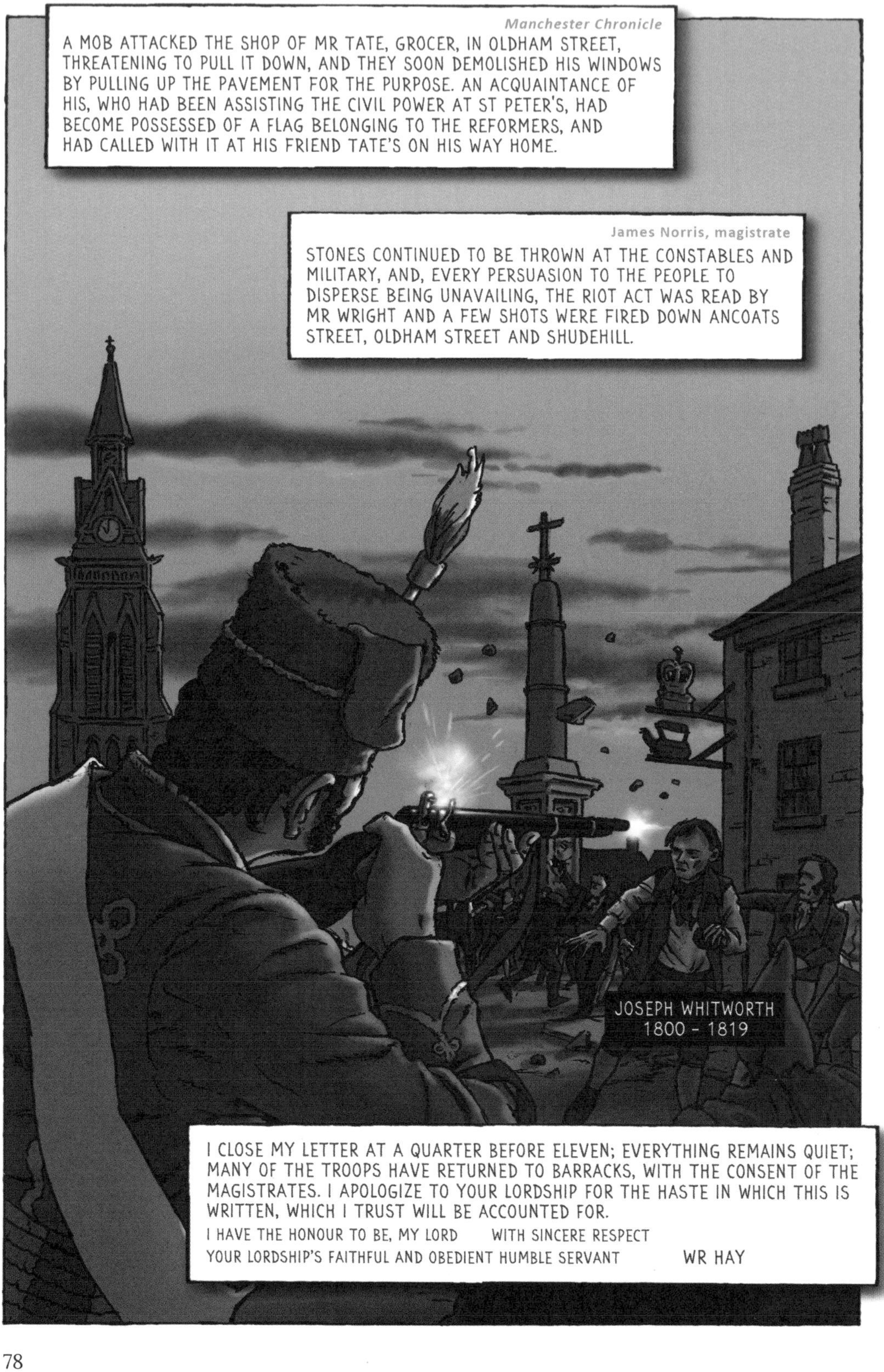
Manchester Chronicle
A MOB ATTACKED THE SHOP OF MR TATE, GROCER, IN OLDHAM STREET, THREATENING TO PULL IT DOWN, AND THEY SOON DEMOLISHED HIS WINDOWS BY PULLING UP THE PAVEMENT FOR THE PURPOSE. AN ACQUAINTANCE OF HIS, WHO HAD BEEN ASSISTING THE CIVIL POWER AT ST PETER'S, HAD BECOME POSSESSED OF A FLAG BELONGING TO THE REFORMERS, AND HAD CALLED WITH IT AT HIS FRIEND TATE'S ON HIS WAY HOME.
James Norris, magistrate
STONES CONTINUED TO BE THROWN AT THE CONSTABLES AND MILITARY, AND, EVERY PERSUASION TO THE PEOPLE TO DISPERSE BEING UNAVAILING, THE RIOT ACT WAS READ BY MR WRIGHT AND A FEW SHOTS WERE FIRED DOWN ANCOATS STREET, OLDHAM STREET AND SHUDEHILL.
JOSEPH WHITWORTH
1800 - 1819
I CLOSE MY LETTER AT A QUARTER BEFORE ELEVEN; EVERYTHING REMAINS QUIET; MANY OF THE TROOPS HAVE RETURNED TO BARRACKS, WITH THE CONSENT OF THE MAGISTRATES. I APOLOGIZE TO YOUR LORDSHIP FOR THE HASTE IN WHICH THIS IS WRITTEN, WHICH I TRUST WILL BE ACCOUNTED FOR.
I HAVE THE HONOUR TO BE, MY LORD WITH SINCERE RESPECT
YOUR LORDSHIP'S FAITHFUL AND OBEDIENT HUMBLE SERVANT WR HAY

IV

I understand I have a right
to tell all I saw?

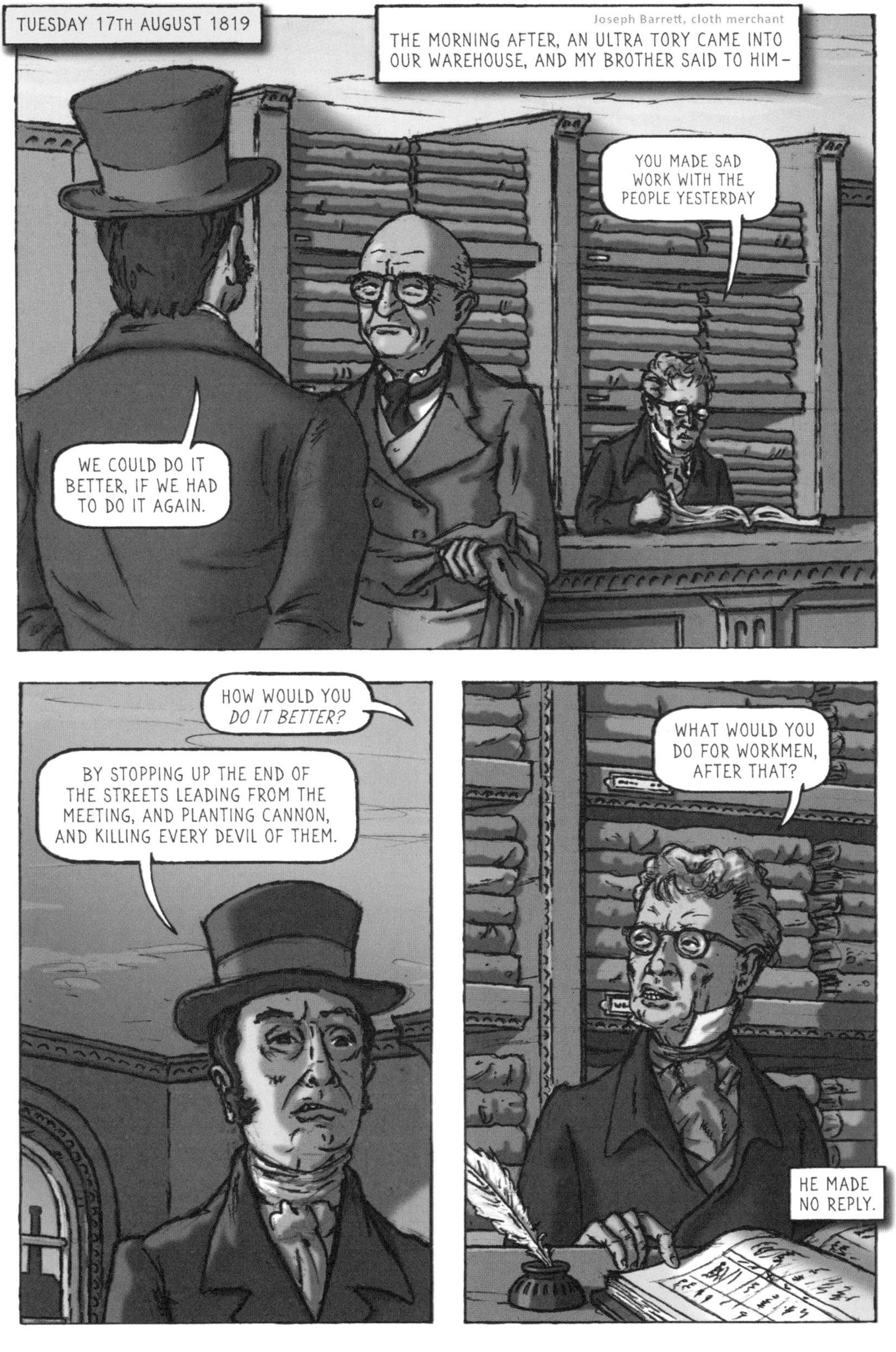
TUESDAY 17TH AUGUST 1819
Joseph Barrett, cloth merchant
THE MORNING AFTER, AN ULTRA TORY CAME INTO OUR WAREHOUSE, AND MY BROTHER SAID TO HIM–
YOU MADE SAD WORK WITH THE PEOPLE YESTERDAY
WE COULD DO IT BETTER, IF WE HAD TO DO IT AGAIN.
HOW WOULD YOU *DO IT BETTER?*
BY STOPPING UP THE END OF THE STREETS LEADING FROM THE MEETING, AND PLANTING CANNON, AND KILLING EVERY DEVIL OF THEM.
WHAT WOULD YOU DO FOR WORKMEN, AFTER THAT?
HE MADE NO REPLY.

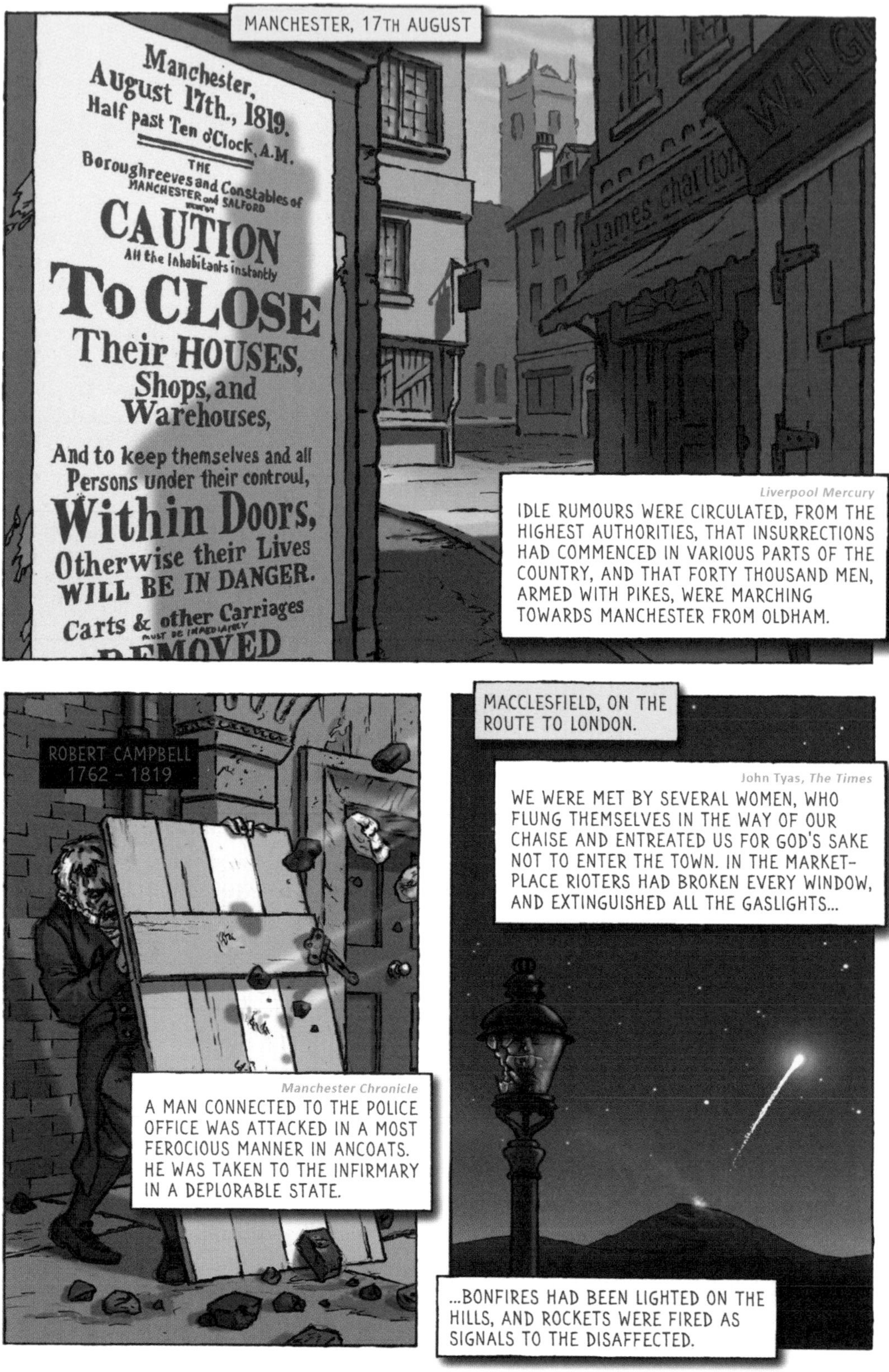
MANCHESTER, 17TH AUGUST
Manchester, August 17th., 1819. Half past Ten o'Clock, A.M.
THE Boroughreeves and Constables of MANCHESTER and SALFORD
CAUTION
All the Inhabitants instantly
To CLOSE
Their HOUSES, Shops, and Warehouses,
And to keep themselves and all Persons under their controul,
Within Doors,
Otherwise their Lives WILL BE IN DANGER.
Carts & other Carriages
James Charlton
Liverpool Mercury
IDLE RUMOURS WERE CIRCULATED, FROM THE HIGHEST AUTHORITIES, THAT INSURRECTIONS HAD COMMENCED IN VARIOUS PARTS OF THE COUNTRY, AND THAT FORTY THOUSAND MEN, ARMED WITH PIKES, WERE MARCHING TOWARDS MANCHESTER FROM OLDHAM.
ROBERT CAMPBELL 1762 - 1819
Manchester Chronicle
A MAN CONNECTED TO THE POLICE OFFICE WAS ATTACKED IN A MOST FEROCIOUS MANNER IN ANCOATS. HE WAS TAKEN TO THE INFIRMARY IN A DEPLORABLE STATE.
MACCLESFIELD, ON THE ROUTE TO LONDON.
John Tyas, The Times
WE WERE MET BY SEVERAL WOMEN, WHO FLUNG THEMSELVES IN THE WAY OF OUR CHAISE AND ENTREATED US FOR GOD'S SAKE NOT TO ENTER THE TOWN. IN THE MARKET-PLACE RIOTERS HAD BROKEN EVERY WINDOW, AND EXTINGUISHED ALL THE GASLIGHTS...
...BONFIRES HAD BEEN LIGHTED ON THE HILLS, AND ROCKETS WERE FIRED AS SIGNALS TO THE DISAFFECTED.

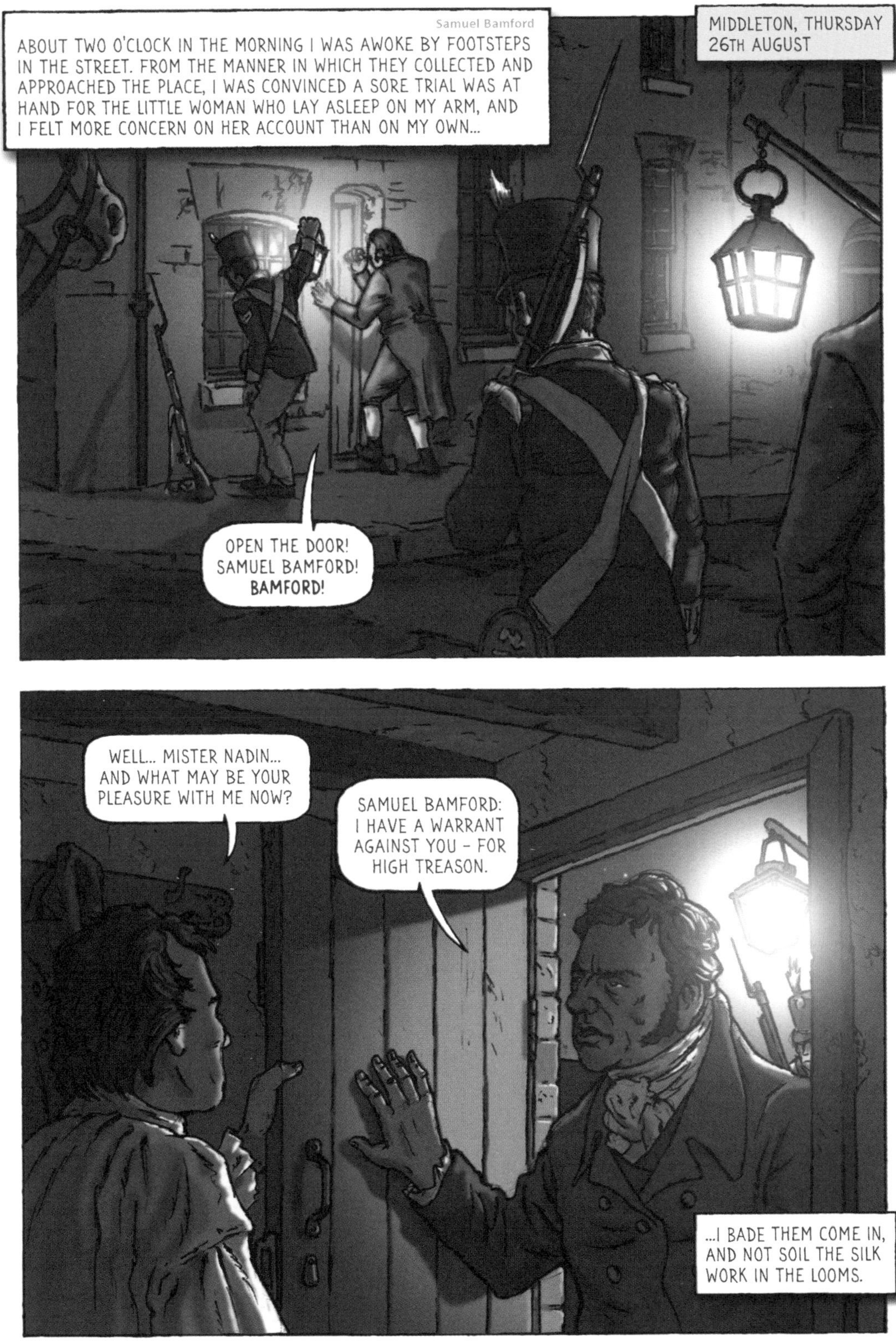
Samuel Bamford
ABOUT TWO O'CLOCK IN THE MORNING I WAS AWOKE BY FOOTSTEPS IN THE STREET. FROM THE MANNER IN WHICH THEY COLLECTED AND APPROACHED THE PLACE, I WAS CONVINCED A SORE TRIAL WAS AT HAND FOR THE LITTLE WOMAN WHO LAY ASLEEP ON MY ARM, AND I FELT MORE CONCERN ON HER ACCOUNT THAN ON MY OWN...
MIDDLETON, THURSDAY 26TH AUGUST
OPEN THE DOOR! SAMUEL BAMFORD! **BAMFORD!**
WELL... MISTER NADIN... AND WHAT MAY BE YOUR PLEASURE WITH ME NOW?
SAMUEL BAMFORD: I HAVE A WARRANT AGAINST YOU – FOR HIGH TREASON.
...I BADE THEM COME IN, AND NOT SOIL THE SILK WORK IN THE LOOMS.

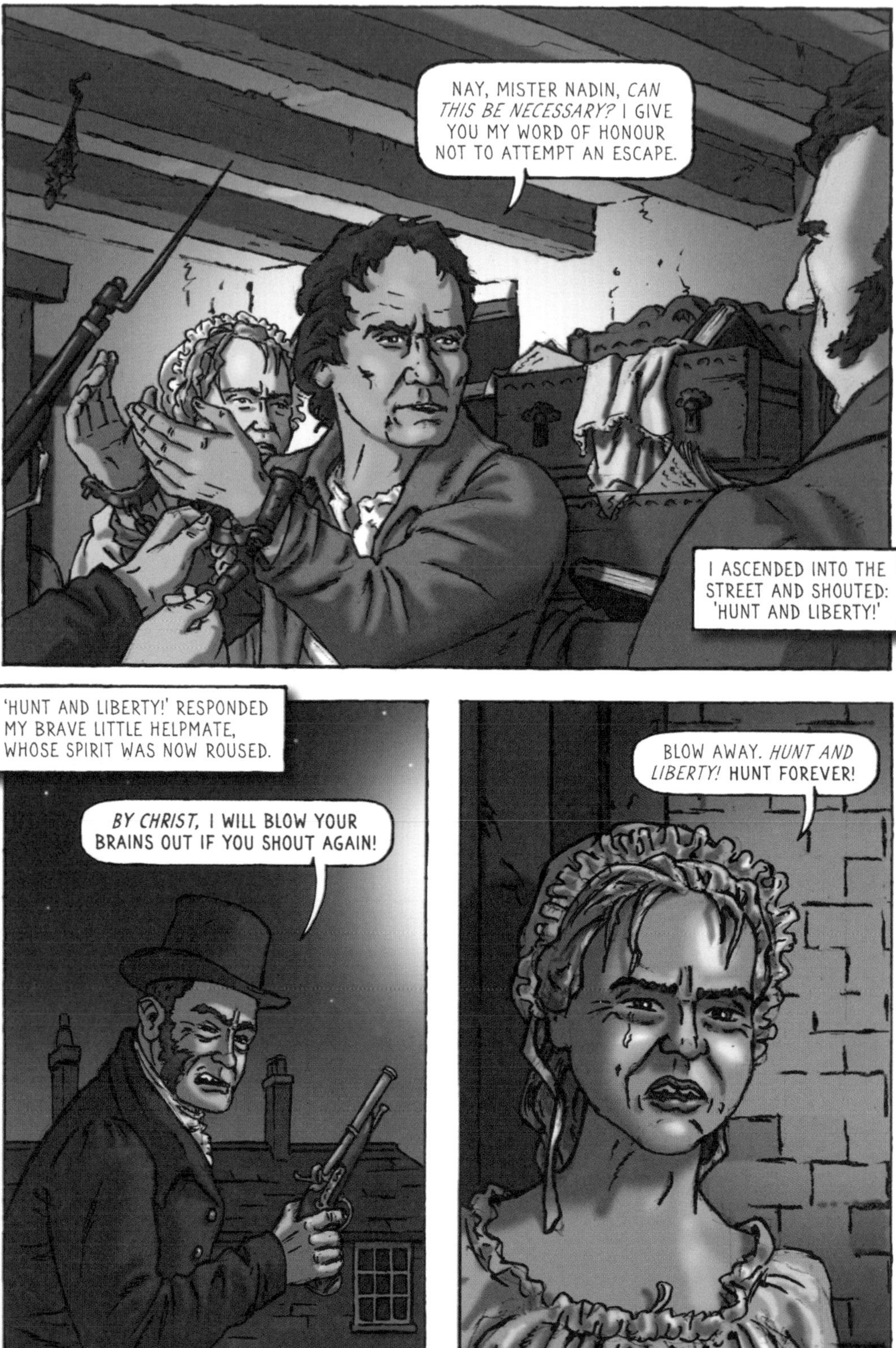
NAY, MISTER NADIN, *CAN THIS BE NECESSARY?* I GIVE YOU MY WORD OF HONOUR NOT TO ATTEMPT AN ESCAPE.
I ASCENDED INTO THE STREET AND SHOUTED: 'HUNT AND LIBERTY!'
'HUNT AND LIBERTY!' RESPONDED MY BRAVE LITTLE HELPMATE, WHOSE SPIRIT WAS NOW ROUSED.
BY CHRIST, I WILL BLOW YOUR BRAINS OUT IF YOU SHOUT AGAIN!
BLOW AWAY. *HUNT AND LIBERTY!* HUNT FOREVER!

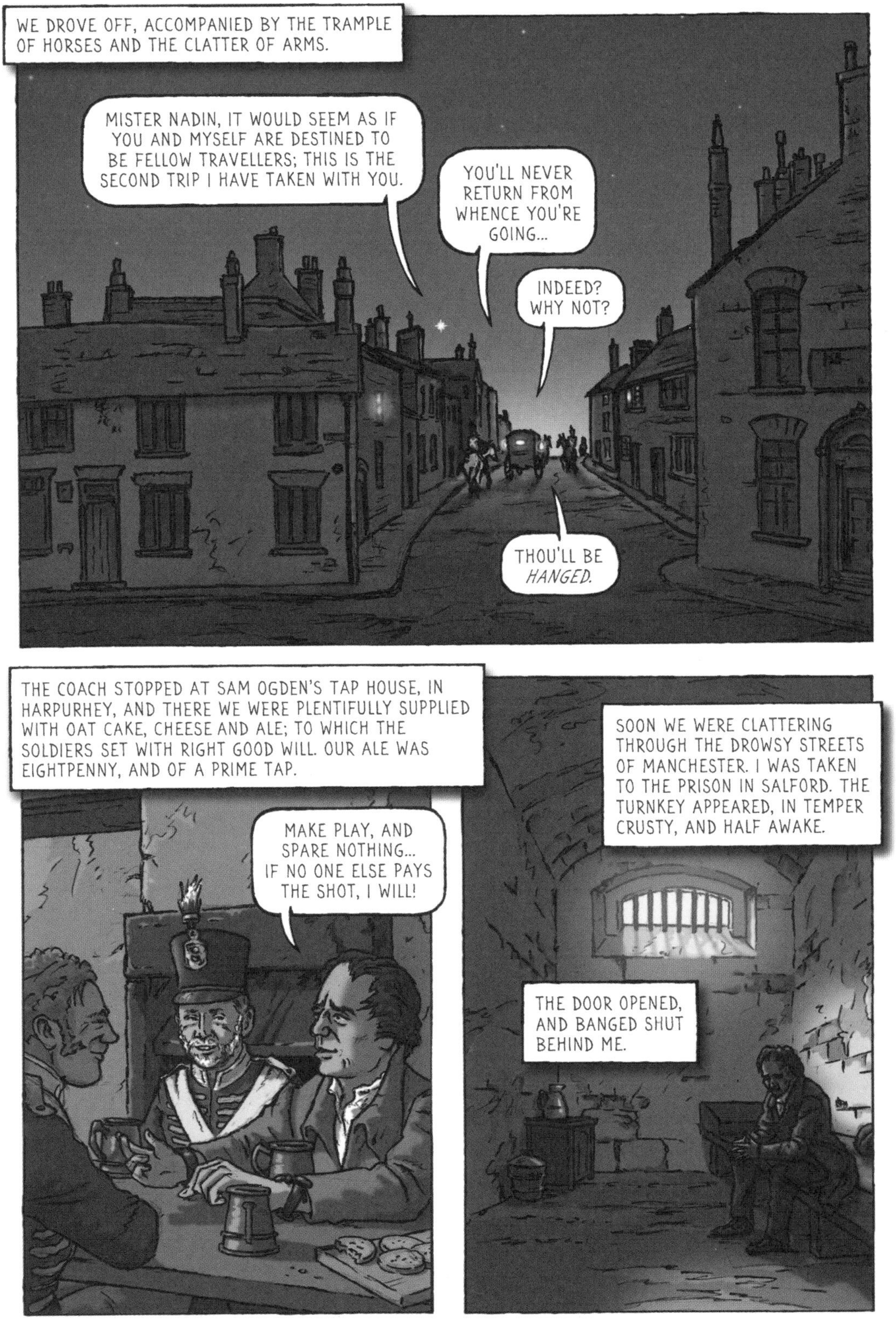
WE DROVE OFF, ACCOMPANIED BY THE TRAMPLE OF HORSES AND THE CLATTER OF ARMS.
MISTER NADIN, IT WOULD SEEM AS IF YOU AND MYSELF ARE DESTINED TO BE FELLOW TRAVELLERS; THIS IS THE SECOND TRIP I HAVE TAKEN WITH YOU.
YOU'LL NEVER RETURN FROM WHENCE YOU'RE GOING...
INDEED? WHY NOT?
THOU'LL BE *HANGED.*
THE COACH STOPPED AT SAM OGDEN'S TAP HOUSE, IN HARPURHEY, AND THERE WE WERE PLENTIFULLY SUPPLIED WITH OAT CAKE, CHEESE AND ALE; TO WHICH THE SOLDIERS SET WITH RIGHT GOOD WILL. OUR ALE WAS EIGHTPENNY, AND OF A PRIME TAP.
MAKE PLAY, AND SPARE NOTHING... IF NO ONE ELSE PAYS THE SHOT, I WILL!
SOON WE WERE CLATTERING THROUGH THE DROWSY STREETS OF MANCHESTER. I WAS TAKEN TO THE PRISON IN SALFORD. THE TURNKEY APPEARED, IN TEMPER CRUSTY, AND HALF AWAKE.
THE DOOR OPENED, AND BANGED SHUT BEHIND ME.

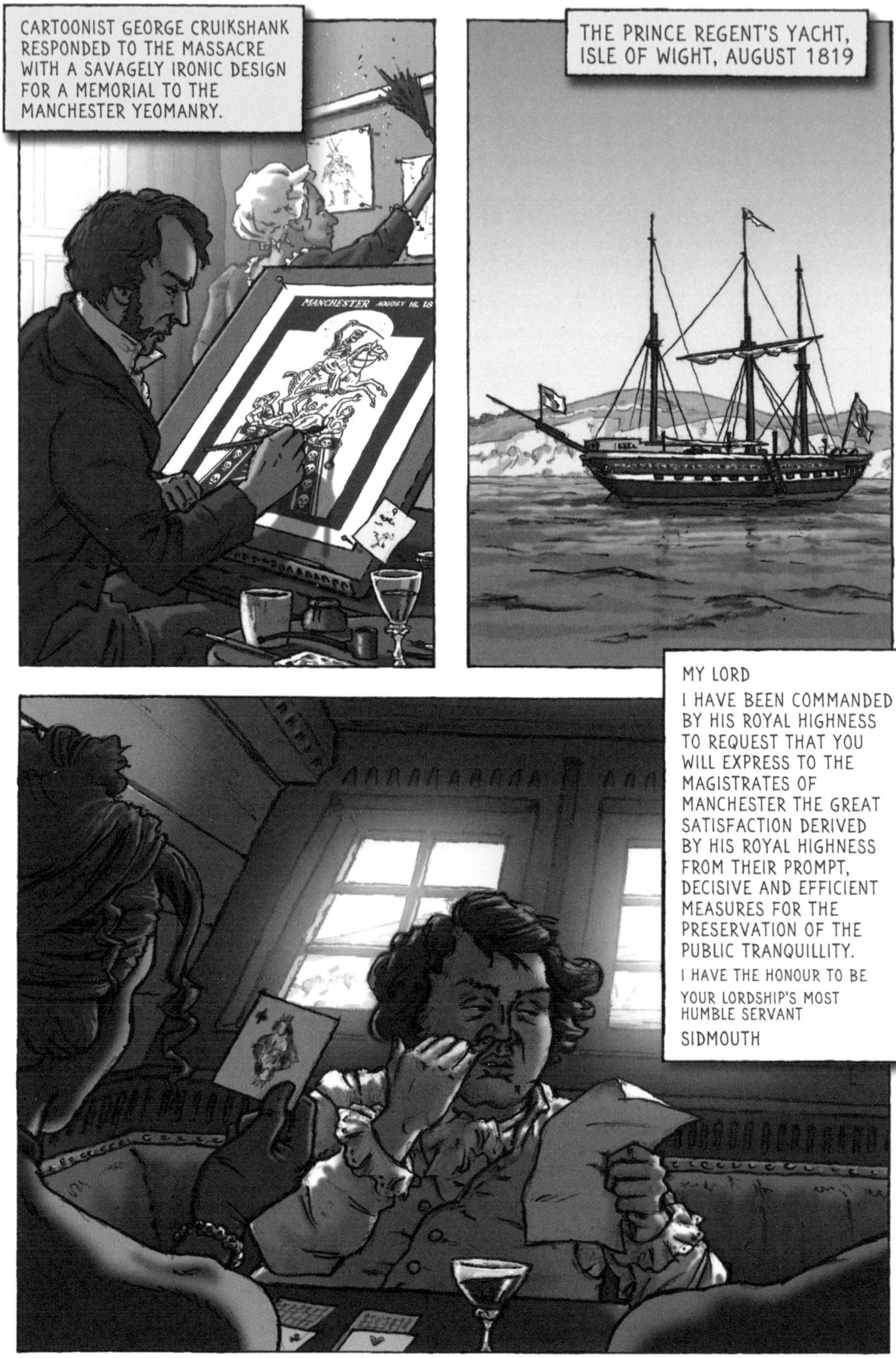
CARTOONIST GEORGE CRUIKSHANK RESPONDED TO THE MASSACRE WITH A SAVAGELY IRONIC DESIGN FOR A MEMORIAL TO THE MANCHESTER YEOMANRY.
MANCHESTER AUGUST 16, 18
THE PRINCE REGENT'S YACHT, ISLE OF WIGHT, AUGUST 1819
MY LORD
I HAVE BEEN COMMANDED BY HIS ROYAL HIGHNESS TO REQUEST THAT YOU WILL EXPRESS TO THE MAGISTRATES OF MANCHESTER THE GREAT SATISFACTION DERIVED BY HIS ROYAL HIGHNESS FROM THEIR PROMPT, DECISIVE AND EFFICIENT MEASURES FOR THE PRESERVATION OF THE PUBLIC TRANQUILLITY.
I HAVE THE HONOUR TO BE
YOUR LORDSHIP'S MOST HUMBLE SERVANT
SIDMOUTH

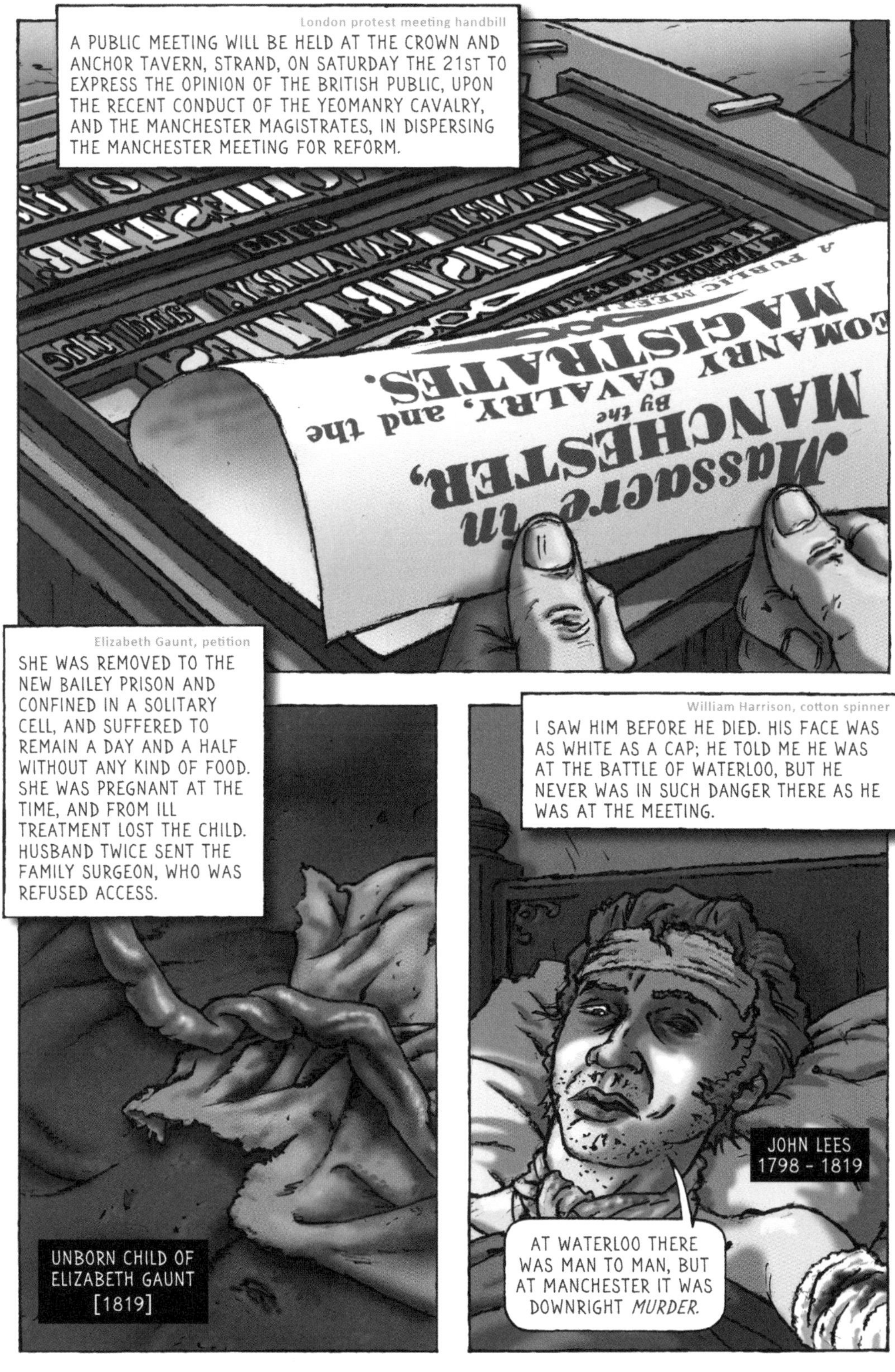
London protest meeting handbill
A PUBLIC MEETING WILL BE HELD AT THE CROWN AND ANCHOR TAVERN, STRAND, ON SATURDAY THE 21ST TO EXPRESS THE OPINION OF THE BRITISH PUBLIC, UPON THE RECENT CONDUCT OF THE YEOMANRY CAVALRY, AND THE MANCHESTER MAGISTRATES, IN DISPERSING THE MANCHESTER MEETING FOR REFORM.
Elizabeth Gaunt, petition
SHE WAS REMOVED TO THE NEW BAILEY PRISON AND CONFINED IN A SOLITARY CELL, AND SUFFERED TO REMAIN A DAY AND A HALF WITHOUT ANY KIND OF FOOD. SHE WAS PREGNANT AT THE TIME, AND FROM ILL TREATMENT LOST THE CHILD. HUSBAND TWICE SENT THE FAMILY SURGEON, WHO WAS REFUSED ACCESS.
UNBORN CHILD OF ELIZABETH GAUNT [1819]
William Harrison, cotton spinner
I SAW HIM BEFORE HE DIED. HIS FACE WAS AS WHITE AS A CAP; HE TOLD ME HE WAS AT THE BATTLE OF WATERLOO, BUT HE NEVER WAS IN SUCH DANGER THERE AS HE WAS AT THE MEETING.
JOHN LEES 1798 - 1819
AT WATERLOO THERE WAS MAN TO MAN, BUT AT MANCHESTER IT WAS DOWNRIGHT *MURDER.*

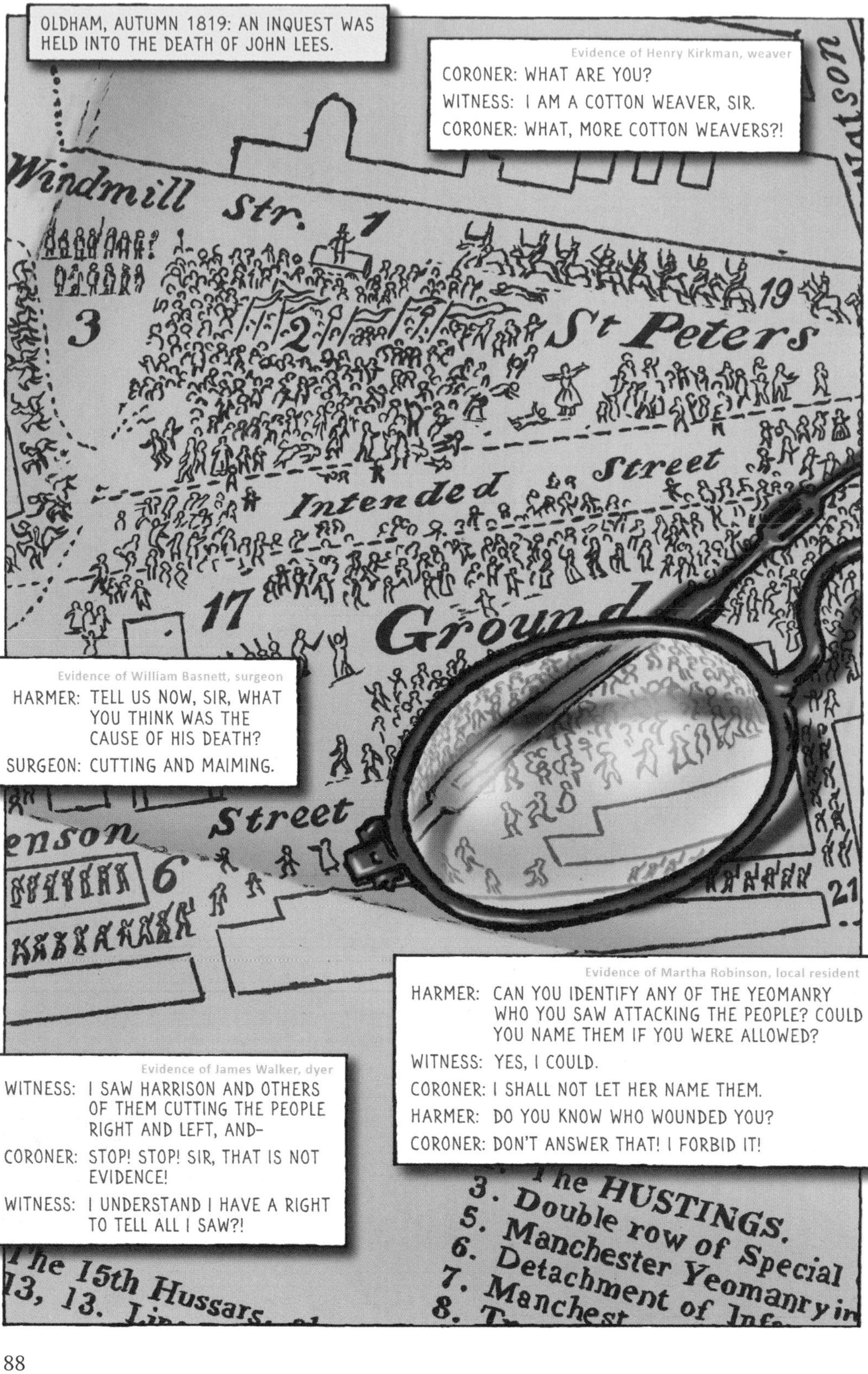

OLDHAM, AUTUMN 1819: AN INQUEST WAS HELD INTO THE DEATH OF JOHN LEES.
Evidence of Henry Kirkman, weaver
CORONER: WHAT ARE YOU?
WITNESS: I AM A COTTON WEAVER, SIR.
CORONER: WHAT, MORE COTTON WEAVERS?!
Windmill Str.
Watson
St Peters
Intended Street
Ground
Street
Evidence of William Basnett, surgeon
HARMER: TELL US NOW, SIR, WHAT YOU THINK WAS THE CAUSE OF HIS DEATH?
SURGEON: CUTTING AND MAIMING.
Evidence of Martha Robinson, local resident
HARMER: CAN YOU IDENTIFY ANY OF THE YEOMANRY WHO YOU SAW ATTACKING THE PEOPLE? COULD YOU NAME THEM IF YOU WERE ALLOWED?
WITNESS: YES, I COULD.
CORONER: I SHALL NOT LET HER NAME THEM.
HARMER: DO YOU KNOW WHO WOUNDED YOU?
CORONER: DON'T ANSWER THAT! I FORBID IT!
Evidence of James Walker, dyer
WITNESS: I SAW HARRISON AND OTHERS OF THEM CUTTING THE PEOPLE RIGHT AND LEFT, AND–
CORONER: STOP! STOP! SIR, THAT IS NOT EVIDENCE!
WITNESS: I UNDERSTAND I HAVE A RIGHT TO TELL ALL I SAW?!
The HUSTINGS.
3. Double row of Special
5. Manchester Yeomanry in
6. Detachment of Inf
The 15th Hussars

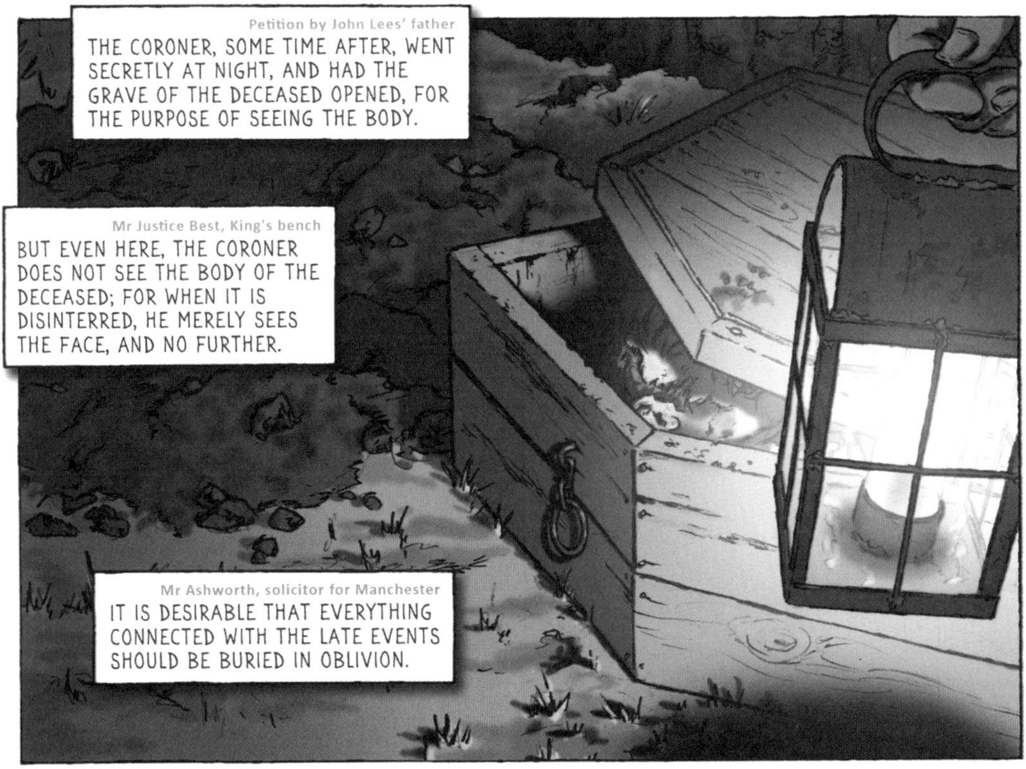
Petition by John Lees' father
THE CORONER, SOME TIME AFTER, WENT SECRETLY AT NIGHT, AND HAD THE GRAVE OF THE DECEASED OPENED, FOR THE PURPOSE OF SEEING THE BODY.
Mr Justice Best, King's bench
BUT EVEN HERE, THE CORONER DOES NOT SEE THE BODY OF THE DECEASED; FOR WHEN IT IS DISINTERRED, HE MERELY SEES THE FACE, AND NO FURTHER.
Mr Ashworth, solicitor for Manchester
IT IS DESIRABLE THAT EVERYTHING CONNECTED WITH THE LATE EVENTS SHOULD BE BURIED IN OBLIVION.

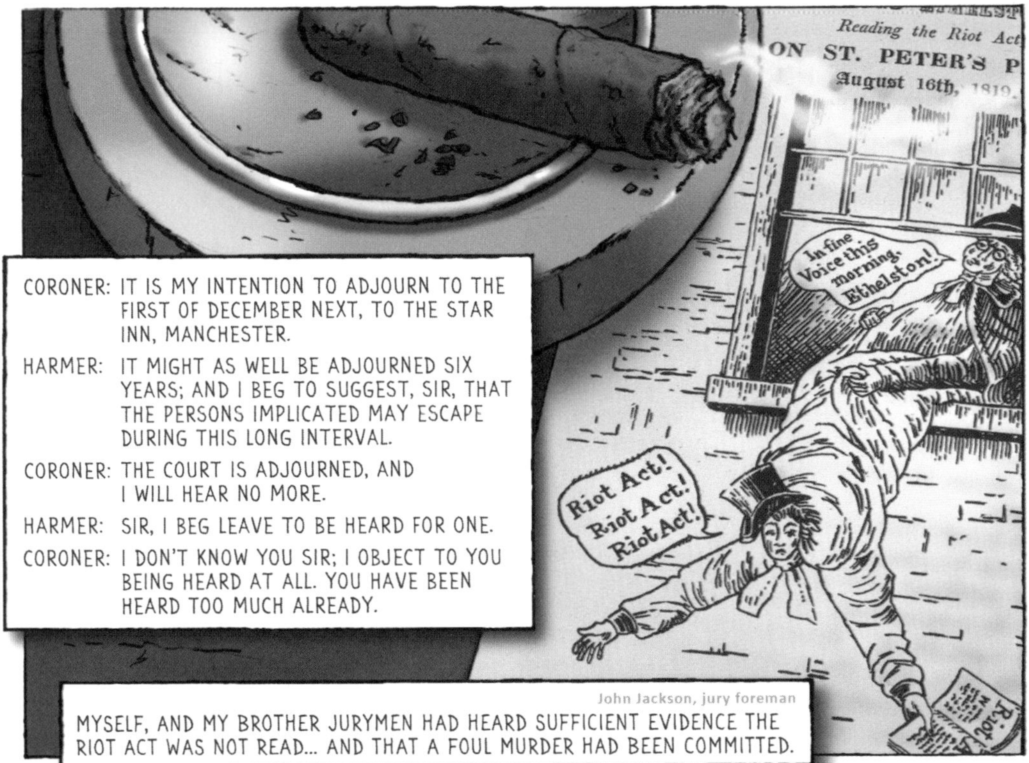
Reading the Riot Act
ON ST. PETER'S P
August 16th, 1819.
In fine Voice this morning, Ethelston!
Riot Act! Riot Act! Riot Act!
CORONER: IT IS MY INTENTION TO ADJOURN TO THE FIRST OF DECEMBER NEXT, TO THE STAR INN, MANCHESTER.
HARMER: IT MIGHT AS WELL BE ADJOURNED SIX YEARS; AND I BEG TO SUGGEST, SIR, THAT THE PERSONS IMPLICATED MAY ESCAPE DURING THIS LONG INTERVAL.
CORONER: THE COURT IS ADJOURNED, AND I WILL HEAR NO MORE.
HARMER: SIR, I BEG LEAVE TO BE HEARD FOR ONE.
CORONER: I DON'T KNOW YOU SIR; I OBJECT TO YOU BEING HEARD AT ALL. YOU HAVE BEEN HEARD TOO MUCH ALREADY.
John Jackson, jury foreman
MYSELF, AND MY BROTHER JURYMEN HAD HEARD SUFFICIENT EVIDENCE THE RIOT ACT WAS NOT READ... AND THAT A FOUL MURDER HAD BEEN COMMITTED.

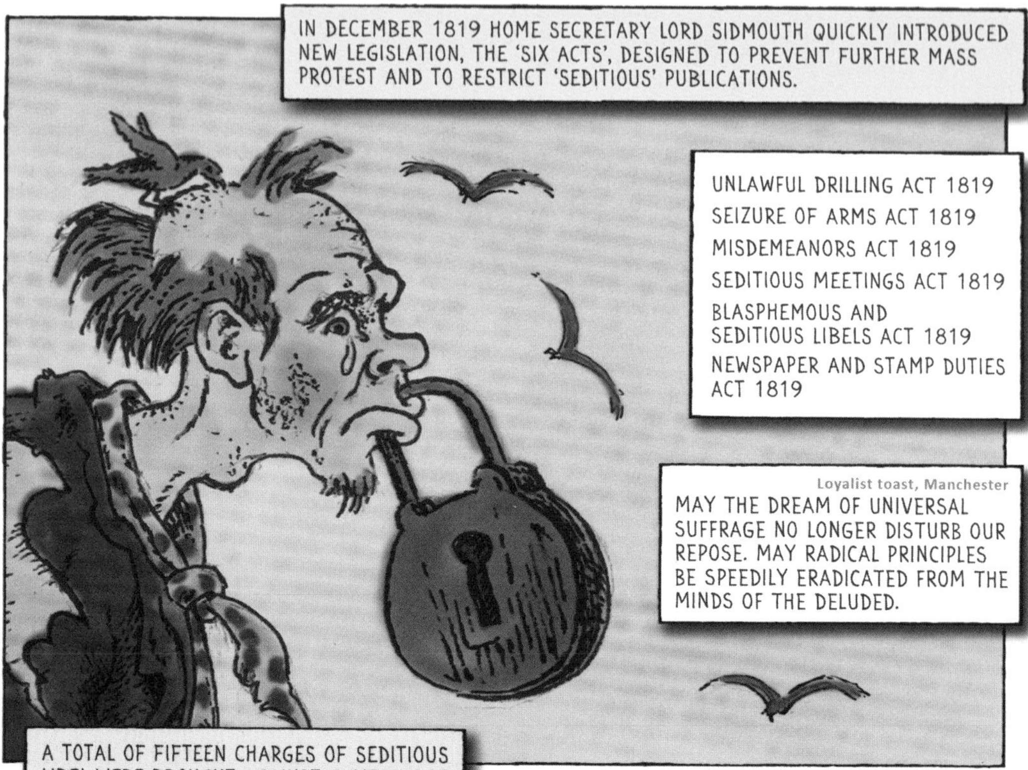
IN DECEMBER 1819 HOME SECRETARY LORD SIDMOUTH QUICKLY INTRODUCED NEW LEGISLATION, THE 'SIX ACTS', DESIGNED TO PREVENT FURTHER MASS PROTEST AND TO RESTRICT 'SEDITIOUS' PUBLICATIONS.
UNLAWFUL DRILLING ACT 1819
SEIZURE OF ARMS ACT 1819
MISDEMEANORS ACT 1819
SEDITIOUS MEETINGS ACT 1819
BLASPHEMOUS AND SEDITIOUS LIBELS ACT 1819
NEWSPAPER AND STAMP DUTIES ACT 1819
Loyalist toast, Manchester
MAY THE DREAM OF UNIVERSAL SUFFRAGE NO LONGER DISTURB OUR REPOSE. MAY RADICAL PRINCIPLES BE SPEEDILY ERADICATED FROM THE MINDS OF THE DELUDED.

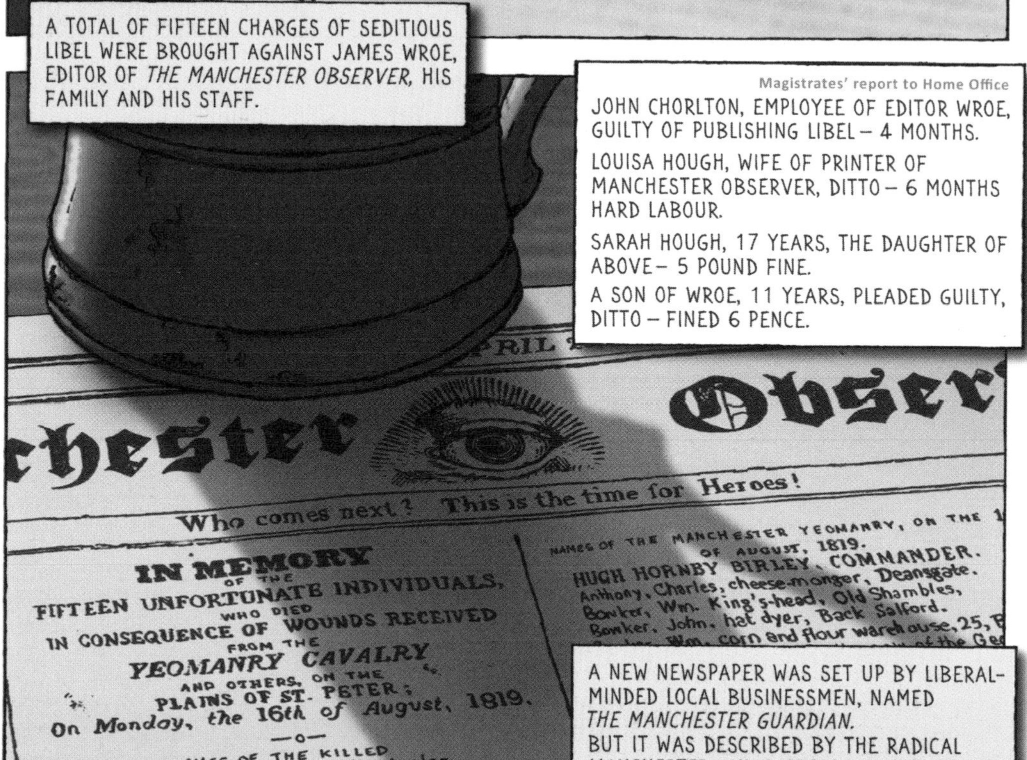
A TOTAL OF FIFTEEN CHARGES OF SEDITIOUS LIBEL WERE BROUGHT AGAINST JAMES WROE, EDITOR OF *THE MANCHESTER OBSERVER*, HIS FAMILY AND HIS STAFF.
Magistrates' report to Home Office
JOHN CHORLTON, EMPLOYEE OF EDITOR WROE, GUILTY OF PUBLISHING LIBEL – 4 MONTHS.
LOUISA HOUGH, WIFE OF PRINTER OF MANCHESTER OBSERVER, DITTO – 6 MONTHS HARD LABOUR.
SARAH HOUGH, 17 YEARS, THE DAUGHTER OF ABOVE – 5 POUND FINE.
A SON OF WROE, 11 YEARS, PLEADED GUILTY, DITTO – FINED 6 PENCE.
chester Obser
Who comes next? This is the time for Heroes!
IN MEMORY OF THE FIFTEEN UNFORTUNATE INDIVIDUALS, WHO DIED IN CONSEQUENCE OF WOUNDS RECEIVED FROM THE YEOMANRY CAVALRY AND OTHERS, ON THE PLAINS OF ST. PETER; On Monday, the 16th of August, 1819.
NAMES OF THE KILLED
John Ashworth, Bull's Head, Manchester.
John Ashton. Cowhill, near Oldham.
NAMES OF THE MANCHESTER YEOMANRY, ON THE 1 OF AUGUST, 1819.
HUGH HORNBY BIRLEY, COMMANDER.
Anthony, Charles, cheese-monger, Deansgate.
Bowker, Wm. King's-head, Old Shambles,
Bowker, John, hat dyer, Back Salford.
A NEW NEWSPAPER WAS SET UP BY LIBERAL-MINDED LOCAL BUSINESSMEN, NAMED *THE MANCHESTER GUARDIAN*.
BUT IT WAS DESCRIBED BY THE RADICAL *MANCHESTER AND SALFORD ADVERTISER* AS BEING 'THE FOUL PROSTITUTE OF THE WORST PORTION OF THE MILL-OWNERS.'

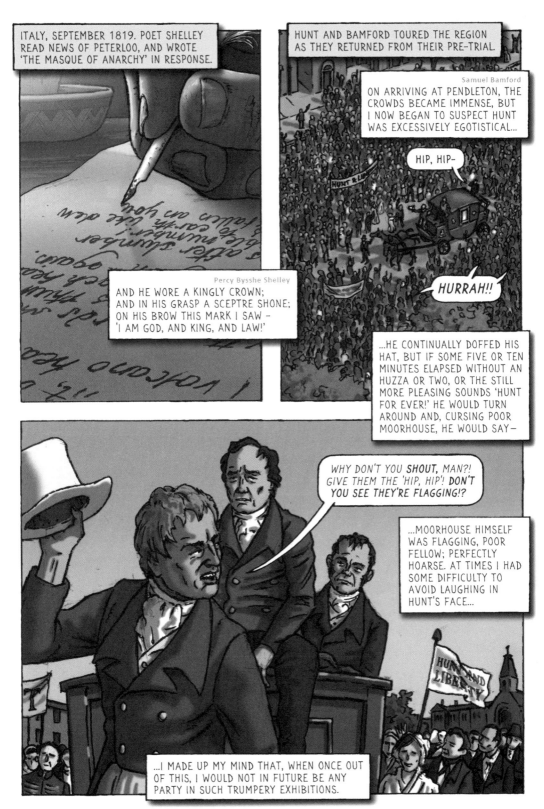

ITALY, SEPTEMBER 1819. POET SHELLEY READ NEWS OF PETERLOO, AND WROTE 'THE MASQUE OF ANARCHY' IN RESPONSE.

Percy Bysshe Shelley
AND HE WORE A KINGLY CROWN;
AND IN HIS GRASP A SCEPTRE SHONE;
ON HIS BROW THIS MARK I SAW –
'I AM GOD, AND KING, AND LAW!'

HUNT AND BAMFORD TOURED THE REGION AS THEY RETURNED FROM THEIR PRE-TRIAL.

Samuel Bamford
ON ARRIVING AT PENDLETON, THE CROWDS BECAME IMMENSE, BUT I NOW BEGAN TO SUSPECT HUNT WAS EXCESSIVELY EGOTISTICAL...

HIP, HIP–

HURRAH!!

...HE CONTINUALLY DOFFED HIS HAT, BUT IF SOME FIVE OR TEN MINUTES ELAPSED WITHOUT AN HUZZA OR TWO, OR THE STILL MORE PLEASING SOUNDS 'HUNT FOR EVER!' HE WOULD TURN AROUND AND, CURSING POOR MOORHOUSE, HE WOULD SAY–

WHY DON'T YOU **SHOUT**, MAN?! GIVE THEM THE 'HIP, HIP'! **DON'T YOU SEE THEY'RE FLAGGING!?**

...MOORHOUSE HIMSELF WAS FLAGGING, POOR FELLOW; PERFECTLY HOARSE. AT TIMES I HAD SOME DIFFICULTY TO AVOID LAUGHING IN HUNT'S FACE...

...I MADE UP MY MIND THAT, WHEN ONCE OUT OF THIS, I WOULD NOT IN FUTURE BE ANY PARTY IN SUCH TRUMPERY EXHIBITIONS.

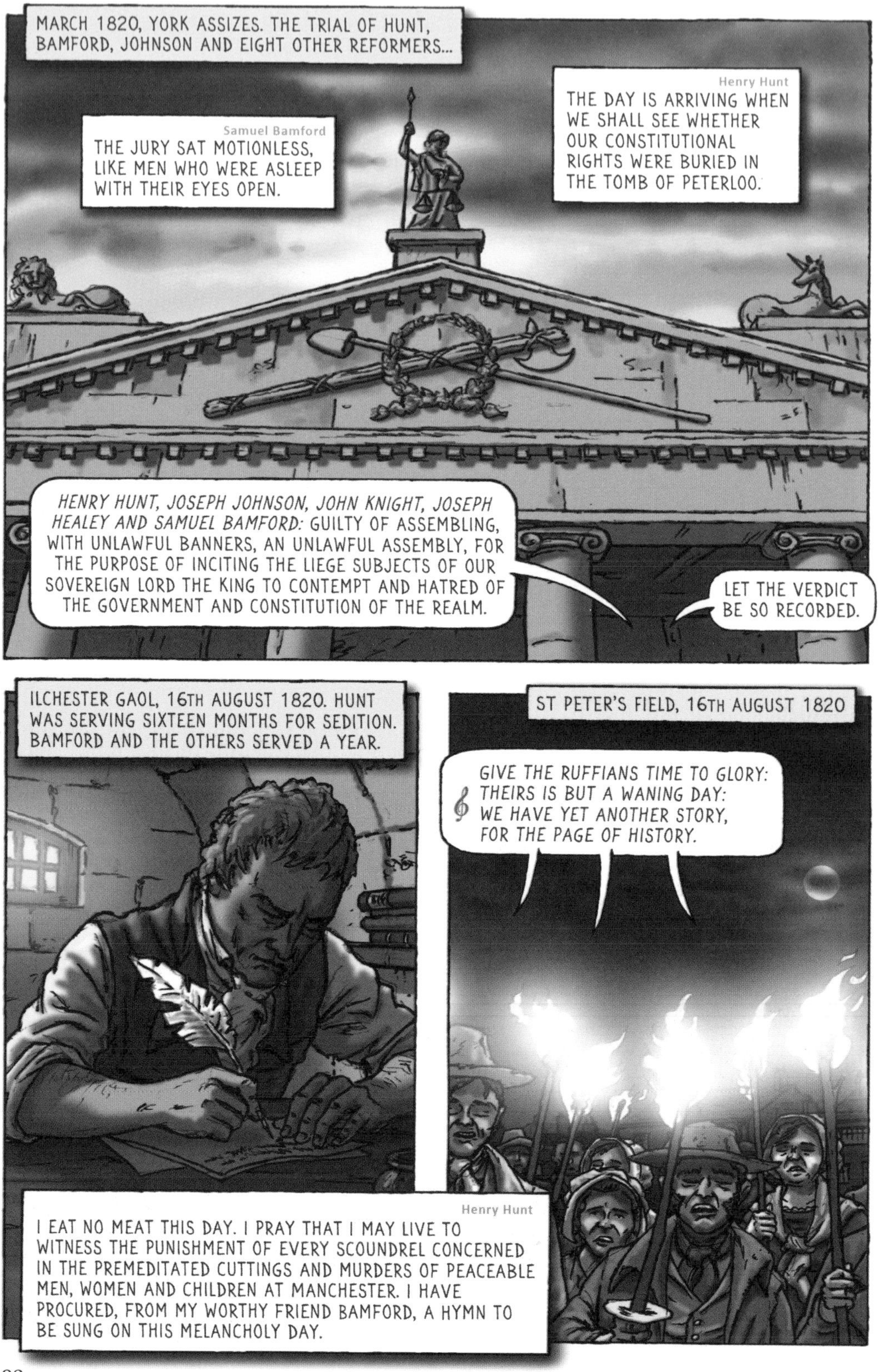
MARCH 1820, YORK ASSIZES. THE TRIAL OF HUNT, BAMFORD, JOHNSON AND EIGHT OTHER REFORMERS...
Samuel Bamford
THE JURY SAT MOTIONLESS, LIKE MEN WHO WERE ASLEEP WITH THEIR EYES OPEN.
Henry Hunt
THE DAY IS ARRIVING WHEN WE SHALL SEE WHETHER OUR CONSTITUTIONAL RIGHTS WERE BURIED IN THE TOMB OF PETERLOO.
HENRY HUNT, JOSEPH JOHNSON, JOHN KNIGHT, JOSEPH HEALEY AND SAMUEL BAMFORD: GUILTY OF ASSEMBLING, WITH UNLAWFUL BANNERS, AN UNLAWFUL ASSEMBLY, FOR THE PURPOSE OF INCITING THE LIEGE SUBJECTS OF OUR SOVEREIGN LORD THE KING TO CONTEMPT AND HATRED OF THE GOVERNMENT AND CONSTITUTION OF THE REALM.
LET THE VERDICT BE SO RECORDED.
ILCHESTER GAOL, 16TH AUGUST 1820. HUNT WAS SERVING SIXTEEN MONTHS FOR SEDITION. BAMFORD AND THE OTHERS SERVED A YEAR.
Henry Hunt
I EAT NO MEAT THIS DAY. I PRAY THAT I MAY LIVE TO WITNESS THE PUNISHMENT OF EVERY SCOUNDREL CONCERNED IN THE PREMEDITATED CUTTINGS AND MURDERS OF PEACEABLE MEN, WOMEN AND CHILDREN AT MANCHESTER. I HAVE PROCURED, FROM MY WORTHY FRIEND BAMFORD, A HYMN TO BE SUNG ON THIS MELANCHOLY DAY.
ST PETER'S FIELD, 16TH AUGUST 1820
GIVE THE RUFFIANS TIME TO GLORY: THEIRS IS BUT A WANING DAY: WE HAVE YET ANOTHER STORY, FOR THE PAGE OF HISTORY.

V

All government rests
ultimately on force.

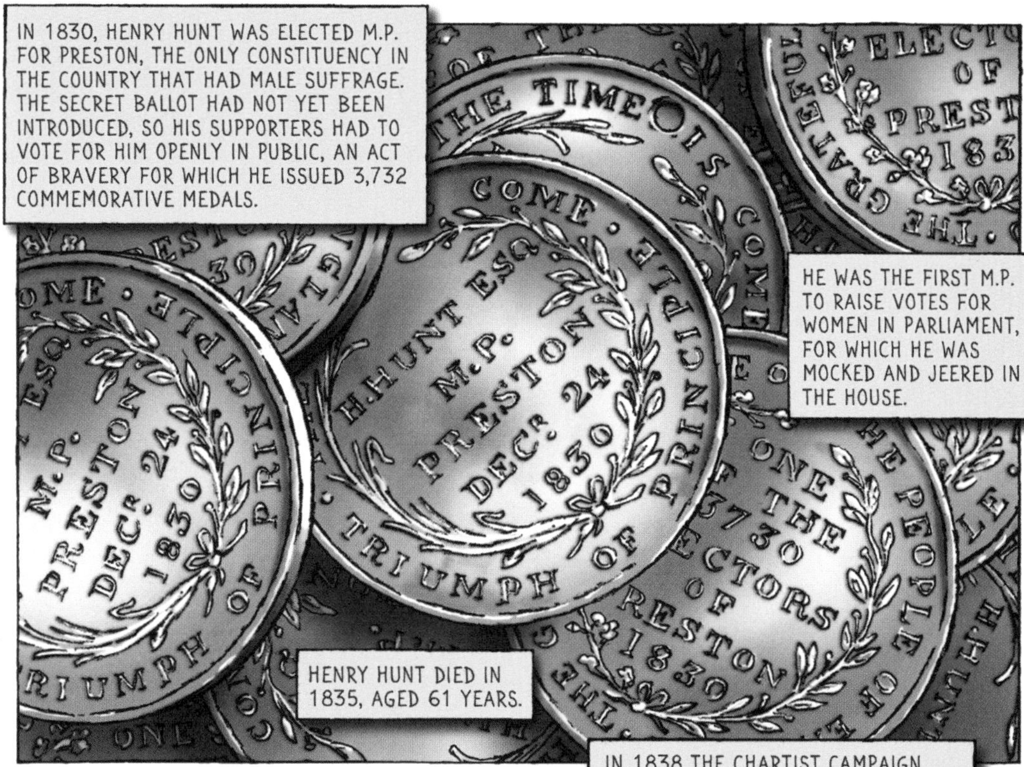
IN 1830, HENRY HUNT WAS ELECTED M.P. FOR PRESTON, THE ONLY CONSTITUENCY IN THE COUNTRY THAT HAD MALE SUFFRAGE. THE SECRET BALLOT HAD NOT YET BEEN INTRODUCED, SO HIS SUPPORTERS HAD TO VOTE FOR HIM OPENLY IN PUBLIC, AN ACT OF BRAVERY FOR WHICH HE ISSUED 3,732 COMMEMORATIVE MEDALS.
THE TIME IS COME
H.HUNT ESQ M.P. PRESTON DEC^R 24 1830
TRIUMPH OF PRINCIPLE
HE WAS THE FIRST M.P. TO RAISE VOTES FOR WOMEN IN PARLIAMENT, FOR WHICH HE WAS MOCKED AND JEERED IN THE HOUSE.
HENRY HUNT DIED IN 1835, AGED 61 YEARS.

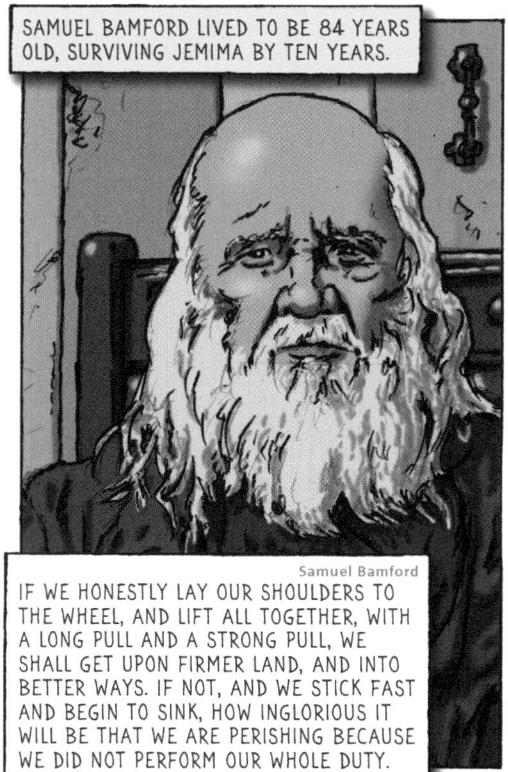
SAMUEL BAMFORD LIVED TO BE 84 YEARS OLD, SURVIVING JEMIMA BY TEN YEARS.
Samuel Bamford
IF WE HONESTLY LAY OUR SHOULDERS TO THE WHEEL, AND LIFT ALL TOGETHER, WITH A LONG PULL AND A STRONG PULL, WE SHALL GET UPON FIRMER LAND, AND INTO BETTER WAYS. IF NOT, AND WE STICK FAST AND BEGIN TO SINK, HOW INGLORIOUS IT WILL BE THAT WE ARE PERISHING BECAUSE WE DID NOT PERFORM OUR WHOLE DUTY.

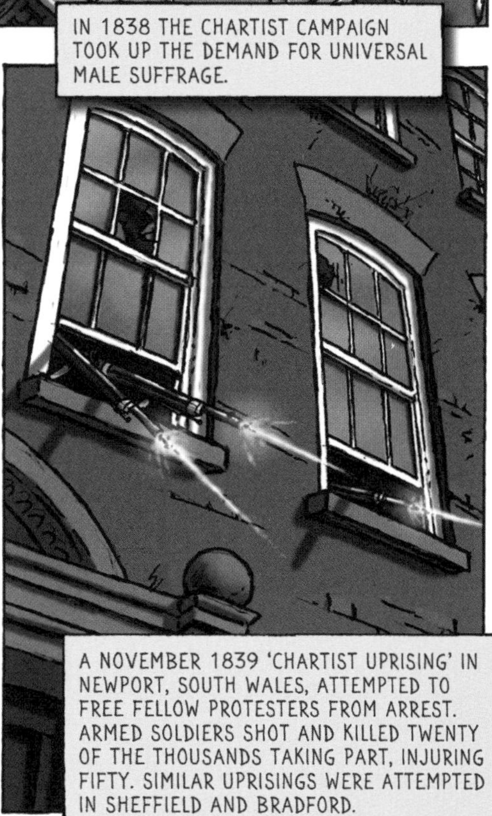
IN 1838 THE CHARTIST CAMPAIGN TOOK UP THE DEMAND FOR UNIVERSAL MALE SUFFRAGE.
A NOVEMBER 1839 'CHARTIST UPRISING' IN NEWPORT, SOUTH WALES, ATTEMPTED TO FREE FELLOW PROTESTERS FROM ARREST. ARMED SOLDIERS SHOT AND KILLED TWENTY OF THE THOUSANDS TAKING PART, INJURING FIFTY. SIMILAR UPRISINGS WERE ATTEMPTED IN SHEFFIELD AND BRADFORD.

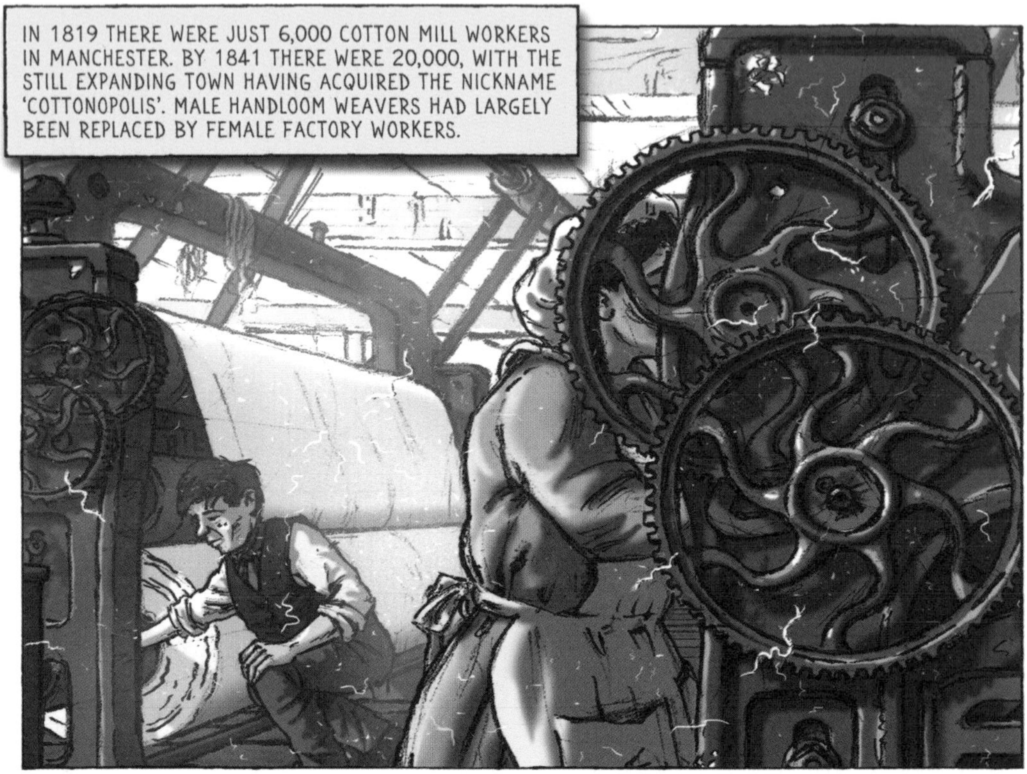
IN 1819 THERE WERE JUST 6,000 COTTON MILL WORKERS IN MANCHESTER. BY 1841 THERE WERE 20,000, WITH THE STILL EXPANDING TOWN HAVING ACQUIRED THE NICKNAME 'COTTONOPOLIS'. MALE HANDLOOM WEAVERS HAD LARGELY BEEN REPLACED BY FEMALE FACTORY WORKERS.

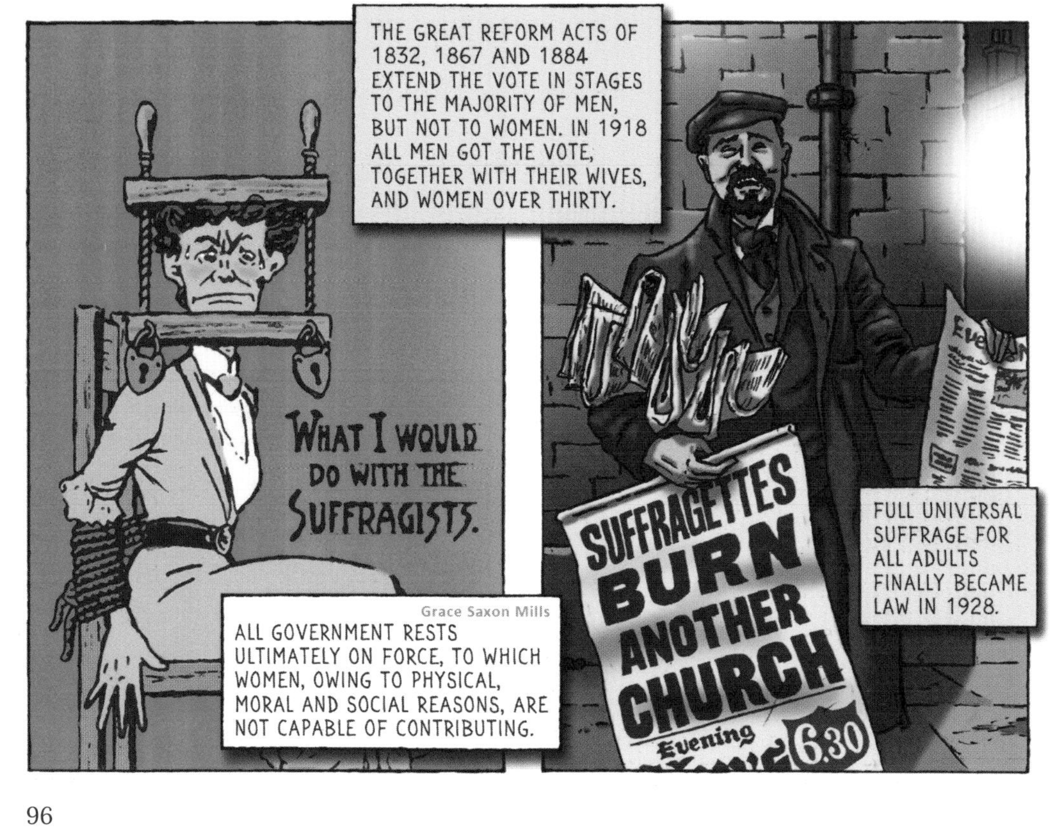
THE GREAT REFORM ACTS OF 1832, 1867 AND 1884 EXTEND THE VOTE IN STAGES TO THE MAJORITY OF MEN, BUT NOT TO WOMEN. IN 1918 ALL MEN GOT THE VOTE, TOGETHER WITH THEIR WIVES, AND WOMEN OVER THIRTY.
WHAT I WOULD DO WITH THE SUFFRAGISTS.
Grace Saxon Mills
ALL GOVERNMENT RESTS ULTIMATELY ON FORCE, TO WHICH WOMEN, OWING TO PHYSICAL, MORAL AND SOCIAL REASONS, ARE NOT CAPABLE OF CONTRIBUTING.
SUFFRAGETTES BURN ANOTHER CHURCH
Evening
6.30
FULL UNIVERSAL SUFFRAGE FOR ALL ADULTS FINALLY BECAME LAW IN 1928.

A MEMORIAL TO HENRY HUNT WAS CREATED BY PUBLIC SUBSCRIPTION IN 1842. BY 1888 IT HAD DETERIORATED BADLY, AND WAS DEMOLISHED.

THE STORY OF PETERLOO HAD BEGUN TO FADE FROM POPULAR MEMORY.

A 1972 ATTEMPT TO RENAME PETER STREET 'PETERLOO STREET' WAS HALTED WHEN LOCAL BUSINESSES CHALLENGED THE PROPOSAL IN COURT. A BLAND AND MISLEADINGLY WORDED STREET PLAQUE FOLLOWED.

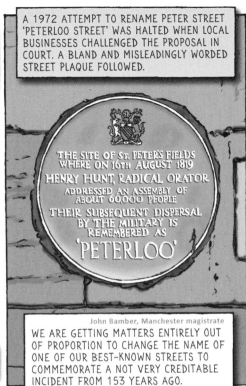

THE SITE OF ST. PETER'S FIELDS WHERE ON 16TH AUGUST 1819 HENRY HUNT, RADICAL ORATOR ADDRESSED AN ASSEMBLY OF ABOUT 60,000 PEOPLE THEIR SUBSEQUENT DISPERSAL BY THE MILITARY IS REMEMBERED AS 'PETERLOO'

John Bamber, Manchester magistrate
WE ARE GETTING MATTERS ENTIRELY OUT OF PROPORTION TO CHANGE THE NAME OF ONE OF OUR BEST-KNOWN STREETS TO COMMEMORATE A NOT VERY CREDITABLE INCIDENT FROM 153 YEARS AGO.

ST PETER'S FIELD, SPRING 2019

The Peterloo Memorial Campaign
PETERLOO ISN'T JUST ABOUT THE PAST: IT'S ABOUT THE PRESENT, AND THE FUTURE AS WELL. ITS MEMORY THROWS A CHALLENGING QUESTION AT US ALL: WHAT HAVE WE DONE TO DEFEND, NURTURE AND SPREAD THE DEMOCRATIC LEGACY THAT THESE PEOPLE DIED TO PASS ON TO US?

Shelley, 'The Masque of Anarchy'
RISE, LIKE LIONS AFTER SLUMBER
IN UNVANQUISHABLE NUMBER!
SHAKE YOUR CHAINS TO EARTH LIKE DEW
WHICH IN SLEEP HAD FALLEN ON YOU:
YE ARE MANY — THEY ARE FEW!

VI

*...being indulged with the company
of another man's wife...*

More detail on the material in these notes can be found in Robert Poole's *Peterloo: the English Uprising* (2019).

The names of the dead
Over the years this list has changed and is continually being updated as new evidence has come to light, or as old evidence is re-examined. This is the official list as of January 2019.

Page 7
The most notorious 'rotten borough' was Old Sarum in Wiltshire, a deserted village site which was represented by two MPs but consisted of little more than just one family.

Page 8
English author and radical Thomas Paine introduced the concept of universal rights to England's working classes in 1792 with his bestselling book *Rights of Man*. Despite his exile from England, Paine had great influence: a cheap edition of *Rights of Man* was widely circulated and discussed.

During the winter of 1792-3 all across the country, effigies of Paine were hanged, broken and burnt by loyalists in imitation of the traditional sentence for treason, including on Deansgate, Manchester.

Anti-Paine open letters were circulated in Manchester and Salford pubs, including one claiming to be from a 'Brother Weaver': 'Do not let us be humbugged by Mr Paine, who tells us a great many Truths, in his book, in order to shove off his Lies.' Even as late as the 1820s, signs saying 'no Jacobins admitted here' could be seen in the pubs of Manchester.

Page 9
Joseph Nadin's self-regard was well known. Magistrates and lawyers took advantage of this fact. The magistrates wrote: 'Nadin is a very useful police officer, whom it is desirable to render cheerful in the exercise of his duty.'

At the trial of John Knight and his fellow reformers in 1812 the following exchange took place:

Q: Your face is pretty well known at Manchester, there is no man so well known.
A (Nadin): I do not think there is.
Q: People are much alarmed at seeing you in the night time.
A: If their deeds are not evil, they have no cause to be alarmed.

Political prisoners from Lancashire were greatly mistreated in gaol. The most notable case was that of 74-year-old printer William Ogden who developed a hernia from the weight of the irons which he had been loaded with by Nadin in Manchester. The irons 'broke his belly, and caused an hernia to ensue... He remained in that dreadful state for more than sixteen hours in the most excruciating torture.'

'The wound in his groin was above seven inches in length'. Ogden told how he 'had his entrails out of his belly in his fingers, like a link of sausages.'

Many prisoners were released from gaol after eight or nine months without trial, and were forced to travel home on the outside of a coach, ill-dressed for winter. John Knight returned home to find his business ruined, his wife ill, and no means to buy medicine.

Another prisoner, John Roberts, wrote to Home Secretary Lord Sidmouth on 6 May 1818: 'You cannot Refuse to [notice] sufferings that as been of the worst I have lost my wife in concequence of my imprisonment and is left with four smoal children and my Self out of imployment totley Destitute of anney meanes of soport and is my Self in a verey Debilitated state of elth.'

Page 12
Just three months after the blanketeer march was intercepted by the Cheshire Yeomanry in March 1817, the Manchester and Salford Yeomanry was formally set up.

It was raised 'for the defence of the towns and neighbourhood of Manchester and Salford', including 'the suppression of riot or tumult or in case of invasion'. (Rules and Regulations for the Manchester & Salford Yeomanry Cavalry, September 1817.)

Yeomanry were usually forces of country gentry, but of the 84 M&S Yeomanry listed to serve in 1819, no more than three were gentry. Six were professional men (attorneys, doctors, a surveyor and a 'dancing master'), 25 were merchants and manufacturers (including 15 in the cotton trade), 31 were traders and shopkeepers, 14 were publicans and five were labourers or servants substituting for their masters.

Captain Hugh Hornby Birley owned Chorlton Mill, near Oxford Road, which was visible from St Peter's Field and is still standing today. Shortly after leading the attack, Birley sacked the entire family of one protester he had seen on the field. Protesters would gather outside his mill on the anniversary of the attack to boo and hiss.

He is buried in a family vault under St Peter's Square, near the cross marking the site of the church.

Page 13
While Hunt repeatedly tried to ensure that the meetings he addressed were peaceful and stayed within the law, Arthur Thistlewood and his fellow revolutionary Spencean activists disagreed. When Hunt agreed to speak at London's Spa Fields in 1816 so as to rally support for another petition to the Prince Regent, a group of Spencean militants broke away from the main crowd before the start, raided a gun shop, and headed towards the Tower of London, hoping to spark a Bastille-style uprising. They were easily defeated and arrested.

It emerged in the subsequent trial that a spy or agent provocateur, John Castles, was involved, bearing out Hunt's description of Thistlewood as 'a dupe of spies'. The 'Spa Fields Riot' was subsequently used as a taunt and accusation against Hunt and other reformers, even though they had not known of Thistlewood's plans.

Hunt briefly owned a brewery in Bristol, but after several barrels were unjustly seized by the Excise, his political enemies used this as propaganda against him, claiming his beer was 'adulterated'.

Samuel Bamford had a somewhat wayward youth, fathering one illegitimate child for whom he paid maintenance, and having another with Jemima shortly before their marriage. The baby was presented to him in church on their wedding day.

Page 14
The weekly Manchester Observer, launched in 1818, was Manchester's first radical newspaper. 'The... only newspaper in England that I know, fairly and honestly devoted to such reform as would give the people their whole rights' (Henry Hunt).

It was a full-stamped newspaper, making it more expensive than contemporary radical publications and, while unaffordable to most working people, there was a network of followers who would pass it from hand to hand, or read it aloud to others.

The editor of the Manchester Observer, James Wroe, fought a long, tireless battle against charges of seditious libel. In July 1819, Nadin strode into the Observer office with a warrant for his arrest. Wroe looked up and said: 'It's what I have been expecting for some time'. He was bailed by wealthy supporters and was back in his editor's chair the same day.

Page 17
Hunt was well known for his distinctive white top hat, a symbol of the purity of his cause. The style was copied by other reformers and was possibly intended as a subversive gesture against class distinctions.

During the theatre brawl court case, Hunt's companion Whitworth explained that they hadn't called the police because Nadin and his group were already in the theatre laughing.

Page 19
Hunt told the Manchester meeting in January 1819: 'Wherever I appear in public, they honour me with the attendance of soldiers – they are become my bodyguard.'

Page 22
The first recorded mention of female reformers was when the 'brave female reformers of Stockport' were toasted, among others, during speeches at the celebratory dinner on the evening of Sandy Brow meeting on 15 February.

Samuel Bamford had first proposed that women be allowed to vote at meetings in 1818. Samuel Drummond responded: 'I think my friend Mr Bamford is more an advocate of the woman than the common cause for which we are met. Women promote the cause, but men must be the substance.'

There is also evidence suggesting that some of the speeches and addresses delivered on behalf of the female reformers were co-written by men. The presence of women on the platform may have been meant, in part, to deter attacks by the military; if so, it seems to have worked everywhere except Manchester.

Page 23
The 'cap of liberty' dates back to Roman times, when it was given to slaves who were granted their liberty. It later became a symbol of political freedom, and was displayed by Britannia on the English penny coin until 1792. When it was taken up by French revolutionaries, who went to war with Britain, Britannia swapped it for a trident. English radicals took the cap of liberty up again after the war as a sign of an alternative patriotism based on constitutional rights and liberties, but the authorities saw it as a revolutionary emblem and were determined to stop it being displayed in public. It appears on the coat of arms of many countries, including Paraguay, Cuba, Argentina, Colombia and Haiti, as well as on the Seal of the US Senate.

Not only did the constables who attempted to capture the cap of liberty and break up the meeting fail in their attempt, they did so pitifully and painfully. An informer reports that the mob cut the reins of the constables' horses and further injuries were suffered later the same evening, including magistrate clerk Lloyd's son being violently attacked and beaten when attempting to break up a rowdy mob in the marketplace.

This occurred after the celebration dinner which was held at the Windmill rooms of a Stockport pub, during which a magistrate burst in and demanded the cap of liberty. The reformers took pity on the ageing loyalist and turned him away politely, reassuring him that if they were to come across the cap of liberty they would faithfully turn it over to the authorities.

The humiliation caused by the Stockport Fray was long lived and deeply rooted. The Stockport troop of Cheshire Yeomanry were present at Peterloo, and no doubt relished the opportunity to take their revenge.

Page 24
The Home Office made it clear that they could not offer relief. Instead the magistrates provided soup kitchens and kept cavalry ready to control civil unrest. John Lloyd: 'I think we shall be able to manage the people & keep them quiet.'

Page 26
16 August was in fact the third proposed date for the St Peter's Field meeting, as the reformers twice postponed and re-advertised it to ensure that they stayed within the law.

Hunt reluctantly stayed a week with Johnson waiting for the re-arranged meeting on 16 August, and later described it as 'one of the most disagreeable seven days that I ever passed in my life'. His dislike for Johnson increased when he learned, two weeks after Peterloo, that his host had let the magistrates see his letters from Hunt.

Page 27
Authority in Manchester's regional towns dwindled in early 1819, while reform meetings were being held almost weekly.

The rebellious atmosphere of Stockport was accompanied by scenes of wretched poverty. Factories stood still and silent while streets were posted with advertisements for lottery tickets and rewards of up to £400 for information about the shooting of a constable named Birch.

John Tyas: 'Poor men are wandering about, with emaciated faces and dejected despairing looks, apparently without employment or the means of support, while their houses seem neglected, their wives and children in rags.'

Page 29
James Murray reports that, following the beating, his attackers made him kneel and said to him: 'You swear never to be a King's man again, nor own the name of a King, nor go a constabling; I will have no more constabling.'

One of James Murray's companions at White Moss, John Shawcross, was well known at the *Manchester Observer* office on 'Sedition Corner': every Saturday he purchased the latest issue for the magistrates and police officers to examine.

Miles Ashworth, an ex-soldier who drilled another group of Peterloo marchers at Tandle Hill, went on to become one of the 'Rochdale Pioneers' who helped to establish the Co-operative movement in 1844.

Page 34
Probably 16-20,000 joined the main marches into Manchester from the surrounding towns: 4-5,000 on the combined Rochdale-Heywood-Middleton march; 5-6,000 on the Saddleworth-Oldham-Failsworth march; 4,000 for the marches from Stockport and Ashton, which merged near Manchester; 2,000 from Bury; and more from Bolton and Salford. Finally Hunt's procession from Smedley Cottage, which attracted supporters as it came into Manchester, was estimated at 3,000. Many more people came shorter distances in small groups, and more again from Manchester attended St Peter's Field to watch the spectacle.

Page 35
John Whittaker, a bricklayer, described seeing the marchers from Middleton and Rochdale setting out and returning on 16 August. In his statement he said he was 'at his work near the road side at Harpurhey, [when he] saw, about ten or eleven o'clock, very large crowds of people going to the meeting at Manchester'. Sceptical at the sight of such a celebratory scene he yelled out to the crowd, 'you will not come back as merry as you go'. They responded: 'We will let you know better than that, we will show you different in a short time.'

Around three o'clock that afternoon Whittaker was still at his work when he saw the crowd return. He reports that he yelled out to them: 'I told you how you would come back, did not I?' They answered: 'We shall come back again and give you some cold steel, we will not come naked as we have done this time, we shall come armed, we have plenty of arms at home and we will fetch them.'

Page 36
Not everyone cheered the female reformers. John Tyas, reporter for *The Times*, reported a conversation in the crowd. 'A group of women of Manchester, attracted by the crowd, came to the corner of the street where we had taken our post. They viewed the Oldham Female Reformers for some

time with a look in which compassion and disgust was equally blended, and at last burst out into an indignant exclamation: 'Go home to your families, and leave such-like as these to your husbands and sons, who better understand them.' The women who addressed them were of the lower order of life.'

Page 37

The husting was still being erected around 11.30am as the first contingent of marchers arrived at St Peter's Field. A body of constables took their positions as the crowd arrived. On seeing the constables, the marchers mistook them for another contingent of protesters and gave them a hearty cheer until they realized their mistake and promptly ignored them.

Page 38

Jemima Bamford described her apprehension about the meeting of 16 August and her fears for her husband's safety. But despite this she was determined to attend, thinking that this way she would at least be with her husband and not alone at home worrying about him. She was separated from him soon after entering the outskirts of Manchester, only spotting him once at the meeting when he got up on the hustings to make arrangements before jumping off the platform into the crowd and out of sight.

Page 39

Several loyalist watchers reported hearing taunts or being directly threatened by marchers as they passed on their way to and from Manchester on 16 August:

James Heath: 'I saw a party of three, and one of those three persons, looking earnestly at me, said: "You will not sleep under that house tonight"'.

John Ashworth: 'Many called out to me by name to go with them, but I said they were a week too soon for me and I could not go till Saturday. One of them also said they would make a "Moscow" of Manchester before they came back.'

The reformer and stagecoach owner James Moorhouse had brought passengers as usual to Manchester that morning, his pregnant wife among them. Afterwards he got into Hunt's carriage as it made its way along Deansgate and somehow managed to get his hand slammed in the door. When they arrived at St Peter's Field he needed to leave so that he could dull the pain with spirits in a nearby pub. He was still at the pub a short time later when the Yeomanry arrived and began to attack the crowd, at which point he decided to make his escape. He was arrested on his way home later that day.

Page 40

The text of the arrest warrants reads: 'Whereas Richard Owen hath this day made oath... that Henry Hunt, John Knight, Joseph Johnson and – Moorhouse, at this time (from a quarter past one o'clock) have arrived in a car, at the area near St Peter's Church, and that an immense mob is collected, and that he considers the Town in danger, and the said parties moving thereto, these are, therefore, in his Majesty's name, to require you forthwith to take and bring before us... the bodies of the said Hunt, Knight, Johnson and Moorhouse.'

Page 42

The number of protesters gathered on St Peter's Field on 16 August is thought to be 40-50,000. Eyewitnesses' estimates varied between 40,000 and 100,000.

Page 44

Chief Magistrate William Hulton was only 32 in 1819, but had already been involved in the prosecution and hanging of local Luddite 'rebels'. His family had owned Hulton Park since the 12th century, and had established a set of profitable coalmines on the estate. When his unionized mine workers went on strike in 1831, he issued a pamphlet addressed to them, complaining: 'You have wantonly injured me to the full limits of your ability, in my purse...'

Page 47

William Fildes' mother was not a protester, nor was she any known relation to female reformer Mary Fildes. The yeoman who knocked William Fildes out of his mothers' arms rode on without stopping.

Pages 50-1

After Peterloo, Trumpeter Meagher became involved in a confrontation with people in the street taunting him for his role in the massacre. He ended up firing shots from his window at a stone-throwing crowd that had surrounded his house. He was eventually rescued by the military and escorted away. He was charged with wounding but acquitted by the magistrates.

Page 56

The 15th Hussars were regular cavalry who had been in the thick of the fighting at Waterloo, and had since been on public-order duty in England.

Pages 58-9

In total nearly 700 people were injured on the day.

Page 65

The Friends' Meeting House is still there, somewhat modified but surrounded by the original brick wall round its burial ground. This 'democracy wall' is the only completely original structure from 1819 still remaining on the site of the massacre.

Page 66

Most of the flags, banners and caps of liberty were captured by constables and the Yeomanry as trophies. There are reports of men boasting about who captured which particular flags and how they were disposed of. The only original banner known to have survived is the green one from Middleton, which is said to have been smuggled out under a woman's dress. It is now in the collection of Rochdale Borough and is displayed at Touchstones Museum. Samuel Bamford reported that on his way home he saw a torn banner being worn by a Manchester yeoman as a trophy sash.

Page 68

A Manchester Relief Committee was set up to raise and distribute funds to the victims of the massacre. (Although a large percentage also went to legal fees defending those who were put on trial.) The original handwritten account book still exists in the Peterloo Collection at the John Rylands Library, Deansgate. The entries record details of the victims, their injuries and how much they were given in relief. These include:

'Bludstow, Thomas, 7 Back Turner-street [Manchester]: trampled and both arms broken. An old man, but not a good character. 40/- final.

'Booth, William, 63 London-road [Manchester]: sabred in the head. Now a prisoner in the New bailey for a bastard child. 40/- final.

'Harvey, Isabella, Wright-street [Pendleton]: struck with a sabre. The parents are respectable people who would not accept any money.'

Page 70

As far away as Ancoats, workers were reported to have been attacked while leaving their shifts at George Murray's Factory on Jersey Street.

The Portico Library on Mosely Street was there in 1819 and is, to this day, a thriving library and cultural centre. Hugh Birley, captain of the Yeomanry, was a member.

Page 71

The historian Michael Bush (in *The Casualties of Peterloo*) has estimated that, although there were far fewer women than men at the meeting, they were at least twice as likely as men to be injured, and twice as likely to have been injured by weapons. It seems that the Yeomanry and constables felt that women who had stepped outside the customary boundaries of their role had also forfeited the customary right to chivalrous treatment and protection.

Ann and John Jones, residents of 14 Windmill Street, worked hard to assist and treat many of the injured victims who came their way. They were disturbed by the heartless conduct of the constables and the Yeomanry. John Jones reported that, while he and his nephew were attempting to revive an unconscious man with water, a constable came up and knocked the basin of water out of their hands, breaking it.

This was the same house where Jemima Bamford took shelter and Martha Partington died after falling into the cellar and being crushed.

Page 76
Following the promotion of Reverend Hay to the lucrative position of Rector of Rochdale, Samuel Bamford attacked the Reverend in his 1820 poem 'Ode to a Plotting Parson':

Come over the hills out of York, parson Hay;
Thy living is goodly, thy mansion is gay;
Thy flock will be scattered if longer thou stay,
Our shepherd, our vicar – the good parson Hay.
And Meagher shall ever be close by thy side,
With a brave troop of Yeomanry ready to ride;
For the steed shall be saddled, the sword shall be bare,
And there shall be none the defenceless to spare.

Page 78
'Strong bodies of Cavalry and Special Constables patrolled the streets, and the town had every appearance of being in a state of complete insurrection. Sudden alarms from different quarters, the escorts of prisoners down to the New Bailey, occasional reports of fire-arms, the sounds of horses' feet, the rattling of the drum, and the strains of the trumpet, kept the

inhabitants in constant trepidation, and it was not till at an early hour on the Tuesday morning that these things ceased, and temporary quiet restored.' (*Wheelers' Manchester Chronicle*, 21 August 1819.)

Others were seriously injured in the New Cross riots, including: Samuel Jackson of Salford, a 17-year-old on the way to see his aunt, who ended up with his leg amputated; Elizabeth Green of Withy Grove, who had her ankle shattered; George Taylor, a shoemaker of Church Street, who was shot in the shoulder; and Edward Jones, 'a respectable master butcher' of Great Ancoats Street, who was shot in the thigh while standing at his own door.

Page 81
Joseph Barrett and his brother were with Mr Hobson at his house which overlooked St Peter's Field. Mr Hobson 'got some refreshments taken to an upper room in the house', and there the three of them watched the scene. The Barretts, who were respectable businessmen, were reported to have shown compassion towards the reformers, giving them help and money as they passed. Barrett's memoir is highly critical of the authorities.

Page 82
The atmosphere in Manchester remained tense over the following days. A 'friendly caution' was posted by the magistrates: 'The occupiers of Houses, from the windows or roofs of which stones are thrown, must consider themselves responsible for all the consequences.'

The *Manchester Chronicle* reported that at about ten o'clock a crowd gathered outside the house of the special constable Robert Campbell in Miller Street, near Oldham Street. It was rumoured that he had killed a child at Peterloo and there were cries of 'villain!' and 'kill him!' A brewer and a publican who tried to protect him were themselves attacked. Campbell fired a shot from an upstairs window and in the confusion escaped from the house and ran down the street, wrenching a door from its hinges to act as a shield. A military veteran of 20 years, he died in the Infirmary the next day, having been 'literally stoned to death, publicly'.

Samuel Bamford writes about visiting Manchester on 17 August dressed in a disguise to avoid being recognized and arrested. He went to Manchester largely to get information on what, if any, plans for revenge were being made

The unrest in Macclesfield, witnessed by *The Times* reporter John Tyas on his way back to London, began with a crowd of men and boys hissing at the richer inhabitants of the town. With the majority of troops still in Manchester, the unrest increased, and several local gentlemen, ready to assist in putting down the protests, were dismayed to find the commander of the few remaining soldiers was drunk.

Having escaped arrest, journalist and publisher Richard Carlile, managed to beat John Tyas to London on a mail coach which left Manchester at three in the morning of 17 August. He was relieved to be escaping Manchester, hoping to be the first to brings news of the massacre to London, although his relief was short-lived. Soon after boarding the coach, his three fellow gentlemen travellers opened a bottle of wine, inviting Carlile to join them. To protect his identity, Carlile was forced to smile through talk about how Hunt was plotting to depose the Prince Regent and place himself on the throne, and joining in with toasts of 'Down with Hunt' which were given with every glass.

Page 86
Cruikshank produced the familiar images of defenceless women being cut down at Peterloo, but he was a paid artist and only a few days before had published a grotesque caricature of the 'The Belle Alliance, or, the female reformers of Blackburn' from which the image on page 22 is taken.

In 1820 he signed the following receipt: 'Received – the sum of one hundred pounds, in consideration of a pledge given by me not to caricature his majesty in any immoral situation. George Cruikshank.'

Page 87
Before the end of 1819 over 30 public meetings were held in England and Scotland to protest about Peterloo, including open-air meetings of many thousands at Wakefield, Leeds, Bristol, London, York, Birmingham, Halifax, Newcastle, Norwich, Sheffield, Wigan, Leicester, Huddersfield, Dewsbury, Skipton, Burnley and Bradford. The radical movement continued to grow in size until winter weather and the Six Acts put an end to public meetings.

Page 88
The Oldham inquest into the death of John Lees sat for 10 days in the autumn of 1819, with reporters present, including at one stage the editor of *The Times* of London. The local coroner, out of his depth in the public eye, moved the venue repeatedly, trying to stop reporting, refusing to hear evidence and abusing witnesses. In the end he made so many blunders that the inquest was called in and stopped by the courts in London. The Manchester authorities were relieved; no new inquest was ordered, and to this day there has been no verdict.

The Riot Act of 1714 set out a procedure for magistrates to declare an assembly to be a riot, even if no rioting had yet taken place. The following notice had to be read to the crowd: 'Our sovereign lord the King chargeth and commandeth all persons, being assembled, immediately to disperse themselves, and peaceably to depart to their habitations, or to their lawful business, upon the pains contained in the act made in the first year of King George, for preventing tumults and riotous assemblies. God save the King.'

If people were still there after an hour, they could be dispersed with impunity by troops. The Manchester magistrates claimed that this text was read from an upstairs window by the Reverend Ethelston as the Yeomanry advanced, but independent witnesses close by insisted that they hadn't heard it.

Page 90
Editor of the *Manchester Observer*, James Wroe, first coined the term 'Peterloo' in his paper on 21 August, advertising a special weekly publication of evidence called 'Peter-loo Massacre'. 'Peterloo' was a bitter pun, comparing the cowardly attacks by the Yeomanry and soldiers on unarmed civilians to the brutality suffered at Waterloo.

Following years of persecution and numerous court battles for seditious libel, Wroe eventually handed the *Manchester Observer* over to the new editor TJ Evans in February 1820. Wroe spent a year in prison on charges of seditious libel. Despite the impoverished circumstances to which he and his family were reduced following his sentence, he later resumed his career as a radical reformer.

Page 91
The poet Percy Bysshe Shelley was in Italy still mourning the death of his five-year-old son, William, when he read the news of the Peterloo Massacre. He was greatly moved to find that the first victim of Peterloo had also been a child called William, two-year-old William Fildes. He picked up his pen shortly afterwards to write his famous protest poem, 'The Masque of Anarchy'. It was considered too risky to publish until after the Great Reform Act of 1832.

Bamford and Hunt's friendship ended in a dispute over conjugal visits in gaol. Discreet arrangements were made allowing Bamford's wife Jemima to visit him in Lincoln Gaol, and eventually to stay for several weeks. Hunt, who was not allowed visits from his own long-term partner Katherine Vince, wrote to ask Bamford to send a letter setting out his own arrangements in support of Hunt's claim to be allowed the same privileges. Bamford refused, moralising about 'the difference betwixt a man being indulged with the company of his own wife, and being indulged with the company of another man's wife'. He may have been worried that it would put his own arrangement with Jemima in jeopardy. Hunt was infamous for his constant disputes and fallings-out with his fellow reformers, but his bitterness towards Sam was irreparable following this incident.

Page 92
Although Hunt and four others were convicted of sedition at York and gaoled, they were acquitted on five out of six charges and the other five defendants were acquitted completely. *The Times* denounced the convictions, saying that the evidence showed 'that the Yeomanry never were assaulted by stones, brickbats, or bludgeons; that there were no stones, brickbats, or bludgeons at the meeting; and that witnesses must have seen if such weapons had been used.' Even the government solicitor secretly agreed, and wrote: 'The evidence uniformly agrees that the people assembled were peaceable in their demeanour, save as to shouting.'

Arthur Thistlewood (of the Spa Fields débâcle) emerged once again in 1820, with another failed attempt at inciting a national revolution. Having been informed by a close confidant (who was a government agent) that a dinner party consisting of the entire cabinet was to take place in London on 23 February, he and a few conspirators made plans to assassinate them all. They hid in a nearby house on Cato Street, Marylebone, armed with guns and allegedly possessing sacks ready for the heads of Lord Liverpool and other ministers, which they planned to mount on sticks and display on Westminster Bridge. They were raided by the police. Thistlewood killed a police officer with his sword.

At his trial he said: 'High treason was committed against the people at Manchester, but the Sovereign, by the advice of his Ministers, thanked the murderers... Insurrection then became a public duty.' Five of the conspirators were executed by the axe, the last English people to suffer beheading for treason. In case of trouble the authorities had prepared placards, bearing the words: 'The riot act has been read. Disperse immediately.'

In 1822 the reformers made a last attempt to get justice for the victims of Peterloo by suing Birley, Meagher and other members of the Yeomanry for the assault of Thomas Redford, who was sabred in the shoulder while holding the Middleton banner. The action of Redford versus Birley failed, but a great deal more damaging evidence was made public.

Page 96

Some suffragette banners echoed those held aloft at Peterloo: 'TAXATION WITHOUT REPRESENTATION IS TYRANNY'.

Page 97

The euphemistic blue 1970s plaque was eventually replaced in 2007, after protesters from the Peterloo Memorial Campaign climbed up a ladder and stuck their own appropriately worded version on top of it on 16 August, at the same time of day as the massacre had taken place.

Peterloo veterans, photographed in 1884 by John Birch (photo courtesy of Gallery Oldham).
Back: David Hilton (79).
Back row: Thomas Chadderton (81), John Davies (78), Thomas Ogden (81), Jonathan Dawson (82).
Middle row: Susannah Whittaker (81), Mary Collins (83), Catherine McMurdo (88), Richard Waters.
Front: Thomas Schofield (81), Alice Schofield (79).
The youngest of these veterans would have been only 13 years old in 1819, and the oldest just 23.

For more information about the background to Peterloo go to: peterloo.org

Peterloo: the sources

Everything in a white panel or speech bubble was written or said at the time, with the exception of two throwaway lines in the speech bubble on page 14 and the second speech bubble on page 52. A significant number of them have been edited for length or clarity, without altering their meaning or character. This section gives the sources. Frequently cited items are listed under 'Main Sources', and one-off items are listed under 'Sources Page by Page'. Dates are 1819 unless stated. Letters, statements etc are mostly from the Home Office Papers, National Archives, and some from the John Rylands Library's online Peterloo collection. Many are available at the websites listed below. This graphic novel is based mainly on Robert Poole's *Peterloo: the English Uprising* (2019), where most of the original material and references can be found.

Main sources

Bamford: Samuel Bamford, *Passages in the Life of a Radical* (1841), Book 1 chapters 24-41, Book 2 chapters 4, 19, 40.

Barrett: Joseph Barrett, *Memoir*, Manchester Archives and in *Return to Peterloo* (below).

Bruton: FA Bruton, *Three Accounts of Peterloo* (1921).

Carlile: Richard Carlile, in *Sherwin's Political Register*, 21 August 1819.

Chippendale: William Chippendale, militia captain, Oldham.

Dyneley: Major Dyneley, letter, 4pm, 16 August 1819.

Ethelston: Reverend Charles Ethelston, magistrate, Manchester.

Fletcher: Colonel Ralph Fletcher, magistrate, Bolton.

Hay: Reverend William Hay, magistrate, Manchester.

Hunt, *Memoirs*: Henry Hunt, *Memoirs*, volume 3 (1822).

Hunt Trial: *The Trial of Henry Hunt and Others* (1820).

Hunt, Prosecution brief: National Archives, TS 11/1056.

Jolliffe: William Jollife, Lieutenant, 15th Hussars, in Bruton.

Leeds Mercury, 21 August 1819.

Lees Inquest: *Inquest into the Death of John Lees* (Manchester, 1820).

Liverpool Mercury, 20 August 1819.

Lloyd: John Lloyd, magistrate's clerk, Stockport.

Manchester Observer: the newspaper is available online in the Peterloo Collection at the John Rylands Library, Manchester.

Magistrates' statement, 7 October 1819, in *Return to Peterloo*.

Peterloo Massacre (*Manchester Observer*, 1819), issues 4 and 6.

Petitions: all in House of Commons, *Votes and Proceedings*, 21 May 1821.

Prentice: Archibald Prentice, *Historical Sketches* (1851).

Redford v Birley: Report of the Proceedings of Redford v Birley (1822).

Return to Peterloo, ed Robert Poole, *Manchester Region History Review*, vol. 23.

Smith: John Benjamin Smith, cotton manufacturer, in Bruton, op cit.

Stanley: Reverend Edward Stanley, Rector of Alderley Edge, Cheshire, in Bruton.

The Times, 19 August 1819.

Other sources

p 7 Robert Southey, *Letters from England*, 1802; Francis Place, London reformer, in EP Thompson, *The Making of the English Working Class* (Penguin, 1968), 751.

p 8 William Chippendale to Home Office, 23 Apr 1812.

p 9 Magistrates' notice, 9 Aug; John Knight, in Prentice, chapter 5.

p 10 The Creature, in Mary Shelley, *Frankenstein* (1818).

p 11 'Advice Addressed to the Lower Ranks of Society', Anon. (1803); Petition to the Prince Regent from 'A Poor Petitioner and a Loyal Subject', 9 Mar 1815; Handbill, London, 2 Dec 1816; Lord Liverpool, Prime Minister, to Lord Sidmouth, Home Secretary, 29 May 1819.

p 12 Samuel Drummond to the Blanketeers, 10 Mar 1817; Thomas Wooler, *Manchester Observer*, 19 July 1819; *Manchester Observer*, 7 Apr 1821.

p 13 'We have it in our power...': Thomas Paine, *Common Sense*, 1776; James Dronsfield, *Incidents and Anecdotes of the Late Samuel Bamford* (1872); Bamford, book 1, ch 4; William Cobbett, 1808.

p 14 Rules and Regulations, Manchester and Salford Yeomanry, Sep 1817.

pp 17-19 All: *Manchester Mercury*, 25 Jan.

pp 20-21 *Manchester Observer* 23 Jan; police informer 'no. 2', 18 Jan.

p 22 Bamford, book 1, ch 28; *Manchester Chronicle*, 10 Jul; anon informer, Middleton, 26 Jul; Manchester Female Reformers' Address, *Manchester Observer*, 31 Jul; *Manchester Gazette*, 7 Aug.

p 23 Lloyd to Home Office, 16 Feb; *Black Dwarf*, 24 Feb; Manchester magistrates to Home Office, 20 Feb.

p 24 Fletcher to Home Office, 10 Aug; Magistrates to Home Office, 1 Jul; Home Office to Major-General Byng, Northern region military commander, 24 Jul; Home Office to Magistrates, 2 March; Hunt, *Memoirs*.

p 25 *Manchester Observer*, 10 Jul; Home Office to Magistrates, 18 Jun.

p 26 Hunt to Joseph Johnson, 6 Jul; Hunt, *Memoirs*; Home Office to Magistrates, 17 Jul.

p 27 Ethelston to Home Office, 19 Jul; Magistrates to Home Office, 31 Jul; Home Office to Lloyd, 5 Jul; Magistrates' statement, 7 Oct, in *Return to Peterloo*; Magistrates to Home Office, 6 Jul; Home Office to Magistrates, 18 Jun.

p 28 Bamford, book 1, chs 32 & 30; Capt Chippendale, Hunt Prosecution brief; Chippendale to Home Office, 16 Aug.

p 29 Thomas Jackson, Manchester Police Office, 7pm, 16 Aug; James Murray, special constable, & John Walker, attorney, Hunt Trial; 'And now I consider...': Richard Owen, attorney, 1.15 pm, 16 Aug; Bamford, ch 33.

p 30 Hunt, *Memoirs*.

p 33 Home Office to Magistrates, 3 Jul; Thomas Worrall, statement, 18 Apr 1820; Carlile, *Sherwin's*

Political Register, 21 Aug; Henry Hunt, 'To the Inhabitants of Manchester', 11 Aug.

p 34 Bamford, ch 34; William Morris, Middleton, *Hunt Trial*.

p 35 Bamford, ch 34; Lawrence Fort, statement, 16 Aug; Mary Yates, *Hunt Trial*; John Whittaker, statement, 9 Nov.

p 36 John Tyas, *Hunt Trial*; Manchester Female Reformers' Address, *Manchester Observer*, 31 Jul; anonymous informant, 31 Jul 1819 (*Papers Related to the Internal State of the Country*, no 24).

p 37 Henry Horton, reporter, *Hunt Trial*; James Scarlett, prosecution barrister, *Hunt Trial*.

p 38 Bamford, ch 39 (Jemima), ch 34 (Samuel).

pp 39-40 Robert Mutrie, *Lees Inquest*; Samuel Morton, manufacturer, John Tyas, *Times* reporter, Roger Entwisle, solicitor, all *Hunt Trial*; Edward Owen, statement, 6 Nov 1819.

p 41 Roger Entwisle, *Hunt Trial*; other statements 16 Aug by John Walker, Richard Clogg, Thomas Blackwall, Richard Owen.

p 42 Bamford, ch 39 (Jemima), ch 34 (Samuel).

p 43 Hunt, *Memoirs*; Jonathan Andrew, *Redford v Birley*; Prentice, ch 11.

p 44 William Hulton, *Hunt Trial*.

p 45 Conversation: Magistrates' statement, 7 Oct.

p 46 Thomas Padmore, Portland St, *Lees Inquest*; William Hulton, message to Major Trafford.

p 47 Ann Fildes, statement, 12 Nov; William Hay, comment.

p 48 Henry Horton, *New Times* reporter, & Roger Entwisle, attorney, *Hunt Trial*.

p 49 *Annual Register*, 1819; Mary Yates, *Hunt Trial*; Magistrates' statement, 7 Oct; William Harrison, *Lees Inquest*.

pp 50-51 James Weatherley, bookseller, *Memoir*; *The Examiner*, 12 Sep; John Edward Taylor, *Notes and Observations* (1820); *Manchester Chronicle*, 21 Aug. Other quotations from *Lees Inquest*, *Peterloo Massacre*, & press reports.

p 52 'Sir, I have a warrant' etc: *Manchester Chronicle*, 21 Aug; Henry Horton, *Hunt Trial*.

p 53 *Annual Register*, 1819.

p 54 Nathan Broadhurst, *Lees Inquest*; Mary Fildes, petition.

p 55 *Manchester Gazette*, 21 Aug; Magistrates' statement, 7 Oct; William Hulton, *Hunt Trial*.

pp 58-59 Bamford, ch 25.

p 61 Edward Owen, statement, 6 Nov.

p 62 *New Times*, 18 Aug; *Examiner*, 12 Sep; Joseph Brierley, petition.

p 63 *Manchester Chronicle*, 21 Aug.

p 64 Sir Charles Wolseley, letter, 3 Sep; Charles Pearson, 5 Sep, *Peterloo Massacre* no 6.

p 65 Edward Owen, statement, 6 Nov.

p 66 William Butterworth, weaver, *Hunt Trial*; *Report of the Metropolitan Relief Committee* (1820); *Examiner*, 12 Sep; *Reminiscences of James Fellows*, Thomas Tonge, 1883; John Stavely Barratt, statement, 30 Jan 1820.

p 67 Mary Dowlan, charwoman, *Redford v Birley*; 'Damn you', Nathan Broadhurst, *Lees Inquest*; Major Cochrane, *Manchester Observer*, 25 Dec.

p 68 Bamford ch 36; John Brierley, *Peterloo Relief Fund Book*, John Rylands Library.

p 69 Bamford, ch 39.

p 70 Carlile; Samuel Allcard account, 9 Sep.

p 71 John Jones, James Mills, Jonah Andrew, *Lees Inquest*; William Leigh statement, in Charles Pearson, letter, 5 Sep, *Peterloo Massacre* no 6.

p 72 Henry Hunt, letter, 31 Aug; 'This is Waterloo': Anne Jones, Windmill St, *Lees Inquest*.

p 73 Bamford, ch 35.

p 74 Bamford, chs 39 (Jemima), 36 (Samuel); 'Ode to Jemima', 16 May 1820.

p 75 Elizabeth Gaunt, petition; Hay, *Redford v. Birley*.

p 76 Joseph Barrett; William Norris Buckley, *Lees Inquest*; Ethelston to Home Office, 16 Aug; Magistrates' statement, 7 Oct.

p 77 Charles Pearson letter, in *Manchester Observer* 25 Dec; James Chisnell statement, 1 Nov.

p 78 *Manchester Chronicle*, 21 Aug; John Moore, Constable, to Home Office, 19 Nov; Hay to Home Office, 16 Aug.

p 79 *Manchester Chronicle*, 21 Aug.

pp 83-87 Bamford, ch 41.

p 86 Home Secretary to Earl of Derby, 21 Aug.

p 87 Elizabeth Gaunt, petition; William Harrison, *Lees Inquest*.

p 88 Henry Kirkman, William Basnett, James Walker, & Martha Robinson, all *Lees Inquest*.

p 89 Robert Lees, petition; letter from jurors to coroner, 2 Jan 1820; *Lees Inquest*.

p 90 Manchester Pitt Club minutes, 1817; Magistrates to Home Office, 27 Jan 1820.

p 91 Bamford book 2 ch 4.

p 92 Bamford book 2 ch 19; Hunt's letter to the Reformers, 19 Oct; Hunt, Ilchester gaol diary, 16 Aug 1820; *Hunt Trial*.

p 95 Bamford, book 2, ch 40. Ashton Chartist: *Northern Star*, 17 Nov 1838.

p 96 Grace Saxon Mills, *Against Woman Suffrage: Some Reasons*, 1912.

Websites

peterloomassacre.org – Peterloo Memorial Campaign site.

peterloo1819.co.uk – Peterloo 1819 commemorations site, including the VR web app and links to many online sources.

peterloowitness1819.weebly.com – Peterloo Witness Project, transcribed documents and transcripts of trials and inquest

luna.manchester.ac.uk/luna/servlet/ Manchester~24~24 – The University of Manchester Library, Peterloo collection online.

manchesteruniversitypress.co.uk/journals/bjrl/ Robert Poole, 'The *Manchester Observer*: biography of a radical newspaper', *Bulletin of the John Rylands Library* vol 95 no 1, 2019 (free online).

vimeo.com/209772068 – the Peterloo animation.

revjosephharrison.wordpress.com/the-peterloo-era-1819 – press reports, letters and biographical information from the Peterloo era.

spartacus-educational.com/PRpeterloo.htm – overview of the massacre, biographical information and press commentary

This graphic novel was made possible by the generous crowdfunded support of:

Shaun Walls

Nick Massey

Teresa Day

Elizabeth & Stuart Bailey, Harriet Monkhouse, Jeff Kaye, Michael Sweeney, UNISON Queen Elizabeth Hospital.

Anne Brunton, Arthur Chapman, Brian Booker, Jacqui Burke, James Schlunke, Jonathan Chambers, Katrina Navickas, Kevin Ball, Lauren Jaye Gradwell, Malcolm Chase, Michael Sanders, Peter Castree, Sarah Hardstaff, Shaun Corkerry, Steven Stokes, Thomas Kearney.

Andrew Walker, Anna Thomas, Antony Quinn, Backer 139, Backer 207, Ben Walsh, Brian Candeland, Chris Smith, Christopher John Green, Dan Harris, Janice Finn, John Ossoway, Margaret Burke, Martin Gittins, Michael Wignall, Paul Monaghan, Steve Poole, The Society for the Study of Labour History.

Aidan Broderick, Amanda Parker, Andrew Marsden, Backer 189, Barry Clavin, Belinda Holmes, Corinne Ford, David Carey, Dr Andrew Beck, Gillian Davies, Graham Chard, Hazel Draper, Ilene Dawn Alexander, Jayne Gosnall, Jean Horsfall, Jerry Elsmore, Jerry Hinds, John Brown, Ken Jepson, Kim Tunstall, Kit Watson, Laura Mackey, Lyn Schlunke, Mark Crail, Michael Skazick, Mohamed Ghalaieny, Neale Cresswell, Nick Pyfrom, Paul Brian Edwards, Paul Herrmann, Quiet Loner, Rajesh Patel, Richard Kerridge, Sachiko Oswald-Tashiro, Scarlett & Sophie Rickard Gluepot Books, Scott & Helen Murray, Simon Ball, Stephen Longstaffe, Suzanne Bradshaw, Tom Webster.

Adrian Lobb, Adrian Spink, Adrienne Walker, Al Franco, Alan Franco, Alan Lomax, Alan Weaver, Alastair Martindale, Angie Farrand, Anne Marie Clift, Alexandra Turner, Alister Black, Amanda Creasy, Amy Kennedy, Andrew Baxter, Andrew Gritt, Andrew Wilkinson, Andy Truett, Ann MacCarthy, Anne Strachan, Arthur Burns, Audrey MacDonald, Backer 12, Backer 30, Backer 109, Backer 239, Backer 275, Ben Dickson, Ben McGarr, Ben Tappin, Benjamin Pflanz, Bernard McGrath, Boo Moorhead and family, Bridie Breen, Bruno Tran, Caitlin Kitchener, Cardinal Fang, Carey Bamber, Carol Talbot, Caroline Derry, Caroline Gonda, Carolyn O'Brien, Cathryn Iliffe, Charlotte Eyraud, Chris & Dave Verguson, Chris Carson, Chris Tucker, Christine Fitzgerald, Chiara Glut, Claire Hewitt, Cllr Victor Chamberlain, CP and Pam Lee, Darren Edwards, Darren Ormandy, Dave Perry, David Howarth, David Hughes, David Jones, David McKeegan, David Rees, David Royle, deadmanjones, Deborah Hind and Jack Wrigley, Deborah Wood, Des Basterfield, Diana Terry, Duncan Harris, Ed Mayo, Eileen Fursland, Elisabeth Kean, Ellen-Arwen Tristram, Fabrice Bensimon, Fiona Marshall, Fiona Turner, Frank Emmett, Gareth Caley, Gary Winch, Gavin Simpson, Geoff Bridson, George Kelsall, Ben Kelsall, Chetham's Library ,George Vickers, George Waterhouse, Gillian Lonergan, Graham Phythian, Hannah Berry, Heath Olive, Henrik Gustafsson, Howard Kistler, Hunt Emerson, Iain Peacock, Ian Berry, Ian Phillips, Jackie Dooley, Jacqueline Riding, James Hobson, James Jefferies, Jamie J, Jane Angel, Jane Hartley Jacques, Jane Lawson, Jane Miller, Janette Martin, Janine Cottingham, Jessica Charles, Jim Howell, Joan Crystall, Joanna Gait, Joe Cozens, Joe Smith, Johanna Wilson, John Belchem, John Bevan, John Crumpton, John Dempsey, John Eaden, John Gardner, Josh Steiner, Joy Hallsworth, Karen Chamberlayne, Karen Shannon, Kate McCarthy, Katie Hall, Kathleen Cosgrove, Keith-Tom Roache, Kevin Duffy, Kirsten Watson, Leesa Chester, Leon Sea, Leonard Baker, Lilly Lane, Lily Paulina, Lindsay Porter, Lis Golding, Lisa Perella, Louise Bolotin, Louise Ina Rowe, Luke Blaxill, Lynda Winton, Maria Moore, Mark Greer, Mark Hodgkinson, Martin Story, Martyn Amos, Matt Winfield, Mel & Jude Rowley, Michael Hill, Michael J Perry, Michael Slater, Morag Rose, Natalie Lee, Nathan Jackson, Neil Evans, Ness (Dickinson) Wojkiewicz, Nichola Potts, Nicola Holt, Nigel Woodcock, Nina Gerrard, Noel Hulse, Norman Boyd, Olivia Glasser, Pam Foster, Patricia Hornby Atkinson, Paul Harnett, Paul McGovern, Paul Rippon, Paul Rutland, Paul Quinn, Paul Williams, Paul Wolstenholme, Paula Millward, Peter Allen, Peter J LaPrade Jr, Peter Morgan, Peter Trumper, Phil Barker, Phil Henry, Phil Hyde, Rachel Coleman, Rachel Wise, Red Saunders, Reuben Wright, Richard Galpin/Kennington Chartist Project, Richard Holland, Richard Huzzey, Rick Whiting, Rob Arcangeli, Rob Ettey, Rob Harrison, Rob Marston, Rob Porter, Rob Shaw, Robert Mortimer, Roger Miles, Ronny Worsey, Rosie Griffiths, Ruth Mather, Saffron Gardenchild, Sam Kimmins, Sarah McNicol, Sean Pelkey, Sheila Tarpey, Sid Sondergard, Simon Walker, Siôn Hopes, Steph Parker, Steph Taylor, Stephen Crossley, Steve Foxen-Durnien, Steve Roman, Steve Taylor, Steve White, Steven Lindsay, Stevie Carroll, Sue John, Susan E Ferner, Susan Stokes-Chapman, Tal M Klein, Tim Cockitt, Tim Gwilt, Tim Mundy, Tim Twelves, Tom Blacker, Tom Hawkins, Tom McNevin Jones, Tony Terry, Tracey Annette, Two Silver Denarii LLC, Vanessa Hall, Victoria Evans Kitchiner.